I0825150

PARTIALLY DEVOURED

ALSO BY DANIEL KRAUS

Novels

Angel Down

Whalefall

They Set the Fire

The Ghost That Ate Us

They Stole Our Hearts

They Threw Us Away

Bent Heavens

Blood Sugar

The Death and Life of Zebulon Finch, Volume One: At the Edge of Empire

The Death and Life of Zebulon Finch, Volume Two: Empire Decayed

Scowler

Rotters

The Monster Variations

With George A. Romero

Pay the Piper

The Living Dead

With Guillermo del Toro

The Shape of Water

Trollhunters

With Shäron Moalem

Wrath

With Lisi Harrison

The Joker's On You

Season's Eatings

Scream for the Camera

1-2-3-4, I Declare a Thumb War

Graphic Novels

Athanasia

The Cemeterians

Trojan

Year Zero: Volume 0

The Autumnal

PARTIALLY DEVOURED

How *Night of the Living Dead*™ Saved My Life and Changed the World

DANIEL KRAUS

COUNTERPOINT • CALIFORNIA

PARTIALLY DEVOURED

First Counterpoint edition: 2026

Library of Congress Cataloging-in-Publication Data
Names: Kraus, Daniel, 1975- author
Title: Partially devoured : how Night of the Living Dead saved my life and changed the world / Daniel Kraus.
Description: First Counterpoint edition. | San Francisco : Counterpoint, 2026. | Includes bibliographical references.
Identifiers: LCCN 2025044923 | ISBN 9781640097155 hardcover | ISBN 9781640097162 ebook
Subjects: LCSH: Night of the living dead (Motion picture : 1968)—Criticism and interpretation | Night of the living dead (Motion picture : 1968)—Influence | Kraus, Daniel, 1975- | LCGFT: Film criticism
Classification: LCC PN1997.N5215 K73 2026
LC record available at https://lccn.loc.gov/2025044923

Jacket painting © Barnaby Edwards
Book design by Laura Berry

COUNTERPOINT
Los Angeles and San Francisco, CA
www.counterpointpress.com

Printed in the United States of America

1 3 5 7 9 10 8 6 4 2

Dedicated to the Image Ten:

Dave Clipper

Marilyn Eastman

Karl Hardman

Richard Ricci

Rudy Ricci

George A. Romero

John A. Russo

Gary Streiner

Russell Streiner

Vince Survinski

The first time you see a movie you say, "I like it." You're not quite sure why. Watch it a second time. You will either like it again or not like it. If you like it again, you will start to look at *why* you like it. That's where the understanding comes from. I tell you, I promise you, the fourth time you watch it, you weep. The fifth time you watch it, you're analyzing. The sixth time, all of a sudden, you get it.

GEORGE A. ROMERO

Night of the Living Dead has been released countless times with varying lengths of preamble. To cue your copy with this book, consider the first frame of the film's first shot as 00:00:00.

00:00:00

EERIE HEAVY ECHO

I CAN'T IMAGINE A DEADER SHOT TO START A MOVIE about the undead, a shot more drained of life, urgency, and momentum. The black-and-white photography will carve like a knife later, but here it's gray-and-gray, a dreary murk familiar to anyone who grew up in middle America. This shot was filmed in November 1967 on vertiginous Franklin Road outside Evans City, Pennsylvania, seven hundred miles due east—only one degree of latitude lower—from my hometown of Fairfield, Iowa.

From this shot, the two towns might as well be one: a dirt road (today paved) winding along a nondescript hill, a fungal growth of timber (today knotty woods), fence posts and telephone poles planted at apparent random, and a couple houses in the distance, the sort of dilapidated rural homes I knew so well as a kid. Lawns sun-fried and acid-burned by dog piss. The guilty dogs bony, skulking, and leashless. Vehicle carcasses besmirching driveways.

In other words, a trap—I knew it even back then. Such traps tended to relax briefly after high school graduation, your best opportunity of escape, or else you might never. Even us escapees never truly got away. Our towns ghost about in our nightmares, and the only exorcisms available are movies like this.

"It is an ordinary dusk of normal quiet and shadow." That's

how this shot is described in *Night of the Living Dead*'s screenplay. It's accurate. It's also ugly. Given the eye and instincts of the film's twenty-seven-year-old director, George A. Romero, I'm tempted to say the ugliness is on purpose. Actually, I'll just say it: It's on purpose. That it's also the widest shot in the whole movie provides us a user manual on how to interpret the rest of the film. *Night* is going to begin *wide* in every sense of the word—broad, banal, boring—before paring down its picture of America like a butcher.

By the film's final shot, there will be nothing left but bones.

Injecting caffeine into this oatmeal opening is a musical track. It begins with the film's fade-in, if not a shade before. It's really good. All the music in the movie is really good, and more surprising when you learn that it came from a can. Romero and his cohort cashed in every favor possible to shoot their flick for $60,000 and finish it at a total of $114,000 (breaking down at $14,000 for preproduction, $20,000 for actors, $60,000 for production, $20,000 for postproduction). It's a steal for a 35mm feature even in the 1960s. Sadly, their considerable artist circle did not include a composer who happened to have their own orchestra.

The score is instead drawn from prepurchased library cues, the old-timey version of the musical stingers that come prepackaged with today's video-editing software. Back in 1997, when editing a 16mm student film at the University of Iowa, I used library cues drawn from dozens of 33⅓ albums in nondescript yellow sleeves. There was no artifice to the track titles; they used pure description to assist the search efforts of radio producers and industrial filmmakers. But there were diamonds in all that rough; I still recall the winsome tune of a needle drop with the vapid title of "Guitar Melody."

The song we hear over *Night*'s first shot is "Eerie Heavy Echo." Thanks to Jim Cirronella's herculean efforts in reconstructing the film's soundtrack for a 2010 album called *They Won't Stay Dead!*, we know a hell of a lot more about the film's music than we used to. This cue, also known as L-1204 (the "L" stands for "Light"), attributed to Spencer Moore at least a decade before

Night, came from the Capitol Library Services Hi-"Q" Series (which, the center label of each LP assures us, can be played using "either standard or microgroove stylus"). I use "attributed" on purpose: Some of the Capitol "composers" were the producers who owned or commissioned the cues.

Scot W. Holton, producer of the film's first (if only partial) soundtrack release on Varèse Sarabande in 1982, notes that, if you perk up your ears (and, I'll add, lower your standards), you'll hear several of *Night*'s cues in forgotten drive-in fare like *The Hideous Sun Demon* (1958), *Terror from the Year 5,000* (1958), and *Teenagers from Outer Space* (1959). Once you're deep into this shit, hearing a *Night* cue in a different film sparks a similar glee to spotting an actor doing a bit part before they were famous.

"Eerie Heavy Echo" begins with eleven notes blasted in syncopation by strings and brass before trailing off into what, I admit, can only be described as an eerie heavy echo. Listened to apart from the film, the track evokes aliens with big plastic heads struggling in ungainly foam suits. Romero was arguably the first director to pair this sort of sci-fi warbling with a visual image too dull for a "Visit Evans City" postcard.

"If the boogie man had a ghetto-blaster," Romero writes in the Varèse Sarabande liner notes, "this was the stuff he'd boogie to."

The effect of *that* music plus *this* image is magic. It's also a microcosm of the film writ large: mundanity tweaked just enough to be unsettling. A car appears on the dirt road at 00:01, unless you're watching a shitty copy of the film, which you probably are, considering that *Night* has been released on home media over *one thousand times*, according to Geoff Turner, who monitors this data for his *Night of the Living Tapes* project. Turner tracks about $1,000 worth of *Night* physical media bought each month on eBay, from Blu-ray, DVD, and VHS to the esoteric formats of LaserDisc, Betamax, Video8, PC CD-ROM, Video 2000, VHD, Betacam SP, and Super 8. (As a kid, I found an 8mm copy at a local secondhand store called the Bargain Box, six 8mm reels inside a wilted box that puzzlingly featured no zombies, only crude sketches of stars like John Wayne and Bette Davis.)

As Romero scholar Adam Charles Hart writes, "*Night* is very possibly the most watched horror film ever made." Which means you might not notice the car until 00:06. If that's the case, buy a better copy. Ideally, the 2018 Criterion edition, pristinely restored by the Museum of Modern Art and the George Lucas Family Foundation.

The car in question is a brand-new two-door 1967 Pontiac LeMans, linden green in actuality with black vinyl roof and interiors. The bland vehicle fits right into the weaponized blandness of the image. The LeMans takes its sweet-ass time crawling along Franklin Road. The shot lasts thirty-six seconds, making it the single longest take in the film. It's interminable. Brilliant, too. With "Eerie Heavy Echo" along for the ride, the LeMans's slow progress is chilling in the way a stray dog walking toward you is chilling.

In America, few things are more ominous than an unknown car rolling your way. It very well might contain news of a death, if not death itself. No one knows this like country folk, who see vehicles approach from miles off by clouds of dirt-road dust. If one defines "country" by Hollywood standards (i.e., not L.A. or New York), *Night* is our most famous country blockbuster. It wasn't made by a "system." It was made by flesh-and-blood outsiders, an unmitigated piece of Americana.

The film *is* America. For better and for worse.

00:00:07 AN IMAGE TEN PRODUCTION

If you don't notice the car at 00:00:07, that's because the film's first title overwhelms the screen, a white, lightly drop-shadowed, all-caps sans-serif font (the closest common font is boldface Franklin Gothic Book) that reads: AN IMAGE TEN PRODUCTION.

Image Ten produced exactly one movie. They don't have the

opening-credits recognition factor of a Miramax, Lionsgate, or Pixar. But they're still around (more than we can say for Miramax) and are active in the licensing of their film's title, logo, and likenesses. If you've bought a product with the movie's title on it (and, boy, have I ever), followed by that little TM symbol, that's proof of Image Ten getting their well-deserved piece of the action, and of a licensee having the respect to pay it. Which they technically don't have to do. Long story. Keep reading.

How one gained entry into Image Ten was simple enough: You threw in $600 toward a dubious-sounding movie hatched by founding members of a Pittsburgh commercial/industrial film production house called the Latent Image (a latent image is the exposed picture on a strip of film yet to be made visible by developing fluid) and a sound recording studio called Hardman Associates. For the record, the Image Ten were Dave Clipper (attorney), Marilyn Eastman (actor), Karl Hardman (producer, actor), Richard Ricci (actor), Rudy Ricci (actor), George A. Romero (director, cowriter, editor, actor), John A. "Jack" Russo (cowriter, actor), Gary Streiner (sound engineer, actor), Russell Streiner (producer, actor), and Vincent Survinski (production director, actor). Fans are familiar with all these names except one, Dave Clipper, a true man of mystery.

Mathletes will notice this only creates a sum of $6,000. Correct—that was the film's projected shooting budget, surprisingly naïve for young pros. Ultimately, additional investors were scrounged up at $300 per share to reach the final $114,000, but Image Ten sounded cooler than Image Thirty-Two or whatever. (The original shares are quite fancy: green bank certificates with a foil IMAGE TEN, INC. stamped in the lower left-hand corner.)

With the film's second shot comes the second title: NIGHT OF THE LIVING DEAD. The film's first grace note is the word *night,* which is presented oversize, outline only, all lowercase. This is dread by contrast: It is not, in fact, night. Our LeMans toodles away from us through daylight. Our amygdala activates as we imagine these environs after sunset. The crooked, cruciform electrical poles lording like twenty-foot skeletons, the ditches deadly tarns, the distant stone bridge a harbor of trolls.

It's a bucolic shot, but what you're looking at is the most disastrous title screen in motion picture history. That's not hyperbole. Do you see what's missing from this title? If you watch a lot of old movies, you probably do. In 1976, draconian title screen laws were relaxed, partially due to *Night*'s infamy, according to Dino Castelli and Sean Q. King's documentary *Chronicles of the Living Dead* (2015). But in 1968, if you didn't have a copyright notice under your title, you didn't own the film. I'm not talking about the title here. I mean the whole fucking film.

Image Ten shot their movie under *Night of the Flesh Eaters* until they received a cease-and-desist letter from a lawyer whose client, Vulcan Productions, didn't want this Pittsburgh trifle getting mixed up with Vulcan's 1964 quickie *The Flesh Eaters*. Even though *The Flesh Eaters*, not a bad flick, is about flesh-eating sea microbes, it does include the line "the strange phenomenon which is neither living nor dead," which at least *sounds* like it belongs in a zombie flick.

Not wanting to kick things off with a lawsuit, Image Ten finished their workprint under the title *Night of Anubis*. The latter reveals Romero's highfalutin aspirations and sensibilities (and possibly cowriter Jack Russo's, too, saddled as he was with a recent English degree). Anubis was the Egyptian god of the underworld—which would be news to patrons of the exploitation theater circuit. They were used to films with the kind of titles *Night* would end up playing alongside, most of them with the word "blood": *Blood Thirst*, *Bloodthirsty Butchers*, *Blood Beast from Outer Space*, *Blood Orgy of the She-Devils*, *Curse of the Blood Ghouls*, and *Mad Doctor of Blood Island*.

On June 10, 1968, Image Ten made a distribution deal with a branch of the Walter Reade Organization called Continental Films, which was digging itself out of prestige-film debt with genre acquisitions like *Ghidrah, the Three-Headed Monster* (1964). Footage exists of the original title frame. Beneath *Anubis* are the words COPYRIGHT © 1968 CONTINENTAL DISTRIBUTING, INC. So far, so good.

A final title change was made: *Night of the Living Dead*, the brainchild of either Jack Russo or Walter Reade's Jerry Pickman—and wow, what a great choice, startling and strong. I shudder at how much gravitas would have been lost by future Romero titles like *Dawn of the Flesh Eaters, Day of Anubis*, et cetera.

But a mistake was made. We'll never know who made it. That's for the best. When the final title change happened, the title-adding person neglected to matte in the copyright notice, that all-important encircled *C*. They call it a copyright bug, and it sure acted like a bug, some exotic, virulent spider that laid eggs inside the project like ticking bombs. Once those eggs hatched, everything that had gone right for *Night of the Living Dead* started going very wrong.

Back then, if you didn't own the copyright of your original film, you had no power to stop Joe Schmoe from screening it, or even releasing it on their own and pocketing the profits. Which Joe Schmoes began doing, especially as the appetite for cable and video content ratcheted up in the 1980s. For Image Ten, an unmitigated disaster. But here's where it gets tricky. For the rest of planet Earth, this disaster might—maybe, possibly, perchance—have been worth all the unfairness, all the lost millions.

As Russ Streiner said on a June 30, 2024, panel at the Days of the Dead convention in Phoenix, "All due respect to all the classic films that have been made, but when was the last time you saw a *Citizen Kane* T-shirt?"

If you've ever sat through an interview with me (sorry), you know all too well I first saw *Night* at age five. A five-year-old doesn't request a 1960s horror classic; rather, it appears on a screen before him. People involved with the film have repeated an apparent truism that *Night* is always playing, every second, somewhere in the world. That makes it the movie equivalent to the Beatles' "Yesterday." If you are alive, you will encounter *Night of the Living Dead*. How you receive it is up to you.

It helped to have a mother who aligned to the factory specs of a Midwestern mom of three except for the caprice of loving horror movies. Upon seeing undead shamblers on the tube, my mother didn't turn it off or shoo me from the room. She proved her deep insight into her middle child by inviting me into the experience, poking fun at the characters and their cavalcade of misfortunes.

It started there for me. Everything. My interests, my career. I have no memories any cozier, happier, or more inspiring. The world opened up from beneath a homemade quilt and atop a shag carpet.

Soon my mother invited me to watch *Twilight Zone* reruns with her on Fridays. Meanwhile, *Night* kept playing. I saw it at age seven. Age eight. Age nine. Suddenly I'm watching it more than once per year. Prior to the VHS revolution, it was the only movie I could watch with the semi-regularity of how my mom watched soaps or my younger sister, Julie, watched cartoons, and with the same breezy fragmentation, too, catching only thirty minutes here or twenty minutes there. This discontinuity surely softened the film's impact, as did commercial breaks hawking Doublemint Gum, Diet Shasta, and Speed Stick.

It's doubtful my spongy kid brain could have handled the film without these structural antacids; when digested whole, the movie is overwhelming, upsetting, and disorienting (even more so when you're old enough to appreciate the trampled taboos). The shitty audiovisual quality of my first hundred or so viewings was the biggest distancing factor of all. Nothing disturbs a kid like the stark terror of adults, but the faces in those blurry airings of *Night* weren't defined enough to call "stark." Nor could I identify the guts munched by zombies (or "ghouls" as *Night* calls them) as anything beyond "stringy" or "sloppy."

Once Adventureland Video opened in Fairfield in 1988, forget about it, especially with a mom willing to look the other way. After cheap VHS tapes began popping up in grocery store bargain bins, double-forget about it. My rough estimate is that I've seen *Night of the Living Dead* three hundred times.

Its hold over me is unique; I am not a guy given to fandom. When I'm finished with comic con appearances, I hightail it from the floor. My shelves aren't filled with pop-culture tchotchkes. I own zero Funko Pop dolls. I envy those given to fandom the same way I envy those given to religion; walking through convention aisles must set off a series of endorphin hits. The flip side, I imagine, is the anxiety of the pious. What if you don't obtain that complete set? Will regret consume you if you don't get that autograph?

Night is my sole exception. Without getting up from my chair I can see a *Night of the Living Dead* shirt, cap, poster, art prints, original painting, lunchbox, plastic cup, coffee mug, coaster, refrigerator magnets, soundtrack album, action figure, trading cards, stickers, plushie, several books, two enamel pins, five lapel pins, two board games, a framed photo of myself with George Romero, and, of course, thirteen editions of the two posthumous novels I wrote with him, *The Living Dead* (2020) and *Pay the Piper* (2024). (I nearly counted my Zyrtec and Flonase, both of which share Image Ten's signature green.)

What do I gain from throwing money at this stuff? The fact that Image Ten is making some long-delayed profit is nice, but I'm not that altruistic. It also has nothing to do with signaling to strangers a common enthusiasm. I'm as unlikely to wear a *Night* shirt to a geeky gathering as I am to put a political bumper sticker on my vehicle. I prefer to ninja my way through public settings.

It's just "merch," and I'm afloat in it. When I look at all this stuff, I'm reminded of how I felt when hiding my childhood blankies (Blankie and Zankie) when friends came over, a powerful mix of adoration and shame. The moment I folded Blankie and Zankie like the Stars and Stripes and placed them in a storage room remains palpable to me, on par with the death of loved ones. I know how that sounds, but it felt like saying goodbye to something much bigger.

Blankies, my mother, *Night of the Living Dead*—proxies of safety, happiness, contentment. I wonder if having all these *Night* products around is a substitute for photos of my dead loved ones, which might be too much to take. *Night*, on the other hand, gets just close enough.

00:00:59 CEMETERY ENTRANCE

Let's get our LeMans to its destination. The car drives off under the screenwriting credit, then comes back toward us under more credits. At 00:00:64, we get our first sound effect: tires on pavement. The real world is beginning to bleed through the eerie, heavy echo, telling us, in film language, that the spectral and the everyday are set to collide.

Two shots later, we come to the famous turnoff. Again the LeMans heads toward us only to make a hairpin turn up a steep, slender dirt road that leads into what look like woods. Given how slow the film's first ninety seconds have been, this is downright gripping. The car has abandoned its Sunday-style meandering to make a distinct choice. We're officially off the beaten path.

The camera punches forward to give us a closer look at the LeMans's climb. It's the first shot of *Night* I'd call iconic. It's the sort of shot people who "have an eye" for photography can frame by instinct, a geometric conflux of slanting lines, weights and counterweights, and lights and darks, all of which draw the eye to the diamond-shaped road sign reading: CEMETERY ENTRANCE.

That's sinister enough, but the state of the sign is more ominous still, and Romero gives us thirteen seconds to absorb it. It looks splattered with globs of mud. But how could mud end up that high? Look closer. It's bullet holes. If you've spent time on American interstates, you've seen plenty of road signs shot to hell. Usually the victims are random signs touting off-ramp BPs and Wendy's. Sometimes, though, the bullets have a purpose. There's an unforgettable photo out there of a Dr. Martin Luther King Jr. Expressway sign marred by forty or fifty bullet holes. These are threats from pissants with guns. Our country is packed with both.

The bullet holes warn us the LeMans is heading into a contested space. Of course it is. The living are here, above ground, driving overlarge sedans; the dead are below, melting to goo inside caskets at best, returning to life at worst. Any cemetery is a DMZ as edgy as the Thirty-Eighth Parallel, where we toe up to rectangles of turf to enact rituals that may or may not match what the buried parties wanted, or still want. The sign below CEMETERY ENTRANCE, legible only on the best copies of *Night*, reads NO PARKING PRIVATE DRIVE. Private to whom? The dead, I'd like to think.

At last we're in the boneyard. The trail elevated us; the woodsy horizon is below. The cemetery is, in a word, unimpressive. Rutted dirt path, sporadic pines, patchy grass, a hodgepodge hundred or so grave markers. The LeMans chugs down the path. It knows where it's going.

Over the film's eighth shot comes the final opening credit: DIRECTED BY GEORGE A. ROMERO. No shot Romero ever directed means more to me. As a kid, I knew movies began with lists of names, but this was the first time I wondered about one of them. The shot pans left to right to follow the LeMans, the first delicate camera move of the film, and it tells us there is an author here, a hand behind the camera. There's a pointed difference between the "George A. Romero" named here and the "George Romero" of his screenwriting co-credit. He's giving this credit the gravity of a middle initial, goddamn it.

The shot is foregrounded by one of those mini American flags people jab in the graves of veterans. It's close enough to the camera to be out of focus, and flutters leftward in opposition to the car's trajectory. For a single electrifying instant, precisely two minutes into the film, the LeMans *disappears behind the flag.* A magic trick, all humans erased from the planet. This is, in fact, the message behind Romero's six-film zombie cycle: *Night of the Living Dead* (1968), *Dawn of the Dead* (1978), *Day of the Dead*

(1985), *Land of the Dead* (2005), *Diary of the Dead* (2007), and *Survival of the Dead* (2009). In short, the erasing of people and what that might mean for the world. (Spoiler: It's a good thing.)

It's gobsmackingly prescient for Romero to introduce himself by transposing his name over the flag. It's on par with the great ironic uses of the American flag in art, from Captain America's helmet in *Easy Rider* to album covers like Ice Cube's *Death Certificate* and NOFX's *The War on Errorism*. From this point onward, Romero's work will be about how America cloaks its hypocrisies and inadequacies in the good old (blood) red, (bone) white, and (corpse) blue.

The next shot is forgettable, a six-second piece of adhesive material as the car pulls to a halt. I love it for its flaw: The bottom left corner of the frame is clipped by black. It's part of the camera lens hood, a doohickey used to stop sunlight from making lens flares. Back in ye olde days of shooting on film, these adjustable flanges were common gremlins in student and low-budget cinema. I find this flaw moving, in the same way blurry, off-guard snapshots of loved ones are moving. And there are countless more flaws to come.

You find the humanity of creators in their imperfections.

00:02:11

THE DAY THE TIME CHANGES

ONE OF THE BEST TOO-WEIRD-TO-BE-TRUE STORIES about *Night* is that Romero asked Betty Aberlin to star as Barbra. You won't recognize the name, but if you're old enough, you'll recognize her namesake role: Lady Aberlin, the principal character of the Neighborhood of Make-Believe that was the best part of *Mister Rogers' Neighborhood*. Aberlin was gentle and unintimidatingly pretty, and because she often comforted a little puppet named Daniel Striped Tiger, I—another Daniel—felt mothered by extension.

It's a shorter road than you'd think from Mr. Rogers's synthetic suburban street to *Night*'s isolated farmhouse. Per Tom Fallows's deep-dive into Romero's business dealings, *George A. Romero's Independent Cinema* (2022), the twenty-two-year-old Romero got a job at local WQED-TV heading up a series of films on "how to entertain youngsters in Pittsburgh." This segued into work on the "Picture, Picture" segments of *Mister Rogers' Neighborhood*, also shot at WQED. (Fellow Pittsburgher Michael Keaton would also work on "Picture, Picture.")

Among Romero's contributions were "How Lightbulbs Are Made," "Things That Feel Soft," and the eleven-minute opus "Let's Talk about Going to the Hospital," in which Mr. Rogers gets a tonsillectomy. Romero often joked it was the scariest thing he ever made. He wasn't totally wrong. There's an eeriness to Mr. Rogers's dreamy narration as he's given anesthetic gas ("And he showed me this mask and said, 'Why don't you try it on?'").

Romero liked to speak of his *Mr. Rogers* work as a pre-*Night* origin story, though in truth the timeline doesn't jibe. According to archival WQED papers, "Hospital" aired in either 1970 or 1971. Romero shot the segment *after* the release of *Night*. I actually prefer this version, as it illustrates how un-rich and unfamous the film made Image Ten; Romero had another decade of gig work still ahead of him. But I can't blame Romero for perpetuating the tale. One, it was a long time ago, and two, hey, it's a better story.

None of this means the story's punch line isn't true. Fred Rogers took Romero aside and politely (I mean, of course) asked Romero not to cast the costar of his children's program in his movie about flesh-eaters. Perhaps a more arrogant auteur would have said "Fuck you, Mr. Rogers!" but George was a go-along-get-along sort of dude.

Judith O'Dea was cast instead. Like everyone else in the movie, she was an unknown, unless you were an obsessive of Pittsburgh musical theater. She debuted in a local production of the musical *Leave It to Jane* at age fifteen (along with her future costar Russ Streiner), and worked as a traffic and weather reporter for WJAS Radio (using the name "Dawn O'Day," which predicted the titles of Romero's next two zombie films). At twenty-two she moved to L.A. to pursue acting, and indeed scored a commercial for Olympia Beer. Shortly after the move, she was called back to Pittsburgh by producer and costar Karl Hardman to audition for his odd little fright flick.

O'Dea then returned to the Golden State, where she continued to be involved in theater. She married the appropriately named Peter Younghusband and ended up at Hughes Aircraft teaching execs how to do oral presentations. O'Dea was pretty. But this was the era of the Elizabeth Taylor and Brigitte Bardot bombshell. The chip in O'Dea's front tooth alone limited her

Hollywood potential. Then there was the question of screen appeal. Of the six major cast members in *Night*, O'Dea often takes the critical brunt. I don't agree—I think she's perfect as Barb—but I concede I don't watch her and think "she could have been a superstar," which is something I *do* think every time her costar Duane Jones is on-screen. Though O'Dea has appeared in many stage productions since *Night*, her sole major film credit is a bit part in the 1978 TV movie *The Pirate*, in which she melts down in a very Barbra-like way.

O'Dea—a.k.a. Barbra—is introduced at 00:02:11, just as "Eerie Heavy Echo" fades out and the LeMans pulls to a halt right where the camera can look through the open passenger window. As the first human we see, there's a lot riding on Barbra. She needs to grab our attention. Instantly, she does the opposite, the character equivalent of the film's opening shot—bland and uninvolving. By now we understand this is intentional. A pattern is being established. It's a ballsy move, boring us on purpose, but it's going to pay off like gangbusters.

Barbra's vacuousness is epitomized by her hairstyle, a smooth, hot-rollered flip parted down the middle, a pair of blonde parentheses framing nothing. (O'Dea kept the "band fall" wig that created this look, until it was lost in a move.) Barb's eyes have the fuzzy focus I associate with shallow thinkers, and the first words out of her mouth, the first piece of dialogue in the film, enunciated in O'Dea's patrician accent, are the kind spoken by people constitutionally incapable of allowing conversational gaps.

"They ought to make the day the time changes the first day of summer."

I mean, what? If I was in that car, I'd groan. Now I have to discuss daylight saving time? The man behind the wheel responds in kind: "What?" Barbra flashes a perky smile that's grating after so long a ride: "Well, it's eight o'clock and it's still light." Like, I don't even know what she's saying. It's mindless chatter.

It does help establish stuff, though. Daylight saving in 1967, the year the film was shot, landed on Sunday, April 30. So that's the day the movie takes place. Or as Barbra (and the film's title) prefers it, the *night*. Eight o'clock p.m., Sunday, April 30, 1967—even documentaries rarely get so specific.

On a broader scale, 1967 sweltered with American tumult. The United States was in its third year of the Vietnam War and on pace to lose over eleven thousand soldiers in that calendar year alone. Martin Luther King Jr. was preaching nonviolence even as the streets were ablaze with race riots and antiwar demonstrations.

When Barbra arrives at the cemetery in her sleeveless dress, making small talk about the time change, *this* is the world she lives in, one of fire and fury and murder, all of it blocked from view, by her hairdo, by the LeMans windshield, by everything. We ought to view the "time change" Barbra mentions through the prism Bob Dylan introduced four years earlier. The *times*—that's what were a-changin'. Romero injected the plasma of these changes straight into the veins of *Night of the Living Dead*, whether he was aware of it or not.

00:02:21 WE STILL REMEMBER

Then there's Johnny. After nearly two and a half minutes of film, during which we've seen not as much as a single other car, Johnny is the spark plug we've been waiting for. In fact, in the first shot of the siblings, Barbra is a little soft. The person the lens is focused on is good old Johnny.

Johnny is a paragon of what today I might call "the angry nerd." White, slender, slicked hair, ostentatious glasses, ridiculous leather driving gloves, radiating a foppish intelligence, but with a cruel curve to his lips. An old Latent Image press binder containing cast breakdowns describes Johnny as "Early 20's. Barbara's brother. Pleasant, informed, interested in girls and cars." I buy the latter two descriptors, anyway.

Johnny's played by Russell Streiner, who cofounded both the Latent Image and Image Ten (as well as Theatre Service

Corporation, a short-lived company that made commercials for drive-ins). As of this writing, at age eighty-five, Streiner remains *Night*'s standard bearer, defender, and living memory. Like everyone in the film, he is perfectly cast. So perfectly cast that it's a relief to see him in behind-the-scenes photos holding clapboards and light meters. He looks perfectly nice—and is, in fact, legendarily convivial in real life. Quite the opposite of Johnny.

A quick word here on spellings. The script calls the character "John," and the closing credits don't award the character with a name at all. Over time, "Johnny" has won out over "Johnnie" or "Jonny" or even the "Johneee!" that appears in the script when Barbra whines. "Barbra," meanwhile, is even more tangled. In the script, it's "Barbara," but the closing credits (authored by Russ Streiner!) misspell it as "Barbra," another lovable error. The spelling elevates O'Dea's would-be heroine into rarefied air, with Streisand as the only other "Barbra" of note.

Barbra's peppy attitude is parried by Johnny's sour one and we swiftly learn why: "You know, we've still got a three-hour drive back. We're not going to be home until after midnight." It's 1967; one assumes Barbra can't drive and her brother was guilted into the job. That's six hours in a car with a brother who can't stop griping ("You think I want to blow Sunday on a scene like this?" he asks) and a sister giving herself an ulcer trying to keep things civil. Shortly, Johnny will ask if there's any candy left and we know why there isn't: The self-centered sonofabitch ate it all.

Finally, we get to the meat of it. Dialogue tells us that Barb and John have come to put a memorial on their father's grave at the behest of their mother, who lives in Pittsburgh. It's worthy to note that "three hours" (or "two hundred miles," as Johnny will soon specify) is not very close to Pittsburgh! In that time, you could make it to Cleveland, Charlottesville, D.C., Erie, or Buffalo. If they are still in Pennsylvania, they are either in the Appalachians (I don't see any mountains) or, more likely, the rolling hills of what is called the Allegheny Plateau.

In the script, Johnny identifies their location as Parkville.

There is a Parkville, Pennsylvania, though it's way the hell out east, near Baltimore. To add confusion, the film later identifies the area as Butler County, a half hour's drive *north* of Pittsburgh (where Evans City is actually located). None of this really matters except as excuse for me to say the following. We are nowhere. We are everywhere. Fitting for the beginning of civilization's end.

Wherever we are, dialogue will soon confirm the siblings grew up here. Johnny has a chip on his shoulder about it; I identify with that. Barbra, though, looks yearnful. There's a deer-meets-headlights quality to Barb that tells me Pittsburgh is too much city for her. Part of her wants to move back here. She has no idea that, in fact, she'll never leave.

I wonder how this setup resonated with the biggest *Night of the Living Dead* fan I knew as a kid: my mom. Susan Laura Kraus (née Jeffrey) grew up in Chicago. In 1980, when she was twenty-seven and I was four, she moved with her young family to Fairfield, Iowa, a town best known for the Maharishi International University, an untraditional college grounded in transcendental meditation that would eventually attract such disciples as David Lynch and Jim Carrey. When I was a kid, it wasn't unusual to hear of S. E. Hinton–style teen rumbles between the "roos" (slang for "gurus") and the "townies" (the rest of us hillbillies).

My mom died at age fifty-two, and years later, my older sister, Jenny, while working on a family history, turned to Susan's childhood friends to understand her thoughts on leaving the city. Susan, she learned, idealized country life and had been excited about the move. So both Susan and Barbra got what they wanted. But what you want is never exactly what you need, is it? In a sense, Susan and Barbra were driven out to rural communities and plunked into houses inside which they would have to survive.

Johnny wants to move the grave to Pittsburgh. This upsets Barbra. Naturally: Disinterring a loved one is a reliably upsetting notion. The funeral industry's night-club-magician sleight of hand, the embalming, the pricey casket, the plot, the stone, the ceremony, the suits and dresses, the pleasant music, the handshakes and hugs—all of it crumbles like soil when the casket comes back up. What's left? Body decomp and the awareness that nothing you did (and paid out the wazoo for) made any difference in the end.

Johnny lifts a plastic cross, festooned with plastic flowers, from the back seat. (If you squint, you'll find Romero and his camera reflected in chrome beside the driver-side window.) Johnny mocks the cross. It says WE STILL REMEMBER but he insists he doesn't. This renunciation of familial respect is jarring. Sure, people had such conversations in 1967, but not onscreen. If first-time watchers were bored by the car ride, now they're sitting at attention. Death isn't being handled with kid gloves, or even leather driving gloves. Johnny has taken them off.

00:03:04 A TECHNICAL PROBLEM

Barbra ends the grousing by rolling up her window and getting out. Johnny follows suit but is distracted by a radio squelch. This always strikes me as odd. I'm pretty sure radios in old cars don't play when keys are out of the ignitions.

In any case, a broadcaster with a stiff transatlantic accent (the voice of costar Karl Hardman) apologizes to listeners for going off-air "due to a technical problem." Johnny shrugs and turns off the (already-off) radio. While not intrinsically creepy, a library-cue sting by William Loose and Jack Cookerly entitled "Night Suspense (JB-33)" begs to differ. A minor-key clarinet scores Johnny, grave ornament in hand, as he catches up to Barbra: "There's nothing wrong with the radio. Must've been the station." Our first hint of sci-fi, and one Romero would work hard to scrub away in his five subsequent zombie films.

It's our first full view of the siblings. Johnny's in a dark suit (blue in reality) with a loud paisley tie, both of which flop as carelessly as his hairdo. The dork's got Flair markers in his shirt pocket. In a commentary track recorded at the Hardman-Eastman facility in Pittsburgh for the 1994 Elite Entertainment 25th Anniversary Collector's Edition LaserDisc (the first release licensed by Image Ten, as well as the first restoration), O'Dea states with authority that Johnny's an engineer. All right. (The gang got an $8,000 advance and 40 percent of receipts for the Elite LaserDisc, but ran into a roadblock that Elite's Vini Bancalari (also known to fans as Zombie Feasting on Fisher's Dead Body in *Day of the Dead*), warned them about in a circa-1995 letter: "The recent announcement of a new 'optical disc' format, DVD (digital video disc), has really caused many buyers to hold back a bit in their buying." Image Ten's luck in a nutshell.)

Barbra, by contrast, is not an engineer. I'll eat my hat if she's employed at all. She's buckled and belted into a tailored poplin raincoat of straitjacket snugness, and she pulls it even snugger, a physicalization of her dutiful, repressed, literally buttoned-up character.

Look at the siblings' left hands. Wedding bands, both of them. This surprised me when I noticed it. Because Barbra and Johnny exist out of time (we never learn anything about them), I always imagined them both as single. But this was 1967. If you weren't married by age thirty, folks might assume you were living an alternative lifestyle. Johnny I sort of get; I imagine him driving some poor wife to popping pills. Barbra, though, seems like the sort who wouldn't shut up about her husband, taking everything he said as gospel. That she doesn't mention him once in *Night* makes me entertain darker options. He's dead and grief has turned Barb into the nervous wreck we see. Or he's an abuser, and that's why she enlisted asshole Johnny today, anything to get away from the monster waiting for her back home.

The forty-acre Evans City Cemetery sits in the southwest corner of Jackson Township in Butler County. Right behind the siblings is the cemetery's only building, a little brick chapel. We glimpsed a reflection of it earlier in Barbra's car window, meaning there's no spatial cheating here; everything in reality is where it is in the film. The white panels over the chapel's windows could be shutters, but I think they are boards, indications the chapel was being used to store gardening gear in 1967. *Night*'s crew used it for craft services.

It makes sense, then, that the 1923 building was scheduled for demolition in 2011 until *Night* sound engineer Gary Streiner (Russ's younger brother, who joined the Latent Image while still in college) raised fifty grand in a Fix the Chapel fundraiser (and then, along with several others, got a tattoo of the chapel). With assistance from Pittsburgh engineer Don Gilmore, the chapel received a new foundation, roof, columned porch, and was bestowed with historical status—all of which helped shift Evans City's perspective on the film that, until then, some locals had scorned. Today you can even get married in the chapel, if necropolis nuptials appeal to you. A photo from the 2014 Living Dead Festival shows nearly all surviving cast and crew on the chapel's new porch, including Judith O'Dea and Russell Streiner. Yes, Barb and Johnny drove all the way back out there, hopefully with a working radio this time.

The duo spends thirty-five seconds searching for their dad's grave and bickering. The fact that most genre films center on romantic couples makes *Night*'s sibling relationship fresh and increased my investment as a child. I didn't care about romance, but sibling rivalries? I had two sisters, and my feeling was that my older one, Jenny, got all the trust and privileges while my younger one, Julie, was the coddled baby. There's truth to this appraisal, but it's also true I, in what felt like caged frustration, was a jerk to both of them. Jenny deflected me with enervating ease. Julie, though, didn't have the tools. Her peaceful play filled me with jealousy; I felt none of that peace. The energy I devoted to snuffing her joy remains one of my life's most stinging regrets.

In other words, I was Johnny.

I'm not being metaphorical. Let me explain.

On March 16, 1991, when I was fifteen, my dad, a southern Illinois farm boy who moved to Iowa to work in soil conservation, inexplicably came home with a camcorder. (Perhaps not so inexplicably: The day before, our dog, Penny, had run away and gotten killed by a car, an incident I, probably unfairly, blamed on my dad. The camera might have been an apology.) The camcorder wasn't VHS, Super VHS, Betamax, or Hi8, but the extremely weird format of mini-VHS. To watch what you shot, you popped a blocky little tape into a VHS-shaped holster before inserting it into a VCR. So, like VHS, but even shittier.

My family toyed with it for a bit, but soon I established squatter's rights. Over the next five years, I spent much of my free time directing a series of increasingly ambitious movies. To wit, my first outing, *Kat Killer* (shot on May 17, 1991, in unedited sequence, as I had no editing equipment) was five minutes long, while my magnum opus, shot in 1993–1994, *The Godfathers, Part Two*, was a soul-crushing two hours and forty minutes. I made these under the cringey moniker "Danman Productions" and aired them on a fledgling public access station broadcasted from the local library with all the pomp and circumstance of a teen employee pressing play on a VCR.

My siblings and friends became an adolescent Image Ten, everyone contributing (poorly but enthusiastically) in front of and behind the camera. If Jami was being stabbed, Julie was mixing the blood he'd spew. If Julie was being decapitated by hedge clippers, Shad was cueing her when to start screaming. Our budgets were less than *Night*'s original $6,000 (typically they were $0), but as we progressed, I began shelling out for props and music.

Once I was too broke to buy a cassette tape I wanted for soundtrack music and told Joe (my most frequent leading man and, perversely, our worst actor) that if he bought it for me, I'd thank him if I ever won an Oscar. The wild thing is, a quarter-century later, a story idea I had as a kid evolved into the Oscar-winning *The Shape of Water*. Sadly for Joe, it didn't earn me a turn at the Dolby Theatre stage mic. (Though I did get to see, in person, George Romero's picture come up in the Oscars' "In Memoriam" section, as Eddie Vedder crooned through Tom Petty's "Room at the Top.")

One of my Danman Productions was *Night of the Living Dead*. It wasn't the only remake in my adolescent oeuvre; I had previously shot mini-versions of *Misery* and *The Blob*. It shouldn't surprise you that my version of *Night* remains the most watchable Danman Production. When my English teacher, Mr. Slechta, showed it in class, the applause was genuine. Love drips off every auto-focus shot. The fact that it's only ten minutes long makes what I chose to include from Romero's film revealing.

Shot on August 8, 1991—two weeks after another rewatch of Image Ten's *Night*—my version begins with me as Johnny and sister Julie as Barbra. Siblings playing siblings. Instead of Evans City Cemetery, we're in our backyard beside a grave marker made from two nailed-together sticks. This "grave" sits between a hay bale my dad used for bowhunting practice and a random cinder block. We're both wearing shorts. This was practically law in Danman Productions: Everyone must wear shorts. I've got chicken legs. I'm wearing a T-shirt from the school tennis team. But just like Russ Streiner, I complain about the long drive.

Several seconds later, my character dies on the grass (right alongside the clearly visible script). I often cast myself as the first character to die; it got me back behind the camera where I belonged. But I like to think there's a little more here going on. As Daniel, I was a jerk to Julie, and as Johnny, I paid for it.

I didn't come to my jackass style of moviemaking out of nowhere. Image Ten was to blame. They instilled within me a profound, lifelong affection for indie filmmaking. I'm not talking about "indie film" as applied to, say, *Pulp Fiction* ($8.5 million budget). I'm talking the real stuff. The shooting-on-nights-and-weekends stuff. The we-might-all-die-if-this-special-effect-goes-wrong stuff. I'm talking *Equinox* ($8,000), *The Battery* ($6,000), *Black Devil Doll from Hell* ($10,000), and *Bone Sickness* ($4,000).

The importance of art like this grows by the day. In a world where AI and CGI create seamless visual media, seeing those seams right where fallible human hands put them is everything—it's proof of intent, of passion, of life itself.

No-budget filmmaking is an especially American folly-slash-miracle, the dreams of the anonymous cauldroned in backyards and basements in hopes of acknowledgment. Of what? That their designs matter. That *they* matter. Much of this cinema falls into the horror genre, for horror is our equalizer. Cancer, car crashes, school shootings, they pluck us out at random. Horror fiction cancels out our IOUs of existential dread. That must be why I write it. Especially when you consider what a nervous, fearful child I was.

Conversely, the emotion generated by no-budget horror is rarely terror. It's joy. Delight. Admiration and love. Every cruddy prosthetic (*Night* has several) and substandard effect reveal our dreams to one another. It doesn't matter if it's Steven Spielberg and Tobe Hooper building extravagant *Poltergeist* effects on an MGM soundstage, Image Ten splattering chocolate-syrup blood in Pittsburgh, or Danman Productions doing god knows what in Iowa.

Call it Don Quixote Disease. Or just call it the American spirit. It's not the finished product that matters, it's the chase of it. *Night of the Living Dead* is a literal and symbolic chase all the way through, and that's why I love it.

00:04:07 CHURCH WAS THIS MORNING

At last, Barbra spots her father's grave and the siblings approach a low, wedge-shaped headstone. We can't see the engraved names, but if you visit Evans City Cemetery, you'll find the stone marks the resting place of Grace and George Cole. We would be within our imaginative rights to call Grace and George the mother and father of Barbra and Johnny. Barbra Cole? Johnny Cole? I like the sound of it. (Anyway, it's better than "Ozarowski," as suggested by the unofficial and not-too-good comic book spinoff *Rise*.)

The larger stone next to it—tarnished today from all the fans who touch it—belongs to Samuel Q. Blair, 1836–1909, who, as it happens, served as a first sergeant on Little Round Top at Gettysburg. (That's not even *Night*'s closest Civil War connection:

zombie extra Colin Fitch was the great-great-grandson of Union general William Tecumseh Sherman.) There's a tall tree next to the Cole stone in this shot, but it's gone now, a victim of the so-called Beaver Falls Tornado of May 31, 1985, part of "a twilight filled with terror," *The Pittsburgh Press* reported, that "ripped clothes off people's backs, killed at least 46, and injured hundreds in at least 11 Pennsylvanian counties." The F4 twister that hit Evans City knocked down tons of cemetery trees and, according to Jack Russo, pulled *two hundred bodies* out of the ground. (Pretty much everyone else disputes this.)

The post-tornado photos are most easily viewed in *The Farmhouse Seven*, a peculiar coffee-table book self-published by Jeff Moreno in 2022. I'm tempted to discount this text for both its shoddy grammar and the fact that it's plastered throughout with roughly seventy celebrity quotes Moreno apparently obtained at fan conventions—and rather comically, over half these celebs, from Anthony Michael Hall to the Soup Nazi, admit to never having seen *Night*! Yet the book is rich in arcana, and due to the contributions of Richard Ricci and Judith O'Dea, must be contemplated.

Farmhouse Seven's cemetery pictures are insane, with headstones rolled like dice, trees spilled like toothpicks, and caskets exposed by collapsed mausoleum walls. When trees that big fall, their root systems can upchuck almost anything. In 2024, Pennsylvania Cable Network released *The Living Dead Reunion*, a documentary on the film's fifty-fifth anniversary, in which Romero historian Lawrence DeVincentz walks viewers through the film's cemetery scene versus how the joint looks today. All the trees that *aren't* there is shocking.

Anyway, it's a lovely shot, the two stones creating negative spaces that Barb and John perfectly fill. Each hides their discomfort in a specific way. Barbra, in another smart bit of business by O'Dea, toys with the leaves of a dangling branch. Johnny kneels to stab the plastic cross into the grave. He remains brash, but brashness in a graveyard is bluster. You can't be surrounded by that many dead bodies and sustain a belief that you're special. The dead will wait you out. They'll get you. Johnny has no idea how soon.

The bluff he chooses is sarcasm about the plastic cross. "Yeah, a little spit and polish, [the caretaker] can clean this up, sell it next year. Wonder how many times we bought the same one." Another clever joke; Barbra has no hope of keeping up with her brother. To some viewers, that makes her a simp, but it makes me like her all the more.

Johnny steps to the side and so begins *Night*'s first immortal sequence. It's like a switch gets thrown, like the wire prongs of the plastic cross have plugged into a spectral outlet. Suddenly, the foregrounded Johnny pops so crisply that the cemetery looks like Old-Hollywood rear projection. The audio choices are similarly stunning. Aside from a twitchy reproach from Johnny ("Hey, come on, Barb, church was this morning, huh?"), there's suddenly no dialogue. Romero instead lays a bed of sound effects: a breathy wind, the grumble of a developing storm. The moment *feels* like a storm, queasy and anticipatory, the world gone thin enough for something otherworldly to soak through.

It goes on like this for forty seconds, an eternity of screen time. That's ten seconds longer than the camera lingers on Michael Corleone's face before he plugs Sollozzo. All the action is at the grave with Barbra, yet Romero affixes us to Johnny so we can sense his loosening grip on a situation he's tried to keep at ironic arm's length.

Abruptly there's a jump cut, probably because Romero couldn't match the shots in editing, but maybe, just maybe, to disrupt a film that thus far has been naturalistic. It steals a breath from your lungs: One frame, Johnny's looking down to the right, and the next, he's looking up to the left, and we've punched into a close-up, Johnny's face saturated in white light, a nuclear blast or alien landing, we assume, until our brain registers the thunderclap.

It's lightning. But from where? It's odd enough to be a dream sequence, except this dream will last for the remainder of the film. For the remainder of *all* Romero's zombie films. The first two sequels, *Dawn of the Dead* and *Day of the Dead*, begin with their heroes waking up. Over and over, Romero's protagonists try to rouse themselves from their nightmare present, but they never do.

It's no secret how Image Ten made the lightning. A disproportionate amount of production stills (and pretty much all the color ones) depict this scene, which makes sense, as it was, for the most part, the final scene shot. That's usually when harried indie filmmakers realize, oh shit, we didn't take enough photos. One of these stills shows the janky-looking Colortran light (the Latent Image owned two sets of lights, Colortran 1000s and Colortran 750s) that the crew turned on and off for the lightning effect. I have a distrust of these lights. My experience with them shooting 16mm film in the 1990s was that they turned scorching in seconds and periodically exploded. White-hot glass shards once melted a carpeted apartment floor my broke ass had to pay for.

Come to think of it, an overheated quartz light is an apt metaphor for this moment: Something is about to explode. *Night* could be the first motion picture you ever saw and still you'd sense it. The full suite of cinema's gears—light, shadow, composition, sound, movement—all turn in harmony, an awesome whole far more than the sum of its dinky parts. For all his nascent prowess, George A. Romero could not have pulled off such alchemy on purpose. No one can.

00:05:11 THEY'RE COMING TO GET YOU, BARBRA

Here it is, then, a shot on par with Bela Lugosi looming on the cobwebbed castle staircase in *Dracula* or Boris Karloff shambling through the laboratory door in *Frankenstein*: the birth of a modern monster. It's only due to an intentional lack of drama that the shot isn't as legendary as those Universal Monster reveals. Romero fills his frame not with sky but with ground—*Night* is highly invested in ground—leaving only the top third of the frame to leafless trees that dangle like sorcerer fingers. It resembles the wide shot of Dracula's staircase right *before* Lugosi's famous close-up. Dracula and this wandering fellow, known to fans as "Zombie #1," are in the same area of the screen and are of equal comparative size. White men in suits, that's all we know of them yet, but honestly, is there any demographic more dangerous?

It's an offhand shot, a distant figure walking slowly amid shrubs and stones. As with the U.S. flag shot, Romero rarely misses a chance to put something notable into the foreground. This time it's a grave ornament shaped like a sheriff's star. I like to think of it as representing law and order, both of which are about to go belly-up.

Despite half a century of crappy-looking transfers that made *Night* look as if shot on 8mm film and dragged through Chernobyl, newer transfers reveal the pristine 35mm negative. Different film stocks have different sizes of grain (*Night* was shot on Plus X, Four X, and Tri X, distinctions I used to understand), and Romero had to expect 16mm copies to be struck from the final master, which would muddy the picture. And yet he's able to place Zombie #1 in the perfect spot to be noticed by viewers while still being too far off to discern details. The only impression I get from his slow gait is that he's not going anywhere in particular. And that's worrisome.

What kind of person is going nowhere in a cemetery?

Johnny puts his driving gloves back on (a flub: we saw him leave the gloves in the car), a sign that he's ready to skedaddle. Still off-screen, Barbra chides her brother for not going to church, to which he replies, "Well, there's not much sense in my going to church." What Romero might be saying here (and I do believe it's Romero: the line isn't in the Russo-Romero script) is that there's not much sense in *any* of us in going to church, it's not going to help in the end. It's quintessential Romero to put words of wisdom in the mouths of his antagonists. It's a direct lesson I put to use in my own work.

Johnny shares a memory of scaring his sister in the cemetery when they were small, causing their grandpa to admonish Johnny (in a German accent), "Boy, you'll be damned to hell!" Barb, as a rule, is barely holding herself together, and this spooks her enough to bolt upright and stride past Johnny.

I know all about older-brother radar, and Johnny's goes off: He smells his sister's fear. Barbra walks straight at the camera, telling Johnny to stop it. No way. He steps to the center of the frame as Barbra rushes off. To keep Johnny centered, Romero pans the camera a few inches to the right, and at 00:06:03 there's a jerk in the pan, a little lurch akin to driving across a patch of ice. This happens when tripod heads are poorly calibrated, a plague I suffered for a decade as a documentary filmmaker.

Of all the tech glitches in *Night*, this is my favorite. I know this stutter by heart. I wait for it on each viewing. It helps that this is probably the most famous shot in the whole film, as it contains the most famous line of dialogue. Two seconds after the pan, Johnny raises his pitch, adopts a Peter Lorre accent, and says in playful, loony singsong, "They're coming to get you, Barbra."

The line's ambiguity is why it has come to represent the film. Johnny doesn't say the *undead* are coming. He doesn't say *aliens* are coming. He doesn't say what these comers are going to *do*. Just that *something* is coming. No three words better nutshell the horror genre. I say this line as Johnny in my Danman Production version. Not just once. Three times. (The 2004 Romero homage *Shaun of the Dead*, which Romero himself loved, even manages a nod, with the character Ed shouting into a phone, "We're coming to get you, Barbara!")

The line shows up in every horror best-of ever made, including the biggest springboard of my adolescent horror journey, Stephen King's genre study *Danse Macabre* (1981). When I donated my King collection to an Iowa library in 2009, my tattered *Danse* paperback was the only book I kept. I have visceral memories of reading it in spring 1988. I recall reading about *Dawn of the Dead* in the cold plastic seats of the doctor's office where I got weekly allergy shots. I recall sitting on our front steps, squinting in the sun, reading King's fairy-tale synopsis of *Night*, which he ends with Johnny's catchphrase.

My second-biggest horror springboard was the 1984 documentary *Terror in the Aisles*, which, for some reason one October, played incessantly on MTV. Hosted by genre icons Nancy Allen and Donald Pleasence, the doc doesn't have much depth, but as a compendium of clips, it was a revelation. The doc's definition of *horror* is wonderfully liberal, and introduced me to films (maddeningly unlabeled, though) that were filed under "Adventure" at Adventureland Video: *Dressed to Kill, Klute, When a Stranger Calls, Marathon Man, Wait Until Dark, Play Misty for Me, Nighthawks,* and *Vice Squad* (which, surprisingly, has the scariest clips of the whole doc). *Psycho* and *Night of the Living Dead* are the only black-and-white films given significant screen time and were all the more impactful because of it.

(Pausing here to pour one out for Adventureland Video, a place even more influential on me than the public library. From 1988 to 1995, the cramped, 800-square-foot, oppressively brown video store rented us VCRs before we owned one, and Nintendos, too, to my luckier friends. Though part of a chain, the Adventureland Video of 110 S. Court Street felt sui generis, from its brown-pebbled plastic VHS cases—I bought one on eBay but it reeks of smoke and mildew—to its sweet deals: $6 for two tapes, with Saturday rentals not due till Monday, a lifetime away. The joint even had its own lore. One day, a freaking *bat* was found perched on a vampire-flick VHS and handily removed by a garbage worker who happened to be browsing.)

Streiner seems to have partially improvised his famous line. The screenplay dictates the more brutish "They're gonna get you," while the 1974 novelization, penned by co-scripter Jack Russo, narrows it to "He's coming to get you." Both documents go further in describing what, exactly, is coming, with Johnny taunting, "They're coming out of their graves."

Thank god Johnny doesn't say this in the film. For him to magically assess what's happening before it happens would be hugely anticlimactic. Romero's art-film enthusiasms had taught him how opacity pays dramatic dividends. What Romero kept, however, was the postmodernist recognition that we are, in fact, in a horror flick. It's a tactic more revolutionary than anything Wes Craven would do twenty-eight years later in *Scream* (a property Romero turned down).

Being the little sister, Barbra can't handle Johnny. Instead of simply ignoring him, she huffs and puffs. He's "ignorant." He's "acting like a child." This is fuel for the cruel. Johnny spiders his arms over gravestones, looks at the tall man lumbering in the distance, and cries, "Look! There comes one of them now."

The cutaway to the man is closer than before but still reveals little. White or gray hair. Favoring his right arm. Staring straight on despite the sibling ruckus. Johnny goes beyond the pale now, grabbing Barbra and fearfully saying, "I'm getting out of here." He dashes away, right in front of the mystery man, who's suddenly ten feet away. A bad cut (did he teleport?), but one that conveys the sense that things are unfolding too fast.

Technically this is the second handheld shot of the film, but practically it's the first, and that's sturdy directing: The camera is literally and figuratively off the tripod in the same way the audience's feet are off terra firma. The shot lurches alongside Zombie #1, whose suit, we notice, is dirty.

In a feature called "Limitations into Virtues" on the Criterion edition of *Night*, Tony Zhou and Taylor Ramos stopwatch each shot in this sequence beginning with "They're coming to get you, Barbra." Each shot is shorter than the previous: 333 frames, 142 frames, 111 frames, 84 frames, 72 frames. Barbra misses the threat of this accelerated pace. She's mortified. She stuffs her hands into her coat and proceeds past the man with her eyes downcast, probably wishing that she was dead.

00:06:34

HE HAD AN OLD SUIT

NIGHT WAS SHOT ON A USED CAMERA CALLED THE Arriflex 35 IIC. The Latent Image—who, by 1967, had seen its annual gross rise from $10,000 to $400,000—purchased the Arri with the $90,000 they earned from their biggest job yet, a sixty-second Calgon commercial spoofing *Fantastic Voyage*, which was a 1966 special-effects extravaganza about a submarine crew (including Raquel Welch) shrunk down to microscopic size in order to float through the body of a scientist and repair his brain. In the ad, a ship full of "Calgonauts" is sent inside a washing machine and gets trapped in the fibers of a dirty T-shirt, where they proceed to combat "gray, dull-looking laundry." It features three key *Night* actors, Karl Hardman, Judy Ridley, and Russ Streiner. (Note: Some say the gang bought the Arri with proceeds from a tourist-aimed State Department of Commerce short titled *Autumn in Pennsylvania*.)

I used Arris in college. They felt like World War II weaponry: cold, heavy, indestructible, and unwieldy even without the noise-buffering blimp required if you had any hope of recording clean dialogue. Blows to an Arri could, and did, knock the lens from the housing, open the magazine and expose the negative, and a dozen other catastrophes I was unlucky enough to witness. If you went handheld, you had to mean it.

Romero meant it. Production photos show him having a smarter rig than I had thirty years later, one that rests the camera's weight on his left hand while his right hand operates the pistol trigger—"You could completely run-and-gun with it," Romero said. A cable trails backward toward a battery that is stationary unless Romero is shooting "wild" (without sound), in which case the battery is held by someone shadowing his movements, usually one of the two sound engineers, Marshall Booth (who became an esteemed doctor of pharmacology; his final paper was on feline bladder control) or Gary Streiner. Keep in mind that *Night*'s honorifics were, in part, attempts to make the finished film look professional. Everyone did everything.

After a final shot of Johnny looking over his shoulder with an asshole smirk, Zombie #1 grabs Barbra by the throat. We cut to his raging face, super tight, the tightest we've been on anyone, too close, in fact, for the Arri to focus. A white, snarling, blurry face, eyes bugged, a grimace of dirty teeth (they used black licorice), our vision overwhelmed as our ears suffer a loud, sustained, heart-attack musical sting.

The 180-degree rule is a cinematic principle that helps movie watchers maintain directional sanity: When two people in conversation are depicted in alternating shots, one consistently faces right, the other left. It is often betrayed by amateurs overwhelmed with other things to think about, and in this moment, Romero falls prey. Barbra is looking left when she's grabbed. The subsequent close-up of the grabber? Also left.

But there's no lemon *Night* can't squeeze into delicious lemonade. To our cinema-trained brains, a leftward-facing zombie comes out of nowhere, as if he and a twin played a trick on Barb. The error is productively disorienting, upending everything we know about how films work, even if we don't know we know them. (Imagine this chapter required turning pages the opposite direction. You'd notice.)

Until now, *Night of the Living Dead* has been foreboding, maybe. Eerie, perhaps. All at once, it's shocking. A man who showed no interest at all in our siblings is now attacking Barbra, face to her chest like he's trying to get at her throat. Quickies of the era don't operate like this. Every scare is telegraphed a mile out with ponderous foreshadowing, ratcheting music, dramatic angles, and narrative convention.

Barbra's attacker is different in every way.

He's not just the world's first modern zombie. He's the first golem of a frightening new age. This sounds histrionic, but he's Vietnam. He comes out of nowhere. He doesn't fight how we think fights are fought. He looks unthreatening until abruptly he's killing us. He's a terrorist you can't blame for his terrorism, because Barb and John are terrorists too: They pumped their father full of embalming poison and stuffed him into the soil. Environmental terrorism. Organs that could have saved lives going rotten. Name one good thing about the siblings. You can't. They bicker over inanities while the world burns.

Johnny says they're coming to get you?

No. We, collectively, should come and get *them*.

More *Night of the Living Dead* products feature Zombie #1 than any other character, despite that his total screen time is, by my stopwatch, roughly four minutes. Who wants to display a Barbra doll? A limited audience. But Zombie #1? Right now on eBay, you have your choice of a $100 eight-inch figure or a $203 twelve-inch figure. Or, for that matter, a $60 slip of paper the actor scrawled with "I'm coming to get you—#1 Zombie." It's quite the windfall for an actor who was cast because, in Russ Streiner's words, he "was there and old enough and thin enough and he had an old suit."

The old-enough, thin-enough, suit-owning guy was named Samuel William Hinzman, better known as Bill Hinzman, though *Night*'s hapless closing credits misspell it as "Heinzman." Streiner's quote makes it sound as if Hinzman was just wandering through the graveyard that day. In fact, Hinzman was doing photo work with the Latent Image when Streiner hipped him to their horror flick. (Hinzman had also worked as a police photographer, so he was no stranger to filming corpses.) He threw in some money, did camerawork with Romero, and like most everyone else, appeared as a zombie in the farmhouse scenes.

An especially good zombie too. With his bony frame, teetering yaw, and gnashing bottom jaw, Hinzman outshone other ghouls. Years later, he spoke of the "body English" of his portrayal; his inspiration was Boris Karloff in 1936's *The Walking Dead* (which indeed involves a dead man returning to life, via a mechanical heart).

Cowriter Russo was originally cast as Zombie #1, but when it came time to shoot, Russo, still in full zombie makeup, preferred to load film magazines. (Romero had even taught Judith O'Dea to load film—a nerve-racking task that used to make my hands sweat.) Hinzman, though, was the camera expert, and went on to serve as cinematographer for two excellent Romero projects, *The Crazies* and *The Amusement Park*, as well as *O.J. Simpson: Juice on the Loose*, the most notable chapter of "The Winners," a package of sports profile docs Romero directed and/or produced and sold to ABC, all of which are more unvarnished and fascinating than sports profiles made today.

Hinzman got to direct with *The Majorettes* (1986), a slasher adapted from the 1979 novel by (guess who?) Jack Russo. Two years later, Hinzman wrote and directed *FleshEater* (a nod to *Night*'s original title, though the film has also been released as *Revenge of the Living Zombies* and *Zombie Nosh*), as well as starring as the central zombie. Though the role is credited as "FleshEater," Hinzman is clearly playing Zombie #1, a fact that intrigues even leery fans like me. This makes *FleshEater* a sketchy third cousin to *Night*, one lacking Romero's intellect and ambition, but ably delivering teens, tits, and torture. Only in a final twenty minutes that directly copies *Night* does *FleshEater* summon some pathos.

That's the extent of Hinzman's directorial output, though acting cameos persisted through 2016, four years after his death, with the release of *Devil Ant 3: Son of Devil Ant* (directed by my favorite bizarro auteur, David "the Rock" Nelson). In articles about Hinzman's 2012 death, his daughter said, "He always joked with me that if he got buried he would come back."

I never met Hinzman, but he comes off well in interviews—levelheaded, reflective, appreciative, even a little sad. In the 2009 documentary *Autopsy of the Dead* (the first two hundred copies came packaged with a random photo autographed by cast or crew), Hinzman gives full credit for *Night*'s success to Romero ("the nerve center of that film") but also appears to lament the loss of their close relationship. Romero had been best man at Hinzman's wedding. It all seems like such a long time ago.

We can't help what we become known for. I'd like to be known for my largely unread historical epic *The Death and Life of Zebulon Finch*, but far more likely I'll end up as the Guy Who Wrote That Whale Book or as an asterisk on *The Shape of Water*. Hinzman's life was defined by that autumn day he spent lurching around Evans City Cemetery. His big attack scene is not only historic. If you have any sympathy for life's unapologetic whims, it's moving too.

00:06:37 NICHOLAS KRAMER

A thing I like to point out to new viewers of *Night*: The instant Johnny sees Barbra get attacked, he rushes to her rescue, rips the attacker off her, and fights him to the death. Johnny might have been insufferable from the moment we met him, but in the end, he's a hero.

Night is full of reversals like this, bad guys showing unexpected jolts of heroism or wisdom. This had a big impact on me as a young writer, though I don't think the notion solidified until a college film class screened John Cassavetes's *Faces*, the *other* most influential indie of 1968. There's a sequence in which Gena Rowlands picks up a guy at a go-go club, the kind of disposable lug films have taught us to discount. And yet this himbo ends up saving her from a suicide attempt. I didn't see that coming. That, for me, became a major goal of my art. Don't let them see it coming. In real life, people are complicated.

Image Ten employed no fight choreographer. For twenty-six seconds, Streiner and Hinzman go at it, hard, and the second half of their fight plays out sans music and dialogue, the only sounds being clothing and flesh. It's awkward and ungainly as only real fights are. Both go down at some point but get back up and grapple and fumble and flail, and in one particularly realistic moment, Johnny's glasses are torn off.

The whole thing makes you wince. Cemeteries have a lot of hard stones.

That's exactly how the fight ends. Zombie #1 brings Johnny to the ground and Johnny's head strikes a grave marker (belonging to Clyde Lewis Myers, 1903–1966, which means he was buried for a year, max, before his marker became a prop). If you watch it in slow motion (and silent, as the meaty thump, accomplished by striking a honeydew melon, is too convincing), you'll notice Streiner's head never hits stone. But it's too close for comfort, one of many examples of the filmmakers dodging catastrophe.

Anyway, that's a wrap on Johnny.

Actually, that's not *entirely* a wrap on Johnny, but we'll get to that later.

During the fight, Romero cuts three times to Barbra, who (and this is going to be a pattern) doesn't help. Rather, she death-grips a roughly five-foot obelisk. The dramatic angle and O'Dea's horrified expression make this her most famous shot, one that every visitor to Evans City Cemetery is obligated to re-create, myself included, on what my photo metadata tells me was 6:34 p.m. on Tuesday, October 22, 2019.

Adam Hart took the photo. We had a hell of a time finding the obelisk. We consulted all five thousand of Evans City Cemetery's graves before stumbling across the famous stone in what Vol. IV of the *Butler County Cemetery Inventory* tells me is Section Two. It was right near where we parked. We felt dumb for not thinking like low-budget filmmakers. Naturally Image Ten chose a headstone close to their vehicles. Why tow heavy equipment any farther? We also should have noticed the oxidized coins lying atop the famous headstones. It's a custom borrowed from military cemeteries, where leaving a penny means you visited, a nickel means you were with the deceased at boot camp, a dime means you served together, and a quarter means you were with the service member when they died. (Image Ten briefly got into the coin biz in 2018 by licensing one hundred copies of the *Night of the Living Dead Premium 50th Anniversary Coin & Book Celebration Set*, featuring a three-inch silver medallion emblazed with Zombie #1.)

Coins coat the famous obelisk like armadillo scutes.

Highly visible in the shot are the carved words NICHOLAS KRAMER, FEB 18 1842—MAR 17 1917. Kramer accomplished a lot in his seventy-five years. The *Cemetery Inventory* lists "G.A.R." after his name, not a reference to George A. Romero but rather the Grand Army of the Republic—Kramer soldiered in the Civil War and later survived a 1904 shooting attempt as Evans City's police constable. If you visit his gravestone today, you won't notice that it's facing a different way than in the film. Upon discovering the four-sided stone toppled from the Beaver Falls Tornado, fans Dave Burian and Christian Stavrakis (accompanied by *Night* actor Kyra Schon, visiting the cemetery for her very first time!) supermanned the thousand-pound rock back onto its plinth; they mounted it a quarter-turn to the north to hide a damaged back corner.

The next shot of Zombie #1 is the iconic image we've been waiting for: shot from the ground, tight on Hinzman's pasty face as he looks up from his crouch over Johnny while lightning flashes. To paraphrase a line from Romero's *Creepshow*, I'll be dipped in shit if this ain't an homage to Boris Karloff's *Frankenstein* close-up. It's the only time Hinzman looks like what the script and novelization describe as a "huddled figure."

The huddle is brief. The trombone blare of a pulsing library cue credited to William Loose and John Seely called "Heavy Agitato (TC-416)" (that TC stands for "Theme Craft," the tag that dominates the Hi-"Q" Library) gives Zombie #1 the signal to clamber to his feet. This track is also known by the much cooler "The Monster Walks," and pops up in an episode of the old TV show *The Fugitive* as Richard Kimble fights the One-Armed Man.

Barbra's paralysis breaks. She runs. Nine seconds later, Judith O'Dea executes one of cinema's foundational woman-trips-while-being-chased falls. To be fair, women's clothing has never been conducive to fleeing. Heels go sideways and skirts limit stride length. Even underwear can be restrictive: The pistachio-colored underwire bra and Lycra pantie girdle Barb wears in Tim Foley's 2015 novelty book *Scream Queens Paper Dolls* (exactly what it sounds like) are probably pretty accurate. One gets the impression Barbra's upbringing has been traditional; she likely considers it her job to be docile and meek. She probably hasn't run since high school.

The flop of her left ankle totally sells that it's her modest pumps that fail her. Instead of hopping back to her feet, she looks back with an about-to-cry expression. This was where my mother would start yelling at Barb to get up! Get up! It's probably when *lots* of people yelled it. In 2024, Steve Abramson released the unlicensed *Night of the Living Dead: The Fotonovel*, a format popular in the 1970s—sort of a comic book constructed of film frames—and it indulges in just this kind of metatextual fun. "GET UP BARBRA!!!" shouts one caption.

Barb appears to hear us. She rolls onto her butt, kicks off both pumps, and hurtles toward the car. Now she's getting somewhere, or at least it seems like it.

00:07:35 FAST ZOMBIES SUCK

The LeMans again. This goddamn car. Barbra collides with the driver's door, pulls it open, and gets inside. A cutaway shows the car's console, which looks pretty weird today, a row of submarine-like portholes to mysterious gauges, what look like two separate cigarette lighters, and—the relevant detail—an ignition switch lacking its key.

Cutaway: Barbra's hand locks the passenger door.

When we next see Barb's face, Zombie #1 runs full speed into the driver's door. You heard me right: *runs.*

Romero's 1978 thematic sequel, *Dawn of the Dead,* was the capstone of cinema's first zombie boom. Grimy, grungy, crumbly, fleshy, gory shockers, many from Italy, home of Dario Argento, who provoked and produced *Dawn.* The era produced plenty of stone-cold classics: 1972's *Tombs of the Blind Dead* (Knights Templar zombies), 1974's *Deathdream* (Vietnam War zombie), 1974's *Sugar Hill* (voodoo-summoned mafia-killing zombies), 1977's *Shock Waves* (aquatic Nazi zombies), and my favorite, 1979's *Zombie,* known in Italy as *Zombi 2* to capitalize on the success of *Dawn,* which itself was released in Italy as *Zombi.* Clear as mud?

Zombies went underground (so to speak) by the mid-eighties, partly because these foundational texts, while brilliant, were hardly blockbusters. Most people didn't notice or care. That changed in the early 2000s with a zombiegeist Romero credited to video games like *Resident Evil* (a movie version of which he nearly directed), *The House of the Dead, Dead Rising,* and *Left 4 Dead.*

I'm not a video game guy (I have only ever owned an Atari 2600 and a Wii) but it's clear most of these games, by their shoot-'em-up nature, were the antithesis of everything Romero believed in. That didn't stop Universal from licensing a tie-in game to go along with Romero's fourth zombie film. I like to think *Land of the Dead: Road to Fiddler's Green,* was cursed by Romero, who would have had nothing but antipathy for the remorseless first-person shooter. GameSpot calling it the worst game of 2005 was actually a sort of victory.

There has yet to be, by the way, a full-fledged, officially licensed mass-release *Night of the Living Dead* video game. (Though I have seen a letter from Romero's lawyer Barry Gutterman confirming interest in a CD-ROM game proposed by Desert Music Pictures in 1995.) There have, of course, been a number of unofficial games. Endorsed by Romero's son George C. Romero (whose zombie comic *The Rise* was unfortunately promoted with NFTs), a *Night of the Living Dead* download was offered for *Into the Dead 2* for one week in October 2018. There's also *Night of the Living Dead VR*, which I'd love to experience despite being nauseated for a full day both times I tried VR. The niftiest video thingie I've seen is *Night of the Living Dead Pixels* by Les Éditions Volumiques, a gorgeous little choose-your-own-path book you progressively fold open to reveal shots from the film embedded with QR codes that activate an app. Artistically pixelated scenes from the film play on your phone and give you a score for your choice. But it's less a game than a piece of interactive art; it was part of a 2011 MoMA exhibit, which speaks to how much *Night* has transcended cinema.

The zombiegeist became a zombissance as movies like *28 Days Later* (2002), *Resident Evil* (2002), and the *Dawn of the Dead* remake (2004) led the undead into multiplexes. While these films nodded at Romero (Robert Rodriguez, who directed the 2007 zombie flick *Planet Terror*, called *Night* the "Book of Genesis for zombie movies"), they worked off a game-changing innovation. These zombies were *fast*. New fans, especially those raised on video games, loved it. Romero purists gagged.

Brian Keene, whose 2003 novel *The Rising* was part of this boom, recounts meeting Romero at a horror convention and giving him a copy of his novel. Romero good-naturedly reproached him about the illogicalities of zombie speed. The in-joke developed to a point where Romero would wear a shirt reading FAST ZOMBIES SUCK and would send conventioneers to Keene's table to tell him so. Keene liked the phrase so much he used it as the title of a story. Far less congenial was the debate on message boards, and to this day it's a whole thing.

So it's notable Romero's first zombie is shown running.

You can explain it away if you want: Hinzman's zombie, the

first one spotted, is freshly dead with blood uncoagulated and joints still lubricated. The real reason, of course, is that Romero didn't have his zombie rules down pat. Though he should have, considering that every other zombie he'd filmed before this scene had lumbered and staggered.

In the moment, however, it's kinetic and scary. Hinzman is as committed here as he was fighting with Streiner. He pulls at the door handle (anomaly two: this zombie understands handles?) and pounds at the windshield with a palm. He hurries to the passenger door (anomaly three: this zombie understands cars?) and does the same. It's harrowing, the whole car shaking for twenty-two seconds before Zombie #1 stumbles off, picks up a big rock, and smashes it against the window (anomaly four: this zombie understands tools?).

There's no trickery. No special effects. It's all done in a single take: The first blow of the rock scuffs the window; the second scuffs it worse, and the third shatters the glass, sending the rock flying right at Romero and his camera. It wasn't like they had a backup window to shatter. Hinzman had to nail this in one take, and boy, does he. In what is fast becoming Hinzman's gonzo style, he thrusts his upper body into the car, giving not one shit about broken glass, and stretches mantis-like arms for Barbra.

Then Barbra does the cleverest thing she does in the whole film. She reaches down and pulls a handle labeled BRAKE RELEASE. The car begins to roll forward down a slope. Zombie #1 clings to the car for twenty feet but eventually must let go. For a moment Romero frames Hinzman through the car's back window, still snarling, still pursuing. It's a terrifying shot, death depicted specifically for American car culture. Drive as fast as you can, Yankee, but you're not getting away.

Barbra steers the car down a steep incline. An exterior shot shows Zombie #1 still coming, a dogged pursuit that, quite suddenly, feels darkly comic. A gradually drifting car versus an undead pursuer? This tortoise race shouldn't feel so exciting. Fellow obsessives can pause the film at 00:08:45 to glimpse a white vehicle parked alongside the path. Maybe Barb isn't as isolated as she thinks. In reality, I believe it's the Latent Image's company car. Regardless, Barb misses it, same as I did for my first 299 watches.

The goddamn LeMans belonged to Josephine Streiner. She's the third Streiner I've mentioned, and there's actually a fourth involved in the picture, Jacqueline Streiner, who married Russ two years earlier and is credited with "Script Coordination." (In the production's most famous cast and crew shot, Jacqueline wears the tiniest sunglasses you'll ever see; they resemble the shades in the DEAL WITH IT GIF.)

Josephine knew tragedy—her husband committed suicide in 1961—but Russ and Gary's mother was game for whatever her nutty sons dreamt up. My mom was the same: If I needed her to play a quick role in a Danman Production, she'd step in, laughing inappropriately the whole while. Mrs. Streiner appears later as a zombie, shambling about in a white housecoat and mussed hair. Josephine died at age ninety-three on February 5, 2012—the exact same day Bill Hinzman died at age seventy-six. And to think, forty-five years earlier, the latter was bashing out the window of the former's car.

Josephine lent her road hog for the cemetery scene, which ended up being a two-day shoot. Improbably, Josephine managed to be the victim of a traffic mishap between those days. She was fine but her LeMans now had a sizable dent in the driver's door. Given how Romero edited this scene, the dent would have been easy to hide. Not knowing that yet, he directed O'Dea to steer her runaway car—her very slow-moving runaway car—so it appears to crunch against a tree. (The tree's gone today, another victim of the Beaver Falls Tornado.)

It's a big reason why people (including me when I was young) think Barbra is a dope. How in the name of all that's holy do you hit a tree on an empty road going ten miles per hour? The script called upon a more logical upward incline to halt the car. On the other hand, the match cut to the dented door does add production value, making it look like the filmmakers had a LeMans to spare. Plus, you know, weird shit happens when you're fleeing your would-be murderer.

Barbra bails out with Zombie #1 thirty feet back but making good time on the downhill stretch. The chase begins. It's the only real chase in *Night*, and all the more impressive for being the first sequence the filmmakers shot. The camerawork is more handheld than ever, the Dutch angles dutchier, and "Heavy Agitato" restarts for a second round, nearly covering the scrunch of weeds under Barb's feet, a sound effect achieved with dried Spanish moss. The long-lens tracking of Barbra through the brambles was the best of its kind until 1974, when Tobe Hooper upped the ante by adding nighttime and a chain saw.

Eventually Barb hits a dirt road (Old Route 68, it's called) and looks befuddled. I know this feeling. Oh, the many signless Iowa byways along which I've been lost! The good news is if you go straight long enough, you'll hit another crossroad. Barbra chooses the direction of the camera, which dollies away in the method still used today by budget filmmakers: Romero squatting in the open trunk of the 1965 Lincoln Continental owned by Karl Hardman.

When the camera pulls too far away, O'Dea runs her heart out. It's like she's been struck by the fear that the crew are going to abandon her.

Zombie #1 is shown picking through underbrush, but he's not such a runner now. Barbra, comfortably ahead, skids to a halt and is caught in heroic focus by Romero's camera, looking lovely: driven, lips parted, hair tossed like Hitchcock-era Tippi Hedren. She sees a place to run. In the next shot we'll see it, too, and once we get there, we'll never leave.

00:09:31 MAKES IT THRU DOOR

The whole deal on the farmhouse is weird. Image Ten needed a place that was a) away from visible civilization, and b) available to be harshly treated. Enter a nearly forgotten hero named Jack Ligo, a skinny, floppy-haired Latent Image intern. Five years prior, Ligo's brother Joe had spent a few days at Camp Deerhead, a ramshackle, two-story, wood-paneled house tucked away off Ash Stop Road along windy Connoquenessing Creek, a seven-minute drive north of Evans City Cemetery. Camp Deerhead was a site for church group outings (and possibly hunters), but Ligo (who tragically died months later at age twenty-two) found out the owner, Gilbert Gass, was fixing to bulldoze the joint for their sod farm, Penn Turf Nurseries.

Gass offered the filmmakers use of it for $300 a month. For a house they could bash to pieces? It was an offer they couldn't refuse. After the final guests departed, the house became a different kind of camp, with Romero, Jack Russo, Gary Streiner, and Vince Survinski living on-site for long stretches despite infestations of rats, snakes, bees, hornets, and mosquitoes, plus a toilet that, due to a busted well, wouldn't flush without water muled in by cast and crew from a nearby well (uphill, of course). Survinski even took baths in the nearby creek.

Barbra's first glimpse, and ours, depicts a humble white farmhouse nestled amid several tall pines along an undisturbed stretch of rolling fields. (There is no farm to speak of, but *Night* tradition dictates I keep calling it a "farmhouse.") In this shot, the farmhouse is just above the middle line of the frame and to the right. If the framing feels familiar, that's because it matches our first view of Zombie #1. See for yourself: 00:05:11 versus 00:09:31.

Both shots adhere to the 1.618 "Golden Ratio," a spiraling nautilus shape that purportedly distills what the human brain understands as beautiful. It shows up all over nature (sunflowers, elephant tusks, hurricanes, galaxies) and all over the human body.

And, apparently, in shots framed by George A. Romero.

We're hardwired to pay attention to such compositions like we're hardwired to see faces in clouds. Both shots also adhere to the photographic principle known as "rule of space," where a void leading an object compels us to imagine that object moving through that void. In the first shot, we imagine Zombie #1 coming toward us. In the second, we imagine Barbra heading for the house. They pull us with expectant motion.

Barbra is thus pulled. She runs for it, pausing for breath at a gas pump. This was a prop borrowed from a local Esso station, but if it strikes you odd that a farmhouse has a gas pump, you haven't spent much time on farms. My father grew up in a farmhouse in southern Illinois (on Kraus Road, named because his parents were the first to live there), a place my family visited for a few days every other summer. There wasn't much to do but scale hay bales, stare at cows, fantasize about climbing the silos, and explore derelict outbuildings and machines. These included a gas pump stocked with diesel for tractors, though I always wanted to fill the family truckster with it. It just seemed neat.

In Barbra's case, it's foreshadowing: The gas pump's going to come back in a big way. The next shot of the farmhouse is the clearest look we're ever going to get of it, and it's nearly indistinguishable from the house on Kraus Road. A two-story box. No frills. One chimney. A small, slanted porch. A dead tree that looks like a witch roasted at the stake. The kind of nondescript domicile you barely notice while zooming past them down interstates. Anything at all could be happening inside.

Barbra grabs the porch door, pounds it, gets no response. She sprints off and takes her second spill, this time down a slope. Damn, can O'Dea ever fall! She gets up, circumnavigates the house, and peeks around the final corner. Zombie #1 is fifty feet away. Proper use of the 180-degree rule conveys that Barbra will need to expose herself to the zombie to explore the last face of the house.

One reason her scrambling is so tightly edited is that these shots were "pickups"—footage Romero went back and filmed after deciding the sequence needed more oomph. My guess is Barb's original entry into the house was more direct. Evidence for this lies in Romero's shooting script, the crown jewel of the George A. Romero Archival Collection at the University of Pittsburgh Library System, which is actually three archives frankensteined together:

one from wife Suzanne Desrocher-Romero, one from daughter Tina Romero, and one from business partner Peter Grunwald.

The archive is an incredible—and incredibly accessible—storehouse of Romero's production documents, ephemera, treatments, and scripts, over 150 projects at last count, very few of them zombie-related. Most material requires making an appointment to go see it, but interest, preservation concerns, and the public domain status led the library to digitize Romero's personal copy of the *Night* script. You can go to the library's digital collections site right now and page through it. I have, many times.

I have also handled the script in person, removed from a gray box emblazoned CONTAINS RESTRICTED MATERIAL and nestled into the archive room's foam book supporters. Romero's script, still inside a coffee-stained, flyspecked Latent Image binder, acts as a time machine. I tasted cigarettes smoked in 1967. I saw where heavily applied marker bled through pages. I felt with my fingertips the emphatic ballpoint cross-out of a Barbra freakout on page 82, inked hard enough I could also feel it on page 83. On the back of page 79 is a smashed mosquito.

The script brims with Romero's handwritten notes, most of them lists of pickup shots he needed. For this scene, the list goes like this:

> *Changes—*
> *runs out of wooded area onto paved road*
> *runs up to point where she spots home*
> *runs up to pump—*
> *up to front porch—tries door—it is locked*
> *runs to rear of home*
> *to back door—sees pursuer at pumphouse*
> *makes it thru door.*

Here's what all these well-orchestrated pickups obscure: Barbra never actually enters the house! O'Dea exaggerates a look as if to say, *Hey, a door!* before she exits frame right. Next shot, she tumbles into an interior room, not from outdoors but from an enclosed porch. We skip an entire room. In doing so, we also skip the transition from daylight to darkness.

Of all the continuity miscues, this might be the most impactful. Whether the film was called *Night of the Living Dead*, *Night of the Flesh Eaters*, or *Night of Anubis*, it was always *Night*—this is a film about nighttime, seeded by the movie's first line, Barbra's blather about the time change. We might strut around in the sunlight, but at night we cluster inside protective boxes, safe and smug until that box gets rattled. The farmhouse is such a box, and therefore is a trap.

00:10:13 FREDDY HELL

We don't notice the spatial jump because Romero shocks our senses. The final, crashing, three-second tremolo of "Heavy Agitato" slices off the instant we cut to the house interior. In abrupt silence (except for a roll of thunder from the storm, which, incidentally, will never manifest), Barb slams the door, locks it, and presses her body against it like it's the protective husband suggested by her ring. The pose is striking enough, hopeless and wanton, to be replicated on posters. I own one.

My history with horror posters is checkered. I got into *Fangoria*, America's premier horror film magazine, right on schedule at age eleven. I found it by chance on the racks at Kramer's Books and Gifts, scandalously close to the bagged nudie mags. The first *Fangoria* I had the guts to purchase was the October 1986 issue with David Cronenberg's *The Fly* on the cover. My main memory of it is bringing it on a camping trip with my dad and getting shamed for it (today's equivalent of being glued to your phone). Though my *Fangoria* stint was brief (I tapped out by 1989), the magazine had an oversize impact on me, and thousands of others. It was evidence, out of the blue, that my shameful interest might not be shameful at all.

My timing was perfect. The October 1986 issue kicked off the mag's coverage of *A Nightmare on Elm Street 3: Dream Warriors*, a film it would obsess over for months. *Night of the Living Dead* had sparked my interest in horror, but *Dream Warriors* blew it into a full-blown obsession.

In 1986, I began drawing horror icons in art class. I memorized the ventilation holes of Jason Voorhees's hockey mask and the whorled scars of Freddy Krueger's face. The compulsion bled into other classes. Unobserved by sixth-grade teacher Mrs. Morrone, I began drawing what I dubbed "Pee-Wee Comics," slipping each one over to my friend Nathan to read. With the vibe of *The Simpsons* (still three years off), the comics depicted a sitcom version of Freddy Krueger; his wife, Mrs. Krueger; their Bart-like son, Pee-Wee; and their baby, Baby.

Drawing comics drained terror from terrifying things and helped me attain mastery over them. My memory of Pee-Wee Comics begins and ends with sixth grade. But my memory is faulty, according to a capsule diary I kept from 1987 to 1992 (mostly a dull log of test grades, Cubs scores, movies watched, and crucial observations like "Have over 20 zits" and "Wore shorts"). The diary reveals I privately continued Pee-Wee Comics for another *four years*, concluding with comic #325 on January 5, 1990.

At that same sixth-grade desk, I wrote an entire "book" (one full spiral-bound notebook) of an imagined fourth chapter in the Nightmare series called *Freddy Hell* (a phrase I picked up from the March 1987 *Fangoria*). Nathan had just introduced me to the hair-metal band Dokken, and Dokken had recorded the theme song to *Dream Warriors*. Everything was coming up Kraus and Krueger. (Following Romero, I was the first person to house their archives in Pitt's Horror Studies Collection, which means, if you really want, you can experience the magic of *Freddy Hell* for yourself.)

But I had a secret. *Fangoria* scared me. I hid my collection in a paper bag beneath my bookshelves like a trove of *Hustler*. On July 6, 1987, I upped the ante by buying *Fangoria Poster Magazine*

#1, solely composed of ten sixteen-by-twenty-two-inch posters. I taped one of Freddy and his leading lady, Heather Langenkamp, on my bedroom wall, despite being queasy about seeing Freddy at night.

What made me queasier was the poster printed on the reverse side, a still from a film I had yet to see called *The Evil Dead*. In this image, two thumbs gouged out a man's eyes. It terrified me, and I was careful not to look it at while hanging the poster.

The first night the poster was up, I lay in bed looking at Freddy, wondering if this had been a bad idea. And then the tape holding up the top right corner of the Freddy poster gave way under the basement's moisture. The Freddy poster folded downward, revealing one of the gouged eyes. I hid my head and bore the rest of the night in mortal terror.

Two days later, I stayed overnight at my friend Greg's house. Greg was a fellow horror nut and *Fangoria* devotee. For months I had been drawing a fake horror mag for his amusement called *Gregoria*. That night I gave Greg my entire *Fangoria* collection, including the poster book. Bad move. Instantly he wanted to put them up, and high on sunlit frivolity, I helped. Three of the posters were truly gruesome: *Motel Hell*, *Re-Animator*, and Romero's own *Day of the Dead*. By the time night fell, my regret had turned into panic. No way I was sleeping in that room. I felt too old to call home but knew this was a horror gamble I'd lost.

My mom picked me up. She was a good person. She didn't add to my humiliation.

The incident exemplifies my adolescent relationship to horror. Exciting one minute, intolerable the next. But after each period of relapse, I worked my courage back up and returned to the gauntlet. I'd always been that kind of kid. Around age eight, scared of the dark space under my bed, I didn't only dare myself to look under it. I crawled into the space to see what would happen.

I didn't know then, and certainly didn't know during my early viewings of *Night*, that I was, dare by dare, scare by scare, zombie by zombie, hammering together a suit of armor I would need as the Freddy Hell of grade school gave way to the just plain hell of middle school.

00:10:23 MONSTER FLICK

After the loud, fevered rollick of the chase, Romero gives us twenty-four seconds to study a new tableau. Thus far, the film has been bathed in hazy gray sun. Now the noose tightens. The house interior is impressionistic, blobs of light over ink-black shadow. Explained Romero, "I was trying to do Orson Welles! I was trying to do *Othello*!"

He guffawed this declaration to the indispensable genre documentarian Michael Felsher on an audio recording laid down on February 9, 2016, part of a series of tapes made as Romero watched his own filmography—more or less his final word on his movies. With Romero in good spirits, and the clink of cocktail ice and the cheeps of a cockatiel named Sam I Am in the background, the Felsher tapes are charming. A bit foreboding, too; each time Romero pauses for a phlegmy cough is a harbinger of terrible things soon to come.

What the light blobs reveal: Barb, a linoleum floor, the side of a kitchen counter, the edge of a small table with a checkerboard cloth, and part of a larger table holding a bowl of fruit. Because it so closely resembles Grandma Kraus's kitchen, I'd wager that fruit is ceramic.

Under the soft flute of a Loose-Cookerly cue called "Light Suspense (JB-37)," Barbra cautiously plods into the next space. It's a spacious and tidy dining room. A table with a quartet of chairs suggests a maximum of four residents. Gossamer blinds imbued with daylight (it's daytime again) contrast with the ominous void of an open door.

Barbra retreats to the kitchen, opens a drawer, and withdraws a huge knife. (The script calls it a "steak knife," but I've never met a steak requiring this size of stabber.) A solid choice, but there's nothing solid about Barb's behavior. She cradles the knife against her bosom, lodging the handle under her chin like a teddy bear. She holds the blade itself with her other hand. She's an accident waiting to happen as she exits into a new room.

It took about two hundred viewings before I noticed the clues scattered across the sitting room floor. A dropped newspaper. A lamp broken to pieces. An open magazine sliding off a table. (And in the lower left, the first appearance of a Latent Image binder containing *Night*'s script.) Barb edges around the leavings like they are a sucking tarn. The following shot is filmed from inside the next room. Though it's dark, we can plainly see this room has more character than the others. There's an animal skin rug and a pronghorn antelope head on the walls, some flowers, and enough clutter to indicate people spend time here.

Very, very, very slowly, Barbra tiptoes into the room, crouched low, knife up. Her face sinks into shadow before cresting back into light.

Then something incredible happens.

At 00:11:36, the camera whip-pans to the right for a split second. It's meant as an unintelligible blur of motion, but if you scroll frame by frame, you'll see two pieces of filmmaking equipment: a gobo (a cutout that throws shadow patterns onto a set) and one of the Colortran lights.

It's hard not to sound maniacal when describing the joy I felt upon discovering this. *Night* has always punched above its weight when it comes to analysis, often placed in the film-studies ranks of *Citizen Kane*, *Breathless*, *Vertigo*, et cetera. To turn up anything new is rare. Imagine noticing a detail in the *Mona Lisa* no one else has noticed. If that's too far-fetched, imagine shuffling through childhood snapshots and noticing, in the reflection of a mirror, the carefree face of the photographer, a loved one otherwise only captured in stiff, posed portraits. It's a gift, one that took fifty years to unwrap.

Unbelievably, it gets better. The next shot was supposed to

continue the pan to the right per a note Romero scrawled onto his shooting script: *"need 3 insert CUs of stuffed heads—first one w/ swish pan to right—>."* Romero was unable to execute his swish pan. Maybe the room was too cramped. Maybe it was three in the morning and the camera was locked to its tripod. So a faux pan was improvised by putting a hand over the lens and quickly removing it.

Right about 00:11:36. Freeze the frame. Look. Four fingers. A thumb. A hand. George A. Romero's hand, most likely. It's a literalization of the idiom of seeing someone's hands all over a work of art. And proof, too, of the human hands underlaying an object to which we have grown perhaps too accustomed.

For me, this hand is an obsession within an obsession. I discovered it in 2014 while writing *Empire Decayed*, the second volume in the Death and Life of Zebulon Finch duology. The story follows a criminal who comes back to life after assassination and must navigate a century of American chaos for redemption. Yes, Zebulon is undead. But it's not until he catches a drive-in screening of *Night of the Living Dead* that he sees others of his kind. He, too, becomes obsessed with this glimpse of Romero's hand and believes Romero is transmitting a private message to him à la Charles Manson and the Beatles' *White Album*. (Incidentally, one of *Night*'s zombies is played by Paul McCartney, just not *the* Paul McCartney.)

The fact that we're only eleven minutes into *Night* may have you already suspecting I'm insane. But I'm not insane enough to think Romero's hand is a private message to me. Still, I take a message from it: Any art that I (or you, or anyone) create cannot be controlled. People have the right to draw from it what they want or need. This is why, in general, I don't fault people for enjoying the art of problematic artists. That artwork is part of *you* now. That's the whole point of art.

What Romero's hand reveals is a wild boar head, taxidermied tusks splayed and tongue artfully ribboned. With the four-note opening cry of a Loose-Seely cue called "Dreary Danger

(TC-157)," Romero flash-cuts from the boar to a deer head to a second deer head before returning to shell-shocked Barbra. Romero, born and raised in New York, was right that taxidermy icks out city folk. Not me. Walls of my childhood home were filled with heads and antlers and fishes and fowls, and once you've dared to touch a deer head's marble eyeball, there's not much more horror to be had.

The heads didn't come with the Gass farmhouse. They came from prop man Charles S. "Cha" O'Dato, owner of Trails End Taxidermy, who, in *Autopsy of the Dead*, refers to *Night* as a "spook movie." (O'Dato's wife, Helen, was purportedly considered for the role of Barbra.) I'm sure the taxidermy was mostly meant to connote "country folk," but there's a comparison to be made between taxidermy and zombies, both of which are a version of life after death. It hearkens back to a Jack Russo story idea that became one of *Night of the Living Dead*'s foundational threads: aliens who put corpses inside glass cases to decompose them to their taste. Bodies in cases: That's taxidermy, isn't it?

The heads were part of the set dressing headed up by Vince Survinski, whose name pops up often enough in stories about *Night* to establish him as the unheralded hero holding the Latent Image together and Image Ten's father figure. Survinski did it all, from handling the firm's bookkeeping to building a goddamn bridge so cars could get to the farmhouse, to set-dressing the house on a $50 budget by pulling from Goodwill (uppercase, the store) and goodwill (lowercase, of cast and crew willing to lend their belongings). When the gang first told Survinski they were going to make a movie, the older fellow did what he did for any new project, taking out a manila envelope and writing on it MONSTER FLICK.

Survinski, the spitting image of middle-aged Robert De Niro, owned the Ardmore Roller Palace (you can't make this stuff up) before becoming a Latent Image partner. What does *partner* mean exactly? My guess is he threw in money he'd made from his lumber business. Before that, Survinski had served with the 630th

Tank Destroyer Battalion in the Battle of the Bulge. And he also wrote country-western songs? The dude just generally ruled.

If only Barbra had a Vince Survinski around. Her taxidermic reverie is interrupted by thuds. "Dreary Danger" restarts as we cut outside to find some dreary danger: Zombie #1 staggering around beneath daylit skies. There's a shed behind him. The characters never investigate this shed, a lost opportunity. Barb grips curtains (sewed by Richard Ricci's mother) and peeks out a window into pure night before we leap back to Hinzman in the naked sun, ripping down a clothesline like it killed his dog. He does a real number on it. The hard snap of the clothesline was reportedly one of the toughest sound effects to foley. It's always the little things.

Barbra closes the drapes (the sound effect was achieved, oddly enough, by flapping an umbrella) and turns around. At the risk of trying your patience, show me another movie that turns a character with so much pizzazz. Romero punches into a slightly closer shot of Barbra as she wheels about, hair flying, background and foreground in motion, before dashing for a desk telephone, a metal-and-Bakelite 1930s-era Western Electric 202 with a D1 base. Barb hunches like a raccoon, the whole room behind her slanted like a sinking ship.

She spins the rotary dial once for an operator but hears only . . . well, I'm not sure how to describe it. The novelization says the phone emits "dead silence." The script indicates a busy-signal message. But this isn't any signal I've heard before. I'd characterize it as a sci-fi pulsing. No effect should have been easier to record than a busy signal, so this computerized throb must be intentional. If so, we need to link it to the malfunctioning radio in the goddamn LeMans.

It's the second clue that what's happening to Barbra stretches beyond her environs. Consider again my dark speculations on lonely farmhouses. Disease doesn't respect family acreages or barbed-wire fences. It runs wild, ends up in the groundwater. What's rotting inside these kitchens, bedrooms, and sheds are the same things rotting America's guts.

00:12:28

ROMERO MODE

KNIFE WIELDED, BARBRA RETURNS TO THE SITTING room. Or den. Or second living room? I've never been able to internalize the farmhouse layout, possibly due to Romero taking artistic liberties with entrances and exits. So when two *Night of the Living Dead* board games came out in 2021 and 2022, I was excited. One, because, well, duh, and two, because each game board was an overhead map of the farmhouse.

Designed by Raphaël Guiton, Jean-Baptiste Lullien, Nicolas Raoult, and David Preti, and officially licensed by Image Ten, *Night of the Living Dead: A Zombicide Game* is by far the fancier production. As the subtitle indicates, it's a volume in a series of board games promising zombie slaughter. I haven't played the series' fourteen other titles, and the word "Zombicide" turns me off. I'm too much of a purist to enjoy the mindless, quippy slaughter of reanimated humans, whether it comes in movies like *Army of the Dead* or any of the shoot-'em-up video games.

At first glance, the Zombicide game looks like the same old song. You open the box to a bevy of candy-colored bits and cards featuring weapons that Barbra is not going to find at the farmhouse (spoiler alert), including a chain saw, a Japanese katana, and an Uzi machine gun. The game's nifty compromise is a so-called Romero Mode, a style of play that goes thematically—and literally—black-and-white by swapping the multicolored minis for somber gray models and flipping cards of character abilities to their black-and-white sides. In Zombicide Mode, Barbra's leveling a pump rifle, her mouth lowered in a Rambo bellow. In Romero Mode, she's the Barb we know, death-gripping her beloved steak knife.

The second game, *The Night,* is most assuredly *not* officially licensed—the rulebook goes out of its way to note the film's public domain purgatory. Yet I found Michael W. Kennedy's game to be a loving tribute, and the fact that it's published by minuscule Texas-based White Dog Games adds to the Image Ten–like appeal. The simple black-and-white components and simpler rules make for what is arguably a better game. Plus, the tiny game pieces with portraits of our characters (as well as their zombified versions) are freaking adorable.

Though the art style of *The Night* is primitive next to *Night of the Living Dead: A Zombicide Game,* both boards are nearly identical in their farmhouse layout. I'm inclined to trust them and, in fact, kept the map of *The Night* beside my computer for the writing of this book. It wasn't until I was revising that I came across the "digital 3D environment" created by Daz Sargeant (assisted by Gary Streiner), Image Ten's social-media guru, website developer, and coproducer of the Living Dead Weekend, an annual *Night*-focused event that picked up after Gary's final Living Dead Festival in 2014. Traveling through this digital farmhouse is an impressive, and for me, highly satisfying experience (though I doubt Romero would love the first-person-shooter-style scoped rifle inherent to the point of view).

Romero confirmed these cartographic efforts in 2016, when he set to transcribing/writing a fresh script of *Night* that reflected the finished film and conformed to modern screenplay standards instead of the original's discursive balladry. The idea was chiefly commercial: He wished to sell *Night* scripts at convention tables, along with scripts for *Dawn* and *Day.* But he didn't finish. His attention strayed, and a year later, he was dead. The script stops mid-dialogue on page 52. But back on page 11, Romero understood the need to set the stage: "We realize that there are FOUR ROOMS on the first floor. Clockwise: KITCHEN, LIVING/DINING ROOM, DEN, LIBRARY."

This layout is complicated by a hall between the living room (a more accurate term than Romero's "library") and den that feeds into the dining room (and includes the stairs to the second floor). This facilitated rapid access to any room in the house. The bathroom, one can only hope, is upstairs.

Barbra, fresh from the beeping phone, moves from den to dining room and creeps her way to a window. We still glimpse daylight, which I mention only to contrast with the next, very important shot, which is teased by the gentle harp cascade of a library cue called "Weird Eerie (ZR-87C)" from George Hormel (yes, of the meat-packing Hormels, and who, incidentally, married French actor Leslie Caron).

A brass smash coincides with what Barbra sees. Outside, it's night. Finally night. Dusk was too delicate a process for our film nerds to pull off realistically. Though you can expect a few more daylight leaks (the film's interiors were shot in daytime with black seamless paper coating the windows), the exteriors have at last succumbed to the titular time of day.

Zombie #1 is *right fucking there* on the other side of the window, a jarring surprise. His stagger is identical to how my nephew used to watch TV as a child, swaying arrhythmically eighteen inches in front of the screen. The fierce purpose Zombie #1 displayed in the cemetery has dulled to a confused belligerence. Somehow his bugged eyes fail to see Barbra.

Barb shifts her gaze leftward and Romero shows us two new figures shuffling through the yard. This could be help, right? "Weird Eerie" tells us it's not. With rigor mortis–inspired motions, Hinzman stiffly turns to look at the newcomers before wheeling his body back to the farmhouse. These few seconds establish concepts that will inform the next half century of zombie filmmakers; magician Penn Jillette once compared Romero to the Velvet Underground, who spawned as many bands as Romero spawned filmmakers. So here's what we now know about zombies. Romero Mode zombies, anyway.

Zombies are slow.

Zombies want to kill people.

Zombies know other zombies on sight, maybe even smell.

Zombies, by extension, know the living by sight or smell.

Zombies are equally content to work alone or in groups.

Some bits of nuance are yet to come, but this is all you need to understand *Night*'s ghouls, and we're not even thirteen minutes into the film. There's no needing to learn where, say, Dracula lives, or how he feeds, or what forms he takes, or what kind of soil he sleeps in, or how he reacts to garlic or holy water, or blah blah blah. Humans come factory-set to fear advancing groups. All animals are built that way.

If you, like Barbra, are a woman, there's the additional fear of being alone and seeing a group of men close in. Millions of terrible true stories begin this way, as do hundreds of movies. Just like zombies, the men in these stories—rapists, assaulters, killers—rarely speak as they advance. To speak might lift their shame to unsustainable levels. Better for both their goal and their guilt to glower and shuffle.

Russo's novelization, never a source of subtlety, makes this explicit: "It dawned on her that perhaps her first attacker had gone for reinforcements, and they would return en masse to batter the door down and rape her and kill her."

Barbra runs back through the dining room and into the hallway. For a few seconds, she behaves like Morten Harket at the end of A-ha's "Take On Me" video, bashing herself between the walls as if trying to break back into a sunnier reality. She grabs the handrail and pulls herself up onto the stairs—then slows. Now that she thinks of it, who knows what's up there?

The next shot, looking down at Barbra as she climbs, is as good as anything Tod Browning did in *Dracula*. Harsh light (the only kind Image Ten knows) is blasted through balusters to ripple high-contrast shadows over the pale movie screen of Barbra's face, hair, and coat. For the most part, *Night* is shooting the straightforward techniques the Latent Image ported over from clients like Heinz and U.S. Steel, but this shot is imbued with the expressionism of F. W. Murnau's *Nosferatu* (1922), and thanks to the exaggerated shadows, touches upon the surrealism of Robert Wiene's *The Cabinet of Dr. Caligari* (1920).

It wouldn't work in color. In one of cinema's great near-misses, Image Ten crunched enough numbers to determine shooting on color 16mm would, in fact, cost no more than black-and-white 35mm. Thankfully, this revelation came after a full week of shooting, and as tantalizing as color was from a commercial standpoint, no way were they going to scrap all that work. Even actor cosmetics had been calibrated to black-and-white. O'Dea's makeup card reads: *24 BASE / SHADOW - grey 1st—then small blue—then white / JAW LINE—outlined w/ grey #3 / NOSE - V down w/ deep red to ½way tip / CHEEKS - #5 rouge / LIPS - #1.*

The stark staircase lighting would be purposeless if not for the terror about to explode upon Barbra. A quick close-up of her horrified face precedes a zoom—the film's first zoom, and cinema has yet to devise anything more startling than a surprise zoom—into a close-up of a gory skull.

00:13:12 SEVEN PINES

"Gory skull" doesn't do the prop justice. If it still existed, it might be displayed in a climate-controlled case beside Dorothy's ruby slippers in the Smithsonian. Though Romero had met future special effects maestro Tom Savini by this point, Savini was unavailable to work on *Night* when something even more horrific came up: the Vietnam War. Savini's combat photography would greatly influence his later career, which would intersect with Romero on *Martin*, and then, more legendarily, on *Dawn of the Dead*.

This left special effects to the Image Ten collective. As legend has it, Romero trekked over to the local hobby shop, Bill and Walt's (unbelievably, still in business today), and bought a couple Renwal model kits: Human Skull and Visible Head, the former reissued by Revell in the 1970s. As model kits went, this was no Allison Prop-Jet Engine. A dozen or so large plastic pieces and a few sprues of polystyrene teeth were all you got. Romero built the thing, added a wig, and used modeling clay for skin. The head was then attached to one of the mannequins the crew had assembled for zombie group shots. (This particular dummy has been dubbed "Manny Quinn.")

The best way to get a clear look at the apparatus is to freeze the film a split second before the zoom. The skull hits the uncanny target only low-budget physical props ever do: the deformed babies of *Combat Shock* and *Eraserhead*, Belial from *Basket Case*, the Zuni Fetish Doll from *Trilogy of Terror*. *Night*'s head looks like nothing before or since. The glossy skin resembles the waxy adipose of actual decomposing flesh. Instead of bridging the model kit's bottom jaw to the top with clay, Romero leaves the fissure between them, which gives the jaw the detached awfulness of a ventriloquist dummy. The teeth are janky. The eyes look as soft as poached eggs. The head's most chilling feature is its liplessness, "as if the corpse had been eaten by rats," the novelization says.

The image, a T-shirt mainstay, still makes me shudder. Gary Streiner felt the same. "One of the only things that really scared me about *Night of the Living Dead*, making it, was that head at the top of the stairs," he said. "It just sat up there for pretty much the whole shoot, as I can remember." Meanwhile, I'm still the kid who crawls under his own bed: I own a life-size replica of the gory skull designed by Brian McGuire and Christian Stavrakis. But I can tell you one thing: I don't keep it at the top of my stairs. Jesus Christ.

I didn't realize two different skulls were made until the November 28, 2023, installment of Image Ten's *Night Talk*, a periodic series of live-stream chats that are manna for super-fans (especially when Gary Streiner broadcasts from his Tacoma in the Evans City Cemetery). In this episode, Jim Cirronella and John Scoleri reveal an astonishing trove of never-before-seen behind-the-scenes photos left behind by cast and crew member Marilyn Eastman. One depicts a gory skull that didn't satisfy Romero, though a photo of it ended up in the *Night* trailer. A rediscovered shot of this first skull is high-octane nightmare fuel, more appalling than anything in the finished film. This head connects to a column of vertebrae that feeds into a fleshy ham hock of shoulder. It looks so real, I might have called the cops had I been the photo's developer. Search it out at your own risk.

The revelation reminds me of shuffling a deck of *Dawn of the Dead* playing cards at Suz Romero's apartment and noticing, on the three of diamonds, a robed skeleton I didn't recall seeing in the film. Matt Blazi (cohost with Eric Kent of *GARF 247*, a YouTube show for the George A. Romero Foundation Network) later showed me the skeleton in the film's housing complex scene. But here's the wild part: It's a real skeleton. No one on set knew it until the skeleton was back for rent at Costume World and identified by a coroner for what it was: the century-old remains of a mid-thirties woman, originally used in Odd Fellows Lodge initiation ceremonies (don't ask me how). In 2013, indie filmmaker William Sanders successfully raised headstone funds for "Dawn Doe."

Night has so far hammered home its shocks with bombastic musical stings, and the gory skull is no different. Barbra's scream duets with what author Randall D. Larson, in the 128-page one-off magazine *The Scream Factory Presents: Night of the Living Dead 25th Anniversary Tribute* (1993), calls "a raging electrical stinger"—a shriek of music similar to the one we heard when Zombie #1 attacked Johnny. Few films dare to sonically punish their audience—nothing upsets people like terrible noises—but this shimmery pulse lasts for an interminable *thirty-one seconds*. It's a brilliant gamble. By the time Barb stumbles down the stairs, streaks through the dining room, and hurls open the front door, you are every bit as rattled.

It's a perfect sequence, a genius way to get Barbra out of the house, no matter how many men await her.

A new man has, in fact, arrived.

The second Barbra's foot hits the outside porch, blinding light engulfs her. It's a spectral enough effect that you half expect a twist out of *An Occurrence at Owl Creek Bridge*, Barb awakening from a farmhouse daydream as Johnny's LeMans jerks to a stop in the cemetery. Instead, the light resolves into headlights, bright as cat eyes, before a face swoops into view from above, somehow.

It is the character the script identifies as "Truckdriver."

"He is large and crude," Russo and Romero write, "in coveralls and tattered work shirt. He looks very strong, and perhaps a little stupid."

This in no way describes the man we see. But let's take a moment to imagine *Night of the Living Dead* if it had proceeded with its original casting. The role was originally slated for Image Ten's Rudy Ricci. Ricci met Romero when acting at the Pittsburgh Playhouse. A childhood illness gave Ricci a leg of fused bones and a tendency toward fever spells, both risky qualities on a theater stage.

Romero cast Ricci as the lead in numerous early experiments, including the pretty much never-seen *Time Present*, and the duo cowrote *Whine of the Fawn*, a feature set in fifteenth-century England that the group, under the alias Duquesne Productions, tried to produce prior to *Night*. The investor package for *Whine* is my favorite object in the George A. Romero Archival Collection, filled with cute artist renderings of cast and crew that make Romero look like the Orson Welles he wanted to be. The cast was to include an actor they had spotted in a high school play: Tom Savini. For a semi-pretentious Bergman love letter, *Whine* is pretty dang good and noteworthy for how closely its ending foreshadows *Night*. These kids were playing for keeps.

Speaking of Ingmar Bergman, written onto the cover of Romero's shooting script binder is what appears to be an epigraph. Naturally, it's of interest to scholars—what quote did Romero intend to tee up his film? But those scholars have so far been frustrated by the indecipherability of the faded ink. Trumpet fanfare: I believe I have decoded it. And it's no epigraph, no profound excerpt of Ovid or Euripides. Rather, it's an opening title screen Romero considered that evinces his Bergmanesque aspirations for *Night*:

> *The Improbable occurrences*
> *That befell a weary group*
> *of Travellers, and the*
> *various circumstances*
> *that followed at Seven*
> *Pines.*
>
> —*tentative title*

It wasn't something Romero penned onto the binder months or years later. In one behind-the-scenes photo, the stanza is already there on Romero's binder. Although this is the first I've ever heard of "Seven Pines," it must refer to the farmhouse, which is surrounded by pines. To be sure, I texted screenshots of the trees to my forester father, who instead of replying "Yes," texted a two-hundred-plus-word deep dive into white, blue, and Norway spruce, their sizes and number of needles per fascicle. Meanwhile, just seven miles down Franklin Road (on which *Night*'s opening shots were filmed) is a borough called Seven Fields, which might have inspired the name. It's enough evidence for me.

(Also barely readable on the binder cover: *B's Copy*. My guess is the binder first belonged to Betty Ellen Haughey, who did the thankless and frankly impossible task of scene-to-scene continuity before presumably turning the binder over to—if not hurling it at—Romero.)

So back we go to the most important new resident of Seven Pines: Truckdriver. A role that sure seems to have been written expressly for Rudy Ricci, who had the beefy physique of a truck drivin' good ol' boy. Though the script doesn't mention Truckdriver's race, come on. Of course Truckdriver was white. Ricci was destined to star. Already he was rehearsing scenes.

All that went out the window when Duane Jones auditioned.

00:13:34 IT'S ALL RIGHT

Of all *Night* documentaries, *Reflections on the Living Dead* has the lowest profile. First released in 1993 as *Night of the Living Dead: 25th Anniversary Documentary*, it's a loose conversation between the "four giants" of *Night*—George Romero, Jack Russo, Russ Streiner, and Karl Hardman—interspersed with testimonials from eminent film folk. (In one shot, *Film Threat*'s Chris Gore drinks a Snapple, possibly the most 1990s thing ever caught on tape.) Boxed inside what looks like a wood-paneled rumpus room (but is probably a TV studio), the foursome, clad in woeful 1990s men's fashions, sit in blue plastic chairs and shoot the shit over the headache of a student-video hum.

The doc has an oddball charm. Amazingly (to me), it was produced and edited by J. R. Bookwalter. When Bookwalter was barely out of his teens, he directed one of my sentimental horror favorites, *The Dead Next Door* (1989), a spunky zombie flick shot in Akron, Ohio, famous for being the most expensive 8mm film ever made at a budget of $125,000 ($11,000 more than *Night*). *Reflections* exposes the weirdest *Night* merch of all time during a separate interview with Karl Hardman and Marilyn Eastman; stacked on their table are cans of *Night of the Living Dead* Devil Pet Food and bottles of *Night of the Living Dead* Zombie Blood Barbecue Sauce.

The gem of the conversation comes from Russo: "Duane just assumed [about Rudy Ricci], 'Well, you're white, you're a shareholder, and you're a close friend of these guys, and I'm not going to get the part.' And he was actually shocked when he got the part." It shouldn't be minimized how awkward it must have been for the gang to jettison Ricci (who, to his credit, eventually voted for Jones too). But the gang was in their late twenties. It was the sort of tough call adults had to make.

It was the best decision Image Ten ever made. The entire tenor of the film changes when Duane Jones steps on-screen. Not with a line of dialogue. Just a look. One look. Judith O'Dea, Russell Streiner, and Bill Hinzman have done fine work moving the ball this far. Ultimately, though, they are reading lines, having fun, going off on a lark.

There's a frisson to the amateur actor, a palpable awareness of the camera, the people crouched behind it, the thrill of being in the spotlight. The greats, however, look like they would be doing what they're doing even if the crew hadn't shown up. The ability to disengage from the apparatus yet still engage the intellect required to hit beats, marks, and lines is a talent I'm not sure can be taught (thousands of acting teachers to the contrary). It's a compartmentalization on par with a child la-la-la-ing with her dolls to block out Daddy hitting Mommy. There's a nobility to trauma victims doing what they must to survive, and we bestow that nobility upon actors who simultaneously exist in two worlds—and look good doing it.

I don't mean it as a dig to Judy, Russ, and Bill (and I don't think they'd take it as one) when I say Duane Jones's arrival as Ben is like an adult entering the playroom. In this single shot—a motionless, one-second, three-quarters-angle, head-and-shoulders close-up of Ben studying Barbra for evidence of life or undeath—Jones radiates strength. He is sculpture; the other actors are paper dolls. There's no particular emotion in his gaze, but you can read from his slightly open lips and half-lidded eyes that he is *thinking*. No one so far in the film has *thought*.

Two other things are readily apparent. One, Duane Jones is handsome. He's just underweight enough for us to glory in the planes and valleys the lights make of his face, the flawless skin, the grave eyebrows, the little twist to the top of his ears. There's something bullish to the broad forehead previously displayed in the pages of *Ebony* magazine, where he modeled for Kent and Tareyton cigarettes, Listerine, and Johnnie Walker.

Two, Duane Jones is Black. A cinemagoer in 1968 might have expected a lot of things to leap in front of Barbra—a mutated scientist, a rubbery sea monster, a giant tarantula, a mucousy blob—but a heroic Black man was not among them.

In the script, Truckdriver demands to know if Barbra is one of *them*.

Ben, though, says nothing. Doesn't need to. He looks away from Barbra at Zombie #1, then rushes onto the porch, taking Barbra by the arms and pushing her inside. Ben carries a tire iron. It's a weapon no more lethal than Barb's knife, but do we have any illusions that Barb could use her knife? We do not.

Ben locks the door, sighs, looks at Barb standing numb, and says the best first line he could say: "It's all right." It establishes Ben as a man of control and competence. It's also darkly, hilariously wrong. Nothing will ever be right again. The broken tone with which Jones says this would be a career-best moment for most actors. Fear, bewilderment, stress, frustration, exhaustion, shock, agitation, insecurity, alienation, anguish, acceptance, determination, relief, doubt, empathy, tenderness, gratitude, politeness, care, optimism, pessimism—it's all there in three little words.

For comparison, here's the line in the script (where all dialogue is all-capped): "AWW RIGHT . . . 'TS AWRIGHT NOW . . ." You can't read Truckdriver's cornpone dialogue without picturing it belted by a drunken Texan. I don't doubt it's Romero's doing. Phonetically overworked dialogue (as opposed to simply declaring, for example, "Truckdriver speaks with a country drawl") is a bona fide Romero tic. At its best, it shows a real ear for tone and timbre. At its worst, it's caricature.

"THERE'S PROBLY GONNA BE LOTS MORE OF 'EM . . .

SOON'S THEY FIN' OUT ABOUT US . . . AH GET US SOME GRUB . . . THEN WE BEAT 'EM OFF AN' SKEDADDLE . . ." Truckdriver says/shouts to Barbra. Duane Jones was not about to say this shit. Scribbled onto Romero's shooting script (where he often interposes "Ben" with "Duane") are efforts to upcycle the dialogue. "Ah get us some grub" becomes "Maybe we ought to have some food, is there food in the house?"

Soon thereafter, Romero just let Jones make his own adjustments. "Probably be a lot more of them as soon as they find out about us," Jones's Ben says curtly, crossing the dining room to scope out the joint. Simple, intelligent, capable. Was that so hard?

Apparently yes, for when Russo novelized the movie a decade later, he didn't portray a Ben as filtered through Duane Jones. Instead, he shows fealty to Truckdriver. Russo's Ben is a midway hybrid whose speech is peppered with *ain'ts*. "I ain't one of those creeps." "I ain't going to hurt you." This ain't a good idea and I ain't gonna ever like it.

This perplexing seesaw didn't end with the novelization. The writer Steven Barnes tipped me off to an old audio drama that depicted Ben in a racist fashion. I found it, an old cassette tape packaged in a paperback-sized box with a tie-dyed Zombie #1 on the cover (and stamped with an old $6.00 price sticker). But I shouldn't have looked so hard: The audio file is still being sold. Produced by Simon & Schuster Audio, it's the kind of thing I, at age thirteen, would have enjoyed upon its 1988 release. The hourlong adaptation, written by Michael Brooks, features a full cast, sound effects, music, et cetera. Even with the action shifted to the eighties (there's a Ronald Reagan impression on the radio) and a Barbra who uses the F-word, it's fairly well done. The exception is the depiction of Ben, who's constantly saying things like "Fo' sho'." Barnes correctly guessed the voice actor had to be white. In fact, the actor was Bill Hootkins, best known as Porkins in the original *Star Wars* and the guy who ends *Raiders of the Lost Ark* by saying, "Top. Men." It's hard casting to swallow, even for 1988.

When the Duane Jones version of Ben peeks into the farmhouse den, we get a good look at his attire: a soft-looking double-knit cardigan over a button-up shirt. Behind-the-scenes color photos taken by Hinzman inform us the shirt was pink. Who saw that coming? Our hero in pink. Combined with his dress slacks, one does not get the impression Ben is a "truckdriver." Then again, facts are facts: He's a Black man in 1967 Pennsylvania. His outfit might be aspirational.

Ben imparts info that will be critical later. He's got a truck. It's out of gas. There's the gas pump seen earlier but it's locked. Does Barbra have a key? Ben assumes she lives at Seven Pines and why not? He's not yelling, but met by a silent Barbra, he's getting louder. A vein stands out in his forehead. Ours too.

Ben lurches into the den and tries the Western Electric 202. It's satisfying to see. Barbra hasn't taken a single confident step, but this guy we just met charges around like he owns the joint. After getting the same sci-fi busy signal, he catches up to Barb, who's comatose in the hallway, gawping up at the staircase. Hyper-aware Ben senses trouble and climbs the stairs, this time to the realistic noise of creaking steps.

We get one more look at the Renwal model skull, this time presented not as an object of horror but of pitiful demise. Ben stumbles back down the steps and holds on to the wall. For five seconds, Ben and Barb are equally useless. It could end right here, in fact, the two slumping to the floor until Zombie #1 and his cronies find their way in.

But that's not Ben. "We've gotta get out of here. We have to get where there are some other people." It's notable that Ben's first instinct is to escape, as he will be changing his tune soon.

Ben tells Barb he's off to gather some food before they leave. This leaves Barbra alone for the first of several instances of brain-fried stupefaction. She wanders to the side of the stairs and begins to study the paneling, I guess? She looks zapped. As a study in shock, it's a little silly, until she hears something dripping and discovers blood draining from the body above into a sticky pool, revealed with a shock-zoom to mirror our first sight of the corpse.

The body didn't look fresh enough to drip blood, but what do I know? Because Barb's the luckless sort, blood dapples her hand and she's off to the dining room, beside a piano, to smother her flip-out before joining Ben in the kitchen. He's rooting through an old condenser refrigerator (not Survinski set dressing; it was already there). Very carefully, Barb sets her knife atop the fridge. It's pointed right at Ben.

She tries to assert herself by twice demanding to know what's happening. It doesn't matter that she's barely capable of standing; a white woman's concerns are paramount. Ben's inward sigh tells us he's been here before. You can imagine these actors playing this scene without a zombie threat. O'Dea is a frazzled and pampered lady and Jones is her smarter but socially deprecated servant. He'll do what he must. But there's a revolution brewing. *Yes ma'am. No ma'am.* His limit is fast being reached.

00:16:07

I CAN TAKE CARE OF THOSE TWO

OUR ODD COUPLE IS DISTRACTED BY A NOISE OUTside. Romero cuts to a zombie smashing in the right headlight of Ben's truck. Ben rushes to a window, counts two zombies, and grabs Barbra to ask her if she's seen more. She says she doesn't know, but she does: Neither of the truck zombies is Zombie #1. If she doesn't pull her shit together, she's going to get Ben killed, and that's where our concern has already shifted: Ben. He's so attractively capable. "I can take care of those two," he promises, and we believe him.

Barb does not pull anything together. She repeats "I don't know" until she's screaming it. She flings herself into a flower-print chair, total abdication of will. I'm sure she expects Ben to console her but instead—you gotta love this guy—he goes outside. He just goes outside! This cat doesn't give a fuck. Outside await droning crickets and a tense, flute-heavy cue by Ib Glindemann called "Space Drama."

A low angle gives us our first good, if brief, look at a zombie who isn't Bill Hinzman. Played by Tom Faust, Russ Streiner's brother-in-law, he wears a suit and some kind of textured makeup. It's unclear what this makeup intends to suggest, but I'm going to go with decomposition setting into cheek fat. (There is some evidence in Romero's shooting script that Faust may have been originally cast as Zombie #1.) Faust shields his face from the headlight with a grimace 1968 filmgoers would have associated with Frankenstein's monster. Fire, bad.

A whole mess of continuity errors follow, but what can you expect from filmmakers who could only afford to break things once? Faust shatters the offending headlight, which a previous shot had shown as already busted. There's a slight jump where Romero has extracted a few seconds so we don't have to wait for the puff of smoke. Cut to Ben as the headlight illuminating him—a headlight that should already be out—fades out.

The other zombie shambles toward Ben. While Hinzman and Faust are fairly reactive and spry, I assert that it's this zombie, played by a blond nineteen-year-old named Terry Gindele, who sets the mold for the next fifty years of Romero Mode zombies. (A goofy bonus feature on a 2004 DVD release of *Night* pairs actors in the film with famous doppelgängers and expertly matches Gindele with Ashton Kutcher.) Gindele is super slow. Dead-eyed. Decomposing. He doesn't know how to fear, not even the tire iron Ben swings at his noggin. Or at least the noggin of a seven-foot-tall mannequin that looks nothing like Gindele.

Gindele goes down. Ben gets on top of him and smashes the tire iron into the zombie's (unseen) face, one, two, three, four, five times.

It's a real what-the-fucker. All Ben really knows of these two guys is that they busted his headlights. On evidence, it seems overblown to leap to violent murder. But that presumes Ben's journey has been parallel to Barb's. I'm not talking only of his journey to Seven Pines, but his straight-up *journey*. Everything I mentioned earlier about 1967 would have affected Ben at a different level than *Night*'s other characters. At thirty-one (Jones's age), Ben might have evaded the Vietnam draft by the skin of his teeth, but there were three hundred thousand guys who looked like him fighting and dying over there. In 1965, Black Americans made up 31 percent of the U.S. Army's ground combat battalions (and 24 percent of fatalities) despite being only 12 percent of the

U.S. population. Back at home, there were 158 separate urban riots in 1967, with a riot in Detroit ending in 83 deaths and 17,000 arrests. From April 5 to 11, 1968, in the wake of MLK's assassination, only six months before *Night*'s premiere, Pittsburgh itself exploded into riots that involved 3,600 National Guardsmen, 1,000 people arrested, and 505 fires.

So let's give Ben the benefit of the doubt. He's seen some shit and knows the truck vandals must be dispatched. He easily topples Faust and smashes his skull in six whacks. ("Fuck this. Who wants to sit through this?" Arthur Rubine, director of Walter Reade, recalls thinking when he first saw the scene.) You don't see the impacts, not even a splash of blood, yet the violence doesn't seem bloodless. You feel each strike. Loud and hard, the moist crunch of splintering wood. Ben doesn't look troubled. His expression, in fact, seems one of wonder. Yeah, he's seen this before. The difference now is that he's the one *doing* it.

00:17:13 NUMBER SEVENTEEN

Finally Romero has the chance to escalate tension by cutting between characters. The kitchen door swings open (despite it being locked earlier) and in staggers a heretofore unseen zombie. Another white guy, this one baggy-eyed and draining blood from a corner of his mouth. He's of the Terry Gindele School, pale of face and trancelike of behavior. A wider shot reveals he's got his sights on Barbra. Barbra (sigh) is still in her chair, hands to her face, contorted in emotional agony.

A zombie is in the house! Rather casually, this instant encapsulates the effect of *Night* on the horror genre. We began at a location that had the gothic trappings of Universal and Hammer horror: the cemetery. But the film didn't go from cemetery to castle or laboratory. Instead, it followed the path of Vietnam vets pushed back into domestic sitting rooms, dog tags jangling as they were sat upon clean sofas. Romero knew all about this. He was 4-F, a military classification for a registrant unfit for service for moral, mental, or physical reasons. I suspect the third reason, based on a 1974 health scare Romero minimized as "a little thyroid shtick" in a letter to Richard Ricci, a shtick that pared the beefy Romero to skin-and-bones until gall bladder surgery.

While Romero was goofing off in art school and protesting the Vietnam War, his father was en route to Vietnam as a naval air navigator. The horror of war had come home. We invited it in. The domestic space would never be safe again, if it ever had been.

The actor who plays this crucial invader is none other than John A. "Jack" Russo, cowriter of *Night of the Living Dead*. On the Varèse Sarabande soundtrack, the Capital Hi-Q library cues are thematically renamed; the cue placed here is called "Ghoulish (J.R.'s Demise)," Russo being the J.R. in question. The LP's not-great sonic quality is remedied by the resplendent 2018 vinyl remaster by Waxwork Records (again credit to Jim Cirronella, who this time enjoyed access to the raw audio packaged with the film's work print). The Waxwork release, by the by, comes with two sets of liner notes, one by Gary Streiner and one by yours truly, in which I make a case no one but me cares about, that *Night* influenced Barbara Loden's fantastic and largely forgotten 1970 drama *Wanda*. (Here's Loden describing her biographical inspiration: "I was like the living dead. I lived like a zombie for a long time.")

The Russo zombie is ten feet from Barb when Ben enters. Ben pulls her to her feet and shoves her to safety. Ben rears back with the tire iron but flubs the strike, and a cutaway shows the weapon hit the carpet. So begins a struggle, both men gripping the other's arms. It's tense seeing Ben in danger. He hurls the Russo zombie to the floor so he can reach for his bludgeon. Romero positions us behind Ben's head so it's *us* the zombie's hand grapples for.

Never doubt Ben. He obtains the tire iron, raises it with both hands, and here we go again: He plants it in the zombie's face with what I'll describe as a *splurch*—another honeydew melon sound effect. (An effectively moody, shot-by-shot, black-and-white 1991 comic adaptation by Tom Skulan and Eric Stanway with art by Carlos Kastro and Eric Mehéu, prefers to interpret this sound as *THRUKT*.) Again, no gore, though that's not because Romero's afraid of gore (just wait). It's simply too sophisticated an effect to pull off, especially when it's better avoided: Ben struggles for a couple seconds to dislodge the tire iron from Jack Russo's face.

Russo is dead. In a way, Romero killed him.

To radically simplify their relationship, Romero was the artiste with shaky business sense, while Russo was the businessman who forever struggled with art. While Romero came off as retiring and embarrassed in interviews, Russo dropped truth bombs and could be disarmingly funny. "I think he could have been a superstar but he took the safer route," Romero said of Russo. "He bet the red-black, instead of ever putting it on number seventeen."

Romero, meanwhile, always stacked his coins on seventeen, often to the deficit of his livelihood. He lived as an artist, and flaunted an artist's quirks. At the aforementioned Days of the Dead panel, Judy Ridley reminisced how the young Romero bought used clothing rather than wash the clothes he owned, prompting Russ Streiner to confirm that Romero, at one point, had amassed fifty-two shirts. (I'm reminded of my first trip to New York at age twenty-three and finding in my cab a bag of disposable underwear. *Disposable underwear*—ideal for the busy artist.)

Russo's self-published 2017 autobiography, *My Life with the Living Dead*, affectingly positions him as the child of an abusive father and manipulative mother (a relationship he used as fodder for *Night*'s Harry and Helen Cooper). The book portrays the young Romero and Russo as close as brothers. It has the ring of truth. A sibling can make all sorts of life choices you disagree with, even besmirch the family name, but the deep roots of the relationship makes it hard not to embrace the sibling when he walks through the door.

The issue at the heart of the Russo-Romero imbroglio has its roots in *Night*'s earliest origins. The facts of who came up with what are as convoluted as the copyright battles. The atmosphere evoked by those who were present at *Night*'s genesis is of bull-session brainstorms over cheap food, "bashing around story ideas" (as Russo puts it in his *Complete Night of the Living Dead Filmbook*) without pretensions of ownership. This fits with the collaborative, democratic utopia Romero searched for his whole career.

Here's Russo's version. After convincing the gang to make a damn movie already over a lunch at local joint called Samreny's, Russo wrote a few pages of a horror-comedy, a couple pages of which are public, that starts with two "ghouls" in a cemetery being interrupted by an object falling from space. Russo tweaked the idea into one of aliens storing people to eat. Kickstarted by this idea, Romero wrote forty pages over Easter vacation. Everyone dug them, and while he pivoted to preproduction, Russo finished the script, roping in his flesh-eating concept.

Romero never publicly accused Russo of getting his facts wrong, but then again, neither man was confrontational. Romero quietly asserted in interviews that *Night* originated with a short story he'd written called "Anubis," which purportedly unfolded as a three-act allegory about the dead overthrowing an existing society, all acts taking place in the same farmhouse. Part one became *Night of the Living Dead*, part two *Dawn of the Dead*, and part three *Day of the Dead*. The story was inspired by Richard Matheson's 1954 novel *I Am Legend*, with *Night* being day one of Matheson's scenario. In raw footage for an interview shot for Stuart Samuels's doc *Midnight Movies: From the Margin to the Mainstream* (2005), Romero—as wired as I've ever seen him, perhaps due to the coffee he's clutching—admits, "I ripped it off, to that extent. I've spoken to Richard about it. He says, 'It's okay. If you made a lot of money, I'd be suing you, but since you didn't make money, forget about it.'"

Interviewed at the 2012 Toronto International Film Festival, Romero even remembered the short story's final line, which I honored by making it the final line of our novel *The Living Dead*. But was his recollection accurate? It's possible; even back then, Romero liked his metaphors heavy, man. The biggest appeal of Romero's version is how it satisfies our longing for a genius narrative. But no one has ever seen the "Anubis" story and the idea that a twenty-some kid could, in one deft swoop, plot out one of history's greatest film trilogies is . . . well, it's a lot.

"Jack says my history is revisionist, and I think Jack's history of it is revisionist," Romero sighs in the Felsher tapes. As with most things, the truth is probably in between, and that's reflected by the opening title credit: SCREENPLAY BY JOHN RUSSO / GEORGE ROMERO. The non-alphabetical order all but guarantees Russo had a heavier writing role than Romero. So Russo's frustration is understandable. According to him, he's the one who came up with the idea of the dead attacking the living. He was the one to make the dead people flesh-eaters (while Romero said it was a carryover from *I Am Legend*). He was the one to devise the iconic ending. Even if all of this is untrue, Russo wrote most of the damn script! But ask any horror fan who invented the modern zombie and only one name comes up.

I have nothing but sympathy for this who-came-up-with-what struggle, especially when the *what* is the zombie, the most important new monster archetype created post-Universal. Unless you're able to find inner peace, that slight is going to fester. It did—and eventually helped tear apart the group of friends.

For now, though, Ben pulls the tire iron from Jack. Released, the zombie's head thuds to the floor. There's a deep, ragged, wet black hole is in his forehead. An important pattern involving head wounds is being established, though it's not clear yet if Ben notices.

Before Ben can bask in his latest ass-kick, he notices the door he closed upon entry is magically open again and a zombie in a white bathrobe (Russ Streiner's robe, if you must know) is heading for it. Ben charges and for a second we glimpse the film's lousiest stand-in, one that would have been right at home in Danman Productions: the bathrobe draped over what might as well be a mop.

Ben jams his tire iron into the plastic head, which is matched with the actor gripping his face and staggering backward.

It's in the space of the zombie's backpedaled steps that Romero reveals, with offhand grace, four new zombies plodding through the lawn. It's this gradual agglomeration of threats that supplies *Night* a slowly dripping dread few films can match. The closest I've seen is James Cameron's *The Abyss*, a scene in which Ed Harris (who received his first starring role in Romero's 1981 *Knightriders*) and Mary Elizabeth Mastrantonio find themselves in a sunken mini-sub with a leak. A small leak. Yet, over the course of the real-time scene, they just can't get the pesky hole plugged. What starts as a minor frustration develops into a sickening realization that one of them is going to drown (they only have one diving suit). A master class in incremental doom.

If you haven't seen *The Abyss*, might I suggest, as a third example of trickling dread, life itself? That day-after-day, week-after-week, year-after-year drudge during which your exact moments of fumbling, or failing, or settling are missed for how stealthily they came. One day, your young eyes see multiple paths to what you want; the next, you can't keep your prescriptions straight and every few months someone you know dies. The zombies of *Night* are death—judging by their condition, death by every means possible—inching to our doorstep, surrounding the farmhouse of our physical bodies. Didn't we close that door? We thought we did. But death waltzed through anyway.

00:18:53 DIRTY POOL

If you're a kid and there's a dead thing, you're interested. Once with a neighbor I poked the bones of a dead bird. My dad often had deer he was dressing hanging upside down in the garage with a gut bucket beneath to catch the innards. My most startling encounter was wandering through waist-tall grass with my friend Chris and abruptly coming upon a dead, bloody pig. Piled against this pig, as if suckling, were a number of dead piglets. It made no sense, but there it was all the same. I was so shocked that I didn't even tell Chris. I just stared at it long enough that I still see it today, the pink shock of all that misplaced death.

Because Barbra has reverted to a child's mindset, it's no surprise she approaches the dead thing on the floor the same way. The Jack Russo zombie died (the second time, I mean) with his eyes closed, but now his eyes are open. Problem is, it's hard to play dead with your eyes open. Russo doesn't quite pull it off: His eyes are clearly moving, though today he attests it was meant as a "death twitch."

Russo's ready explanation doesn't surprise me. His dedication to *Night* is lifelong and unimpeachable. It's what he's chosen to do post-*Night* that makes him a figure of controversy among the fandom. Namely, an endless series of disposable at best, salacious at worst, semi-related zombie projects.

This isn't a crime. It's just less than we want it to be.

Russo's zombie projects began with the 1974 novelization of *Night*, an acceptable prose adaptation useful to fans who didn't have access to the script. But the script has been readily available since it was included in Joe Kane's 2010 *Night of the Living Dead* book. This script matches Romero's shooting script with the addition of a cover page that carries the title *The Anubis* and sketchily credits Russo as the sole author. Russo regrets its inclusion in the book, complaining in his autobiography that Kane "had the gall to call me 'deluded' and in other ways insulted me after he had wheedled my permission to reprint the *Night of the Living Dead* screenplay."

Real trouble began when both Romero and Russo wanted to make sequels. The cleanest account of this mess is in Paul G. Gagne's seminal 1987 book, *The Zombies That Ate Pittsburgh*. The men exchanged releases that allowed Romero's sequel to be produced as well as Russo's sequel, cowritten with Rudy Ricci and Russ Streiner. The same year Romero's *Dawn of the Dead* became a smash hit, Russo adapted his own script into a novel. Three years later, *Variety* announced that the novel, *Return of the Living Dead*, had been optioned by Orion Pictures. Out leapt Romero's lawyers to stop the title being used; they had successfully prevented *Messiah of Evil* (great movie, by the way) from using that same title.

This time they lost. "Dirty pool," Romero called it.

Russo didn't entirely win, though. All that got used from his work was the title. The good news was that the end result, directed as a comedy by Dan O'Bannon, was a hit. The bad news was it came out just six weeks after Romero's labor of love, 1985's *Day of the Dead*. The mid-eighties market wasn't big enough for two zombie flicks. Audiences got confused. *Day* suffered. (Domestically, anyway. Globally it was #26 that year with $34,004,262 box office, over twice as much as #58 *Return of the Living Dead*'s $14,238,828.) It would be a couple decades before *Day* got its critical due—a Romero pattern.

You could call Russo's subsequent zombie projects opportunistic. But a guy's gotta eat. It's when Russo's ambition intersects with Romero-identified iconography that fans revolt. Russo's *Night of the Living Dead* comics, for instance, provide backstories to some of the film's characters, but in place of insight or sensitivity we get gore and nudity. There's nothing natively suspect about nudity in horror. But Russo's use of it feels on par with the nudie mag he cocreated in 1993, *Scream Queens Illustrated*: The nudity serves only the nudity, nothing more.

All this said, it's hard to fault Image Ten for licensing projects Russo brings them. The investors are owed a hell of a lot. Then there's the bitterness, the yearning. Half of making it in the arts is sheer luck. Anyone who says otherwise has wealthy parents. Not being the recipient of that luck, especially as Romero went on to be considered one of the greatest horror directors in history, had to hurt, even if you loved Romero like a brother. Which Russo did.

It's okay to love Image Ten (I sure do) and dislike some of their projects. Image Ten's approval of the Russo brainchild

Night of the Living Dead: 30th Anniversary Edition (stay tuned) was the most contentious call they ever made. In many fans' hearts, it closed the book on Russo, which I understand even as I urge them to go easy. Every member of Image Ten had it hard after *Night*—it's a testament to their fortitude that we don't know *how* hard, how many years' worth of sleep they lost—and Jack Russo may have had it hardest of all.

00:19:08 DECEMBER 1966

Let's turn our eyes away from Russo. Ben is on the same wavelength. "Don't look at it," he orders Barbra, with a brassy punctuation mark from a Loose-Seely needle drop called "Black Night (TC-155)." Russo's skull-cracked face slides out of frame as Ben drags him by the ankles. Marvelous shadows intercede as Ben pulls the body across the kitchen and through the back door. The zombie quartet we saw earlier edges closer. Ben arranges the body on the porch. The zombies, closer. Ben squats, lights a match. Closer, closer—come on, man!

The way the Russo zombie mushrooms into flames makes me wonder if he died from gasoline consumption. The zombies shield their faces and recoil. If you look to Ben's right, you'll spy a ladder alongside the house. Left there by the film crew, probably to get high-angle shots of the undead. Let's hope zombies don't know how to climb.

Ben retreats inside. The whole episode strikes me as ill-construed. But Ben's confidence is contagious. Sure, why not? Let's leave a blazing pyre unattended on the old, dry wooden porch. What's the worst that could happen? (In fact, nothing happens. Ben's a genius.)

Ben locks the door, severing the music, pushes the little kitchen table against it, and sits on it, taking another of those long, silent moments Duane Jones is so good at leavening with anguish. He wipes his forehead—and what's this? Another ring, which sort of looks like a class ring, but because it's on his left ring finger, I'm going to say he's married.

Jones himself wasn't married, so this is no accidental accessory. Three out of three of our characters so far are married, but not one ever references a spouse. *Night* is saying something here about the nuclear family. When you're close to dying (or so goes the narrative we've been fed), you say goodbye to loved ones or tell a witness to deliver the message that you loved them. Barb and Ben, however, live a different experience. Marriage, for them, might have served a purpose similar to their vehicles. Useful to a point—necessary, even, to navigate the wilds—but now that those vehicles are incapacitated, there will be no mourning.

The next thing Ben does is turn on the kitchen lights and shout, "Get some more lights on in this house!" That's right, horror hounds, a character who actually turns on lights! Horror films so habitually use darkness as their foundation for jump scares that brightness feels revolutionary. For this reason, some horror fans (raises hand) have a special affection for horror films set in the daytime. *The Wicker Man, Jaws, Midsommar, Session 9, The Birds, Who Can Kill a Child?, Last House on the Left, The Devil's Rejects, Children of the Corn*. Daylit horror is inescapable. You can't hide. It's also often hot, and for me, heat is associated with nausea.

Barbra, following orders, totters away. Barb and the zombies move with the same shambling gait: The line separating *us* from *them* is thinner than we'd like. It's the word *them* that's important. *Them* is zombies, yes, but it's also the cowards, the self-preservationists, the outright villains. Before this film is over, each character will serve their time as *them*, and nothing impresses me more about the screenplay.

Ben digs in a toolbox, finds a screwdriver, and flips it in the air like a drumstick. My dude is thriving. He grabs a hammer and pulls open the exact drawer that contains nails. Hell yeah, he does. He asks Barbra to find some boards they can nail up. Barbra, honestly, acts like she's shit-faced drunk. She caresses her knife and wobbles into the kitchen. Ben proves he's all of us by losing his temper for the first time. He hollers, "Look, goddamn—" only to cut himself off. Scaring this lady more won't get them anywhere.

He takes her by the arms and addresses her like a frightened child. "I know you're afraid. I'm afraid too." He then explains the plan that will occupy the action, and direct the conflict, for the rest of the film. He's going to board the place up. He needs Barbra's help to gather wood. It takes a bit for this to sink into Barb's rattled brain, but eventually she nods.

It's easy not to notice the calendar behind Ben. The month being displayed is DECEMBER 1966. While it's feasible a film shot in 1967 might take place in 1966, Barbra and Johnny's time-change conversation makes it clear this is April. Which means whoever has been scraping out an existence in the farmhouse has neglected to advance the calendar for four straight months.

Maybe the death at the top of the stairs had nothing to do with zombies.

Barbra enters the den. The shot is dominated by the fireplace. (A fake one, actually, but you'd never know it for Vince Survinski's artistry.) Atop the fireplace sits a framed photo of a man. Caucasian. Older. Wearing the full-band white collar associated with Lutheran and Anglican/Episcopalian clergy. That's interesting. If the dead woman at the top of the stairs was the daughter of clergy, the dead returning to life might have signaled to her the onset of Revelation 20:5, which foretells the resurrection of the wicked dead. That's a zombie apocalypse, folks. Hallelujah.

The camera cuts to our old friend the wild boar head, and tilts downward to find Barbra's hand trailing over an octagonal box. She grazes a button, thereby triggering the film's most beguiling (and unscripted) sequence. Lighting supervisor Joseph Unitas (he played pro football, just like his famous cousin Johnny), who spent roughly a week on set, believes he suggested it to Romero. Though routinely called a "music box" by fans, it's really a Roundelay, a lipstick carousel produced in the 1940s by a company called Swiss Harmony. Press the top button and all six sides open like ladybug wings and rotate, each door offering a lipstick.

The Roundelay was on loan from Vince Survinski's sister. She never got it back—someone stole it on the last day of shooting. The plinking melody you hear in *Night* comes from an actual music box still owned today by actor Kyra Schon; it sounds like a variation on Mozart's "Der Vogelfänger (the Bird Catcher's Song)" from *The Magic Flute*. But Roundelays did, in fact, play songs, and when Romero made *Martin*, he used this Roundelay's tune for ice-cream truck music. Factoids don't get more factoidy than that.

The next shot is of Barbra's eyes *through* the Roundelay's revolving doors, an escape into innocence and beauty. It's quintessential Barbra: She lives life with a happy face soldered to her head like the Man in the Iron Mask. A mask that heavy wearies you, and blinkers you too. There's also something pious about this moment, notable in a film that eschews shows of religion beyond Barbra's graveside genuflection. Even that scene was curtailed; the script directed Barb to handle rosary beads, but Romero must have nixed it. (He brought the beads back in *Day of the Dead*, quite pointedly, with the character of Miguel Salazar.)

We are left to wonder what's holy to these characters. For Barbra, it's this: a pretty wheel that should be offering her lovely makeup, one more kind of mask.

The lullaby is undercut by a library cue called "Mysterious Hour." A rising tremolo poisons the innocence. The doors of the Roundelay close over Barbra's face, the eyeholes of her mask filled by smoking pitch. Innocence is worse than gone. It was never really there.

00:22:37

HELL IS OTHER PEOPLE

BEN'S HAVING A FUCKING FIELD DAY. HE DETACHES A door, grabs an ironing board, rips a plank from the bottom of the sink, and gathers the lumber from behind it. (Why someone stored lumber in their kitchen is anyone's guess.) His energy is cathartic. Maybe he *is* a truck driver, not a long-hauler but a local delivery guy, and he sits all day in his cab, muscles vibrated to jelly by the road under the wheels. The only motions he's allowed are slight turns of his head. An October 12, 1968, article in the *New Pittsburgh Courier* says Jones plays a "salesman," a bold claim I found backed up by a press sheet in an old Latent Image binder, which, sure enough, describes Ben as "Late 20's. Negro. Attractive, well-spoken salesman. Powerful but sensitive." Freed from the wheel at last, Ben's a running back called off the bench. This is his time to shine.

The next shot of Barbra is one for the books. Romero frames her in front of the fireplace. Not only does she block the man in the clerical collar, but also the deer head, which effectively gives her antlers. There's no way this pagan image is accidental, but I don't know what to make of it. Romero might be saying that devils, in the form of zombies, have come. He might be saying the opposite, that it's the living who are the devils.

More likely, I think, Romero is comparing women like Barbra

to trophies. She has the requisite tailoring and the dog-show hairdo. But she was never taught the skills necessary to survive without a husband. Remove her from civilization, as *Night* has done, and she's doomed.

The next thing Barbra does always got my mom chuckling. Barb gathers a handful of wood from beside the fireplace. I don't mean firewood. I mean itty bitty sticks that might be useful if they were boarding up a dollhouse. She deposits her useless find on the fridge and plods across the kitchen (there are visible light stands all over this scene) to help hold the loose door Ben's nailing crosswise against the back door. Put "help" in quotation marks. She only gets in the way, then pouts when the hammering gets too loud.

Up until this instant, *Night of the Living Dead* has unfolded in real time. We've been with our characters for every second. That ends with the next shot's dissolve—film code for time passing. (It is one of only five dissolves before the end credits. Dissolves cost money.) We rejoin the action as Ben nails the final board over a kitchen window. Though I admire his effort, he's not done a stellar job. Boards hang in haphazard crisscrosses. The zombies aren't giants; it might have made more sense to focus on the bottom halves of windows.

As Ben segues into the dining room, he removes his cardigan. We loved you, cardigan. He chatters to keep the mood up, though it's unclear if Barbra hears. She picks at her fingernails like she's bored. Ben, though, is on a tear. As he begins disassembling the dining room table, he tells a story that provides lore fans would dissect for the next fifty years.

The truck Ben arrived in isn't his. He "had jumped in" to the truck to listen to the radio. This sounds like a good way for a Black man to get shot in 1960s America (2020s America too), so things must have already gone topsy-turvy. Indeed, Ben describes a "big gasoline truck" being chased by ten to fifteen zombies. He says he had to brake not to hit it. (Now he's driving the truck? Okay, so he definitely stole the truck.)

The scene Ben describes is awesome. The gasoline truck cut across a road, punched through a billboard, and tore over a gas pump, becoming "a moving bonfire." Hot damn. Romero didn't have the budget for such a sequence, but it goes without saying that a modern version of *Night* (produced at the scale of Zack Snyder's 2004 *Dawn of the Dead* remake), would film the hell out of this scene. Actually, Snyder's *Dawn* features an Easter-egg homage: Early in the film, far below an aerial camera, a truck tears through a gas pump and becomes, you guessed it, a moving bonfire.

But budget wasn't why Romero avoided it. He preferred it this way. Of all the revelations in Adam Charles Hart's *Raising the Dead: The Work of George A. Romero* (2024), the biggest epiphany is how profoundly influenced Romero was by Jack Gelber's 1959 play *The Connection* (more widely seen in Shirley Clarke's 1961 film adaptation, which, incidentally, is cinema's first found-footage film, a format Romero would adopt for *Diary of the Dead*).

Romero starred as "Leach" (a gay junkie who ends up OD'ing) in a March 1960 production of the play, which, to boil it down, is about people milling around in an apartment. Over a lunch of Mexican conchas, Hart posited to me that *Night of the Living Dead* is just *The Connection* with some zombies on both ends. Insert mind-blown emoji.

The people of *The Connection* do little but pace and squabble. They consist of Black and white people coexisting with surprising normalcy. The apartment set is as banal as the farmhouse. They await their dealer, just like *Night*'s characters wait for rescuers. Like *Night, The Connection* features jarringly gross interludes: squeezing pus from a boil, the OD scene.

Even the play's pessimistic moral, voiced by the dealer, sounds like something Romero would have written: "They got lousy squares and they got lousy hipsters." It doesn't matter which camp you fall into. Either way, you're doomed. Given all this, I wonder if Gelber felt he was reworking Jean-Paul Sartre's *No Exit* (1944) in which three people's eternal damnation is being stuck in a room together. The play's most famous piece of dialogue, "L'enfer c'est les autres"—*Hell is other people*—might as well be *Night*'s tagline.

In light of these stage origins, *Night of the Living Dead: Live!*, a play first produced in 2013 by Nictophobia Films, feels like closing a circle. The comedy is a bit shrill for a guy like me raised on the understated motion picture, but it pays dividends after the intermission, when the story as we know it ends and the play rewinds *Clue*-style to posit eight additional endings, the last of which, naturally, breaks into what I admit is a fairly rousing song ("If we give it our best / and we do what we said / we will survive / this *Night of the Living Deeee-eeead*!")

A play? Sure. But not in their strangest dreams could Image Ten have predicted Jordan Wolfe's *Night of the Living Dead!: The Musical!* (the slogan: "Horror! Bloodshed! Belting!"). A rock-and-roll spoof in the tradition of the equally implausible *Little Shop of Horrors*, the show has lyrics like "Tonight the world will learn that death is just a start, / The dead are rising up to munch your beating heart." Just don't confuse this with Kevin Frei and Leah Koestner's *Night of the Living Dead!: The Musical* (one fewer exclamation points). I haven't seen it, but I've heard the songs, which include "Karate Rangers" and "Libertarians in Love." So I'm guessing it takes a few liberties with the story. In Romero's archive is a contract for yet another stage license to Pittsburgh's City Theatre Company, for which Image Ten received all of $500.

If even that's not enough, first of all, who damaged you? Second of all, try *Night of the Living Dead: The Opera*, which debuted at Pittsburgh's Microscopic Opera Company on October 31, 2013, with music by Todd Goodman and libretto by Stephen Catanzarite. It's a frequently beautiful work with a sobriety surpassing even that of the original film. Even if you can't dig the lyrics out of the operatic voices (for me, it helps that the lines are often verbatim from the screenplay), the opera reveals the bones of the Russo-Romero script by unfolding as a series of ensembles. For example, so far in the film we've seen a Barb-and-Johnny duet and a Barb-and-Ben duet—but more ambitious arrangements are coming.

The last name you'd expect to hear associated with the opera is Bill Hinzman, but it was, in fact, Zombie #1 who pitched a *Night* musical to Catanzarite—Hinzman, always working the angles, had a ready supply of *Night of the Living Dead* business cards with Zombie #1's face on it. Catanzarite wisely considered the idea too campy, but thought it might work as an opera. It does, and I'm especially fond of how the zombies sit in the theater's front row only to stagger to the stage as needed. This upends the expected staging, suggesting that we, the audience, are in league with the zombies, not the survivors—a position Romero would increasingly take in his films.

All of which brings us back to Ben: He's *telling* his story instead of living it on camera, a choice as affecting and as formally tidy as *The Connection*. The message is that all characters in *Night* will be judged solely on their actions inside the farmhouse. Maybe Ben was a beloved community leader before this. Who cares? Maybe Barbra volunteered at an orphanage. Fuck it. It's meat into the grinder. Let's see what grade of sausage comes out the other side.

By now, Ben's no longer talking to Barbra. He's stopped dismembering the table and is in conversation with himself—with the person he was until today. "Didn't know if the truck was going to explode or what," he says in a tone of apology. This is good writing, good editorial judgment for having no music, and *incredible* acting. This was, in fact, the audition scene with which Duane Jones dropped the jaws of Image Ten. Our minds scramble for what Ben is apologizing for. For stealing the truck? For leaving people to die? It doesn't matter. There's cowardice in his recent history, an intriguing contrast with the capable hero.

Ben says he looked for help at Beekman's Diner (which the script nonsensically places in Cambria County, ninety miles west of Pittsburgh), but the place was encircled by fifty or sixty zombies ". . . just standing there . . . staring at me." If the ghouls we've met so far are any indication, Ben's talking about fifty or sixty white rural Pennsylvanians. Consider the names that might have gone through Ben's mind. Zachariah Walker, for instance, lynched in Coatesville, Pennsylvania, in 1911. Sure, that's fifty-six years earlier. But if you head the other direction, fifty-five years after this scene, up pops another name: Donté Jones (all too close to Duane Jones), found hanged from a set of monkey bars in Blue Bell, Pennsylvania, in 2022, a death ruled a suicide but surrounded by suspicious data points. White neighborhood. Missing wallet. No suicide note. No rational explanation.

Ben's too smart not to understand past as prologue.

00:27:29 LEAVE ME THE HELL ALONE ABOUT IT

Never again will Jones's voice be as vulnerable as when he describes plowing through zombies in his truck. "Just wanted to crush them," he admits in horrified wonder, and who, in their most candid moment, can blame him? The sadness Ben conveys is less for the monsters he killed than for the monster he, in that instant, had become, ravenous for blood.

Jack Russo reports that Duane Jones broke into tears at the end of this monologue, and then went around shaking hands and hugging the all-white crew, at last not feeling like an outsider. "Duane kept suspecting we were going to make him an Uncle Tom or something," Russo said. "It wasn't until we were halfway through that he was convinced he was going to be a hero." It's the sort of scene that wins people Best Actor awards, though there was no way Oscar voters would have given the time of day to a low-budget shocker. The big winner at the 1968 Oscars was *Oliver!*, a grindingly wholesome musical toward which I have a begrudging affection due to having dopily played the Artful Dodger in a high school play. (*Night* didn't win an Oscar, but it did take home an Oscar-sized statuette on October 28, 1990, as part of a TV special called *The Horror Hall of Fame*. The award was handed out by a hulking Jason Voorhees and a pipsqueak Danny Pintauro of *Who's the Boss?* fame.)

Jones could have earned Oscars for each of his three first

films: *Night of the Living Dead*, *Ganja & Hess* (1973, winner of the Cannes Film Festival Critics' Choice prize before it vanished for forty years), and *Losing Ground* (1982, another stone cold classic, lost for thirty-two years). Jones costarred in only one other film, 1986's *Vampires*. He's great in it but can only do so much in a role cobbled from footage from the unreleased *Negatives*.

That's the extent of his starring roles according to the Internet Movie Database (and everywhere else). To learn otherwise, you'd have to spelunk through *The Catalyst*, the student newspaper of SUNY Old Westbury, where Jones taught for the last three years of his life. Amid these fusty old stacks I discovered mentions of four heretofore forgotten TV/film appearances.

Jones appeared in an episode of the CBS series *Black Heritage: A History of Afro-Americans* entitled "Me and My Song" (1969), a poetic dramatization of Harlem Renaissance poets; *Rise: A Love Song for a Love People* (1975), a lost indie film about Malcolm X (I have to assume that Jones plays Malcolm, given their physical similarity); and WCVB-TV Boston's one-hour *Good Luck Mr. Robinson* (1979), which I managed to find. Jones is terrific in it, even if it's an educational film about stress and high blood pressure.

Here's the choicest nugget: Jones spent part of 1969 originating the role of Bert Skelly on the soap opera *One Life to Live*, before ceding the part to actor Herb Davis (who does look a lot like him). Jones did the role under the alias "Wayne Jones." While I can't absolutely confirm Duane was Wayne (the 1968–1976 kinescope copies of *One Life to Live* were lost in a fire), I can't imagine how *Catalyst* writers would have come up with this fact unless Jones told them.

Setting aside these forgotten projects, as well as quick cameos in *Beat Street* (1984) and *To Die For* (1988), Jones boasts a John Cazale–level batting average. So why wasn't Jones catapulted to widespread fame? Because Hollywood already had Sidney Poitier at the time of *Night*, with Harry Belafonte ascendant. What, were they expected to support a *third* Black leading man?

Jones offered a different explanation of his life's trajectory.

He was, in short, an artist of the truest stripe. It was the *process* that mattered—the experience, not the recognition. At the University of Iowa circa 1997, I blundered into a small-group chat with André Gregory. (I, inveterate dummy, had no idea who André Gregory was.) The legendary avant-garde director, writer, and actor spoke with gusto about rehearsing *Uncle Vanya* for three fucking years without giving any performances (though Louis Malle filmed the process in *Vanya on 42nd Street*).

It was J. D. Salinger–style art-for-art's-sake, and it made an impression on me, partially because I, as a budding artist, had brought myself up the same way. Writing for me began as a form of play with my childhood buddy, Ben, and I didn't get serious until around, say, sixth grade, when I started writing for myself—and no one else. It was around then that I had the idea that would become *The Shape of Water.* In middle school I wrote novellas, and in my senior year wrote a fantasy epic with the curious title of *Gator Skin.*

I never tried to get anyone to read *Gator Skin.* Or anything else I wrote. It never occurred to me. I simply adored writing, in my bedroom, in study hall, after fellow employees went home at my after-school job at the movie theater. Little has changed.

I'm still André Gregory, plugging away at *Vanya.*

Among the *Vanya* faithful was Duane Lionel Jones. After graduating from the University of Pittsburgh in 1959, Jones studied at the Sorbonne in Paris and the University of Oslo, was a Phelps-Stokes exchange scholar in Niger, taught lit at Long Island University, helped design Harlem Preparatory School, and created English-language programs for the Peace Corps. He wrapped up a master's degree at NYU while working on *Night,* and afterward oversaw Antioch's lit department from 1972 to 1976, whereupon he became executive director of New York's Black Theater Alliance until 1981. A May 13, 1978, piece in the *New York Amsterdam News* reports Mayor Ed Koch naming Jones New York City's Commissioner of Cultural Affairs, but that sounds crazy to me. Per a scribble in Romero's archives,

Jones lived during those years in the East Village near Tompkins Square Park, specifically at 400 East Ninth Street, a four-story building of beige stucco that today houses the Lime Tree Market on its ground level.

From 1986 on, Jones was the artistic director of Manhattan's Richard Allen Cultural Center and taught theater at SUNY Old Westbury at the Maguire Theater (today called the Duane L. Jones Recital Hall, if that gives you any idea of the impact he made in those two years before his death). He also taught acting at other institutions, and privately.

No *Night* adage is retold more than the one claiming Jones's race was irrelevant to his casting. From Romero on down, everyone swears Jones was just the best actor to audition. I'm sure he was. But look. You didn't cast a Black man as your lead in 1967 unless you were progressive enough to consider it a normal or decent thing to do. The fandom's insistence upon this colorblind narrative is ill-considered. In *With Bloom Upon Them and Also With Blood,* National Book Award–winning poet Justin Phillip Reed, who is Black, takes no prisoners: "If Romero truly cast Duane Jones . . . not at all because he was Black, people oughta be ashamed to say that shit with big grins the way they do."

Romero tried to be sensitive to race relations. In 1963, under the aegis of Ram Pictures, he directed a twenty-one-minute film called *Connection* (shades of *The Connection*?), which follows a Black family's struggle to live a fulfilled American life. Alternately known as *A Man with a Revolver* and *Elegy,* it's the sole surviving excerpt from a two-and-a-half-hour anthology film Romero, Streiner, and Richard Ricci made called *Expostulations,* entirely shot and edited but abandoned before sound was added.

In a 2008 interview, Romero tipped his hand by saying, "We thought we were being very hip" with the colorblind casting of Jones—which tells us they weren't colorblind at all.

Jones knew damn well what it meant to be cast, and that was enough. He was fresh off of starring in a Negro Ensemble Company production of *The Terraced Apartment,* a one-act play by acclaimed playwright Steve Carter, probably staged at the Old Reliable Theatre Tavern, an Off-Off-Broadway stage at the back of a Lower East Side bar. The play dramatizes the discomforts of a Black couple who move to an upscale Harlem neighborhood.

By Jones's account, he advised the credulous young Romero to adjust the racial dynamics of two scenes. "You know what happens to me on the street?" he asked Romero, vis-à-vis a scene where Ben slugs Barbra. Jones also nixed a contemplated sequence in which Barbra saves Ben's life by throwing herself in front of him. Said Jones, "I convinced George that the Black community would rather see me dead than saved."

The most famous of *Night*'s behind-the-scenes photos is a portrait of fourteen cast and crew members lined up on Gass farmhouse land. Taken by Hinzman, the photo has that Kodachrome saturation you don't see anymore. As bright as the sun is, the smiles are brighter. George Romero's smirk. Jack Russo's office-photo stiffness. Keith Wayne's Hollywood pizzazz. Judith O'Dea's awkward beaming. Judy Ridley's natural shine. Karl Hardman's dopey delight. Marilyn Eastman's wanton glee. Only one person isn't smiling: Duane Jones. He is, in fact, looking down at the grass, eyes lost in his brow's shadow. He probably looked away from the sun for an instant. Regardless, it has a powerful effect. Jones alone seems unblinded by the light of youthful optimism. He foresees a different, darker future.

Later in life, only Jones's students and colleagues knew him. Never fans of the film. This was by design, the opposite of the path taken by people like Jack Russo. That doesn't mean Jones and Russo were so different. Either reaction was a valid way of navigating the fraught relationship to the film that defined them. Take it from me: Creators can't love their work with a fan's passion. They know the compromises baked into it; they know the opportunities or relationships it cost them; they know who felt slighted or uncredited; they know the vitriol or diminishment aimed at it, some of it backlash, but not all. Any pride is tainted with poisons only the artists can taste.

You've made it. Art has made you immortal. Doesn't it feel good?

Ask a vampire. The one Duane Jones plays in *Ganja & Hess*, maybe.

Jones attended the world premiere of *Night of the Living Dead* on October 1, 1968, at Pittsburgh's Fulton Theater. (In a bit of backstage drama, the film print arrived from New York mere hours before the show.) Per a local rag called *Lebanon Daily News*, the premiere, attended by over a thousand people, had "all the Hollywood trappings of waist [*sic*]—deep cleavage, black limousines, and a smoky cocktail party in the grand ballroom of the William Penn Hotel." The *New Pittsburgh Courier* ran pictures. One shows a theater banner that reads, THE NIGHT OF THE LIVING DEAD, not the only time I've seen the title led with the word *The*, but considering the event, the most flagrant.

In photos of the event, Jones looks happy with his arms around two young Black women: his sister, Marva (who would become the city attorney of Atlanta, the first African American woman to hold such a position), and "rising young model-actress Nancy Walker." (I can find nothing on this Nancy Walker, and way too much about the Nancy Walker who called Bounty paper towels "the quicker picker-upper" in commercials.) *New Pittsburgh Courier* coverage notes one of Jones's guests as his "aunt Pauline Gordon, prominent mortician of Johnstown."

There's a photo of Jones at the New York premiere, too, looking, if I'm not mistaken, slightly less happy.

After that, he all but disappeared from view of the moviegoing public.

Jones only attended one other screening of *Night*, delivering a lecture on Halloween night, 1985, hosted by New York's American Museum of Black History and Arts (where the film played alongside 1976's *Dr. Black, Mr. Hyde*). He never met fans. He never even saw another George Romero film. That Jones is so damn good in his debut film makes these facts sting. As a classically trained actor, he came to *Night* suspicious of its genre, and that suspicion likely grew with the film's inclusion on questionable double bills. *Night* was often paired with *Slaves*, which came out a year later from Walter Reade. I attribute this to both films having Black leads, though I cannot in my wildest nightmares imagine a worse pairing, *Slaves* being a glacially slow and mawkish slave plantation melodrama starring Dionne Warwick and Ossie Davis.

My hunch is such twin bills offended the hyperaesthete Jones. *Night* is a magic spell conjured by unreproducible alchemy. Jones, on the other hand, is a flawless diamond. No one needs to tell me the pride he took in his work. It coruscates from his steely eyes, two headlights no zombie can smash. Jones grew up in the Monongahela Valley steel town of Duquesne ("Do-CANE"), sibling to Marva and Henry Jr. (the latter disabled in the Korean War) and child to Mildred and Henry, who was one of the state's first Black police officers (he died before he could see his son's first movie). In a June 2020 *Georgia Bar Journal* interview with Marva, she calls Henry "a surrogate mayor for his people in a large section of the state."

Henry's very job was a kind of activism—and the other Joneses followed suit. Against her mother's cautions, Marva attended anti-war protests in Washington. "I had the audacity to hope and dream that I could make it in a profession where almost nobody looked like me," she said. So did Duane, who dabbled in writing, painting, and piano (I wonder if he ever played the farmhouse's piano between takes) before settling on acting.

The amour propre Jones had in his cosmopolitan education and multiple spoken languages is felt in his Shakespearean elocution. All reports from the *Night* set describe Jones as constantly reading heavy literature. ("You didn't have small talk with Duane," Judy Ridley once recalled.) My favorite set photo shows Jones lounging in black sunglasses reading a book that I have finally identified as Ernest Havemann's *The Age of Psychology* (1957), billed as "a layman's guide to the modern science of human behavior." You could describe *Night of the Living Dead* the same way. Maybe Jones was doing character work?

Duane Jones only spoke publicly about *Night* twice.

In 1986, the TV show *Entertainment Tonight* ran a weeklong series of four-minute segments called "Masters of Terror," hosted by seventy-five-year-old Vincent Price. One focused on *Night*. While Price's analysis is iffy (I doubt *Night*'s zombies represent "sixties conformists whose senses were dead," though you could make that argument for *Dawn*), the piece contains the only—the *only*—video of Jones addressing *Night*. In these precious eleven seconds, Jones (in a striped gray blazer over a paisley shirt unbuttoned to reveal an aquamarine tank top) says, "I'm not sure that [Romero] was reaching for deep sociological explanations or symbolism." That's it.

Far more significant is a 1988 interview conducted by journalist Tim Ferrante. With help from Jack Russo (with whom he owned the publishing company Imagine, Inc.), Ferrante convinced Jones to sit for a three-hour audio interview for *Fangoria*, twenty-two minutes of which were licensed as bonus content for various *Night* releases. I revere the Ferrante tapes as others revere the Zapruder film. Interviewed from his home at SUNY College at Old Westbury, Jones sounds relaxed and bemused, though stronger emotions tremble beneath.

Some part of Jones needed to diminish *Night*. It might have been a reaction to a life that had taken him on a path less celebrated than the one signposted by the film's fame.

Jones's key statement comes at the top of Ferrante's interview: "It should never be misconstrued that my enigmatic, mysterious persona that I have in some instances deliberately created just to have the space in which to have a private life, is a lack of gratitude. It's not. But it is my absolute insistence that I be seen as a total human being and not as Ben."

They are words to make you cheer. But they also cloak the umbrage, I believe, of a film career that did not (or was not allowed to) take off. In a January 1975 interview conducted by Gary Anthony Surmacz in *Cinefantastique*, Streiner, Hardman, and Russo are understandably bilious over Romero alone getting credit for *Night*. "I think you feel put upon because of the obvious attempt to copy the glory on a single-handed basis for the production of *Night of the Living Dead*," Hardman says. Jones, to Ferrante, says the same thing: "There are some of us who could have used another kind of boost to our careers."

You feel that bitterness? So did Hazel Garland, who penned the *New Pittsburgh Courier*'s Things to Talk About column in the 1970s. The small-town papers I grew up with featured such columns, in which rural gadflies offered hyper-local news flashes like who was painting their garage, or who was waging war against garden rabbits. In her March 25, 1978, column, Garland describes running into Jones at a party. Re: *Night*, she was told that "nothing had come from it. Duane had not even been approached to appear in the latest film shot on location at the Monroeville Mall." (In an April 18, 2025, episode of the *Matt and Mike Pull Focus* podcast, O'Dea expresses a similar sadness that Romero never called again.)

(The *Courier*, a leading Black newspaper, is *the* place for Jones juvenilia, including an October 24, 1953, report of the sixteen-year-old Jones attending a "wiener roast" at which he "had a very enjoyable time," and July 2, 1955, coverage of Jones and Elsie Howard being elected "Mr. and Mrs. Duquesne High School.")

Richard Ricci noticed this shift in relations. He gave what was likely his final interview for *The Farmhouse Seven*, in which Jeff Moreno reports, "Years after, according to Richard, Duane Jones became very militant, and their friendship went from good to antagonism . . . Richard offered to give Jones half of his [Walter Reade] checks, thinking it might improve their friendship, which unfortunately it did not."

Something's amiss. Romero liked to cast his friends, over and over. Yet never Jones, arguably the best actor he ever worked with, and one who was readily available. There were hurt feelings somewhere. Even if the slight was minor, Romero and Jones were non-confrontational enough to let it fester into a lifelong chilliness. In Ferrante's interview, Jones stresses that if you're a new friend of his, you get to mention *Night of the Living Dead* exactly once: "People who know me and live in the same environment that I do know they need to leave me the hell alone about it." It's no wonder that Ferrante posseses the only Duane Jones autograph known to exist.

These aren't the words of someone grateful. They are the words of someone wounded. In the excellent documentary *One for the Fire* (2008), costar Marilyn Eastman suggests the whole gang knew of Jones's anguish, saying, with palpable regret, "He was a tortured individual." In personal notes, Karl Hardman echoed the sentiment: "He was a very melancholy soul."

Romero spoke of being in touch with Jones only when casting in New York due to Jones's Negro Ensemble connections. A year before Jones's death, Romero and his then-wife Christine ran into Jones at the Pittsburgh airport. Asked about this in *One for the Fire,* Romero nearly tears up with emotion, a rare thing, and speaks with atypical inarticulateness. "I wish Duane was still alive because he would be the guy I'd most want to talk to about . . . you know . . . 'how do you feel about this, that this is happening,' or that this film has become 'important,' in a certain sense." It's clear Romero regrets not taking the time to understand what the experience meant to Jones—in other words, for not being a better friend.

The dignified Jones never would have reached out for this kind of amity. The most sensible reason he gives Ferrante for forsaking *Night* is the peril of stagnating in nostalgia's brine. Makes sense to me. I don't doubt there are people I went to high school with who subsist on a diet of teenage glory. A winning pass. Election to a homecoming court. After a while, most adults stop trying new things. They have kids, which is definitely new, and the experiments begin again. Jones wasn't going to let this happen. He was going to keep progressing, goddamn it, even if it meant shrugging off the most incredible thing he'd been a part of.

The shoot was "great fun," he tells Ferrante. The crew, he says, was "considerate."

00:27:58

SLAP HEARD ROUND THE WORLD

BARBRA KNEADS THE LACY CLOTH THAT USED TO live on the table Ben just annihilated. She's sitting in front of a window. The shades are up. Bothers me every time. What's stopping a zombie from bashing through that window? There's a moth on the glass, the most normal thing in the world. Barbra, too, acts as if all is normal, launching sans preamble into her own story. "We were riding in the cemetery," she begins, a weird way to describe what they were doing. She recounts her and Johnny's travails in a space-cadet voice, like she's mistaken this moment for a social visit. She claims she responded to Johnny's *They're coming to get you, Barbra* by laughing. That's a highly revisionist take.

Ben rolls his eyes. Going by how hard my mom laughed, this was her favorite scene. As Barb continues her pointless account, Ben resumes work on the table. A few babbles later, it's clear he's given up on this white lady. "Why don't you just keep calm?" he suggests.

No chance of that. Barbra reaches the part of the story where Zombie #1 grabbed her and flips out all over again. I doubt O'Dea's clawing at her own clothing was meant to have sexual overtones, but it does, and it's impossible not to be reminded that Barb and Ben are a white woman and a Black man alone together.

It doesn't matter what's happening. What matters is what it *looks* like is happening. Case in point: On April 29, 1970, the Walter Reade Organization mailed Image Ten what the envelope announced as "Actual Screen Transcript." In it, Ben is referred to as "the Negro" until his name comes up. It's what he looked like to the transcriber. What he looked like to nearly everyone.

"I think you should just calm *down*," Ben reiterates. I suppose it's unkind to Barb, who did, after all, suffer a trauma, but I laugh every time. The disparity between the two characters is inherently comic, like Léon having to take care of Mathilda while killing people, or the Mandalorian watching out for Grogu.

Histrionic as it is, it's fine acting from O'Dea in what is basically her showcase monologue. (In a September 30, 2025, episode of the *Bede vs. the Living Dead* podcast, O'Dea says the speech, for which she did two takes, was improvised off suggestions from Romero.) How seldom Romero cuts from O'Dea shows his confidence in her ability to hold our attention. Barb's grating here, but that's why O'Dea is so effective; she's not afraid to shed her leading-lady mantle to become the thorn in our sides. Credit also to Romero. Like all smart directors, he tossed aside what he thought he wanted, or what the script wanted, and mined the actor he had for the actual riches contained within.

Despite this, Romero's most oft-voiced regret about *Night* was Barbra's weakness. This marks a rare place where Romero and I diverge. I love how Barbra is portrayed in *Night*, and O'Dea, for what it's worth, agrees. Her shell-shock is as every bit as likely as any other response. Netflix categories have sanded down the concept of a "strong female lead" as one who "kicks ass." It's frustrating. A strong female lead is one who doesn't operate on clichés. That's it.

What's un-cliché about Barbra is that she doesn't get stronger as the movie proceeds. Character arcs are overrated; I wish more stories had the courage to have characters enter and exit without having learned a goddamn thing. More often than not, that's how the world works. *Night of the Living Dead* is the epitome of this approach. Each character blazes into the movie one way and blazes out unchanged. It's the difference between *plot* and *story*. Keep your plot; I just want to know how this car crash ends up.

And crash this scene does. Barb tells Ben they need to find Johnny. He ignores her; he's got tables, chairs, and ironing boards to nail up. Barbra's white privilege unsheathes like claws and she repeats the demand four more times at increasing volume. Finally she leaps up, and wrests Ben by the sleeve. He's annoyed but calm. "Don't you know what's going on out there? This is no Sunday school picnic." He informs her, not unkindly, that her brother is dead.

A woman like Barbra in a conflict like this? Sorry, she'll need to speak to the manager. She rockets past Ben to try to open the door. Ben pulls her back. Cut to a close-up of Ben's face as Barbra's hand slaps his cheek. His face goes tight and angry—and then he flat out decks Barbra with a right hook.

Discussions of the film's racial dynamics usually center on this scene. While the script states only that Barbra is "slapping at his face" (and the novelization removes the slaps altogether), lore has it Romero instructed O'Dea to slap Jones three times. Jones refused. Per O'Dea's recollection, "[T]his was a very sensitive issue for Duane Jones at that time and he said, 'I can accept being smacked once. But I don't want to play it the way that you've written it.'"

Jones's nonviolence extended both ways: He also didn't want to punch out Barbra. Here, the filmmakers prevailed by insisting the plot required an unconscious Barb. I'm skeptical. Barbra already *looks* faint, so why not just have her faint? My gut tells me everyone in that farmhouse understood the power of that punch. It was the right choice for the character. It was the right choice for the movie. It was the right choice for the time.

In the Heat of the Night, featuring Sidney Poitier's "Slap Heard Round the World," hit screens on August 2, 1967, while *Night of the Living Dead* was filming. The two scenes are fascinating to watch together—*In the Heat of the Night of the Living Dead*, let's call it. Poitier's slap is a lightning-quick reflex to the backhand slap he receives from a genteel racist. Poitier was a big enough deal to have the slap cemented as part of his contract (which paid him $200,000 plus 20 percent of the gross). Jones, on the other hand, was earning jack shit (and 2 percent of the gross, yippee) from a bunch of yahoos somewhere outside Pittsburgh. Still Jones had the foresight to do what smart actors in low-budget films have always done: control as much of their fate as possible.

It was Duane Jones's face going up on those cinema screens.

His right fist too.

Socked, Barb flaps like an inflatable toy. She goes cross-eyed. You practically see the birds circling her head like Wile E. Coyote. She passes out and Ben catches her, and the dramatic blurt of an Ib Glindemann track titled "Curious Danger (TC-158)" tells us Romero appreciates the meta-drama. Ben hoists Barbra into his arms, her legs bared toward the camera, and settles her onto the sofa.

The scene grows more dangerous by the second. Ben unbelts and unbuttons Barb's coat. He throws open the coat, revealing Barbra's dress (she did complain that it was hot), and fairly leaps back so that no viewer gets the wrong idea. No one focuses on Jones's face at this moment, but if you do, you'll see he looks more uncertain than anywhere else in the film. Anywhere else in *any* film he ever made, come to think of it.

00:31:47 A VIRTUAL ARMY

Much of what gives *Night of the Living Dead* its power is the scantiness of dumb behaviors. There's no bathing beauty failing to notice the swamp creature rising behind her. There's no randy teenagers reading from an accursed tome. There's no scientist creating a technology that turns ants into super-ants. The characters in *Night* make ill-advised choices, but choices that make solid sense given who they are. This made it all the more disturbing to me as a kid. That your characters could make consistently smart decisions and *still* end up as zombie feed? It didn't bode well for adulthood.

Here, though, a minor logic lapse as Ben, fresh from boarding up the kitchen, squats before the den radio and turns it on. As we know from the goddamn LeMans, this was the era of car radios, as well as portable radios with lunchbox handles. But the Seven Pines farmhouse is bygone. This 1939 Zenith 7S363 (a family heirloom of Karl Hardman) is the size of a pulpit and looks like something that would issue cigars and bourbon. The two-toned wooden cabinet features waterfall contours and is fitted with Art Deco chrome and a complicated glass dial that looks sourced from an airplane cockpit. Among enthusiasts, the 1939 model (a hefty $70 upon release) was the last gasp of great prewar radio craftsmanship—plastic parts were introduced a year later.

Like vinyl records, the 7S363 is treasured for its sound. What do we like about it? I've seen such sound described as "warm," "resonant," "deep," "rich," "authoritative," and "open," terms that trip over themselves to not say what they mean: It sounds *human*, percolating with the idiosyncrasies and imperfections that make any art feel personal. There are people behind this sound, not only the radio voices but the builders who installed the coils and the operators who slid the levers. This radio, and later a TV, are the lifelines that tenuously bind the farmhouse to the world. Just as this film, also made by fallible but inspired hands, is bound to me.

Naturally Ben wants to reach these distant voices. What doesn't make sense is why he waited this long to do it. He snaps a white dial to the right, then waits six glorious seconds for the thing to warm up. If you grew up in the era of digital TV, you can't know the yawning-awake promise of a cathode-tube device. I see myself in our living room, pajama knees in orange shag, snapping the dial on the family Magnavox like Ben snaps the dial on the Zenith. The thick hum in my sternum, soft snaps like burning leaves behind the glass, the electric dust that dances my arm hairs. The wait. The languorous fade-in, the slow saturation, the evolution from gray ghosts to colorful icons: Papa Smurf, Pee-wee Herman, Zack from *Saved by the Bell.* But when our Magnavox showed *Night of the Living Dead*, the gray ghosts stayed gray.

"Because of the obvious threat to untold numbers of citizens, and because of the crisis which is even now developing, this radio station will remain on the air, day and night!"

The words aren't shouted, but exclamation points are inherent in the tense timbre of old-timey broadcasters. There's a comfort to be found in such invariable voices, whether relating stock prices or the potential end of humankind. The broadcaster tells Ben that hundreds of radio and TV stations are "pooling their resources" to report on "an epidemic of mass murder being committed by a virtual army of unidentified assassins."

In 1967, this would be scary but not unexpected. If you were the establishment, protestors with tangled hair and flower-power trappings felt like a "virtual army." If you were the protestors, the lawmen beating you back might be the literal army; the Kent State shootings wouldn't happen until 1970 but the writing was on the wall. "Eyewitnesses say they are ordinary-looking people," the broadcaster says, and you have to wonder if, while editing this scene, the bottomless potential for zombie metaphor began to solidify in Romero.

One could almost make a career out of it, right? Audio survives of a Romero Q&A from June 16, 1970, after a screening at New York's Museum of Modern Art—a pivotal moment in the critical reassessment of *Night* sparked by the French film journal *Cahiers du cinéma;* as *Newsweek* put it in November 1971, the film "sank into the flickering world of the underground, where it took root like a mutated mushroom." In this recording, Romero asserts he has no plans to make another horror film. He's clearly embracing the cultured take on his debut. He says the word *metaphor* a lot, though, charmingly, pronounces it *mettafer.*

Ben doesn't seem too fazed by the news, but then again, he said he had a radio in the truck. He already knows Beekman's Diner wasn't an outlier. While the radio continues, Ben drives some more nails and looks through an unboarded window at four ghouls, Zombie #1 among them, advancing past his truck. Phil Green's percussive "Dramatic Eerie (PG-190)" accelerates as Ben finds a box of wood, tosses it into the den fireplace, squirts it with Energine lighter fluid, and lights it up. (Romero spent *four nights* at Hardman Associates, where he often slept, getting the foley sounds of that squirt can just right.)

Diegetic sound all but fades out to allow us to revel in Romero's dynamic camerawork and editing. Ben douses an easy chair with lighter fluid while a female voice—the only human tone in the film's score—undulates over the thudding cue. It's one of the soundtrack's most haunting moments, evidence of real artistry hidden in those dusty LPs.

Ben rips down a drape, ties it around a table leg, soaks it in more liquid, and lights it on fire in the fireplace. (Error alert: bright daylight through the window.) With a free hand, he opens the door, slides the chair onto the porch, sets it on fire with the torch, and kicks it off onto the lawn.

I don't know where to start. Of all the risky pyrotechnics in *Night*, this one most sets my teeth on edge. Duane Jones looks terrified. He's running around with a flaming torch handling a chair soaked in lighter fluid. When that chair goes up, it fucking goes *up*, six feet of roaring flame that could have caught the porch roof on fire, if not Jones himself. Then he has to kick the active fireball? Though I'm in awe of all Ben's heroics, I don't see the sense of this one. So he scares off four zombies? Until the chair burns out?

I'd be remiss here not to huzzah poor Gary Streiner, who did, in fact, end up on fire from this effect. Gary was usually on sound, but as this shot was done wild, he ended up tasked with relighting the chair for another take. He lit himself as well. Thankfully, former fireman Bill Hinzman was there to push Gary to the ground and snuff out the flames. (The Latent Image's own H. Cramer Riblett, a former firefighter and zombie extra, might have also been present.)

To Ben's credit, the zombies don't like it. Perhaps it's because, as the script reads, "They are cold, dead things," and heat reminds them of their warm-blooded past. If you listen beneath the music cue—the noirish "Mysterioso (ZR-68)" by George Hormel—you'll hear the undead cry out as they never really do again in a Romero film. A human sound, really, appropriate for a 1980s Magnavox or 1939 Zenith. My best phonetic transcription would be *"EEERRRAAAHHH!"*

00:34:59 MISSHAPEN MONSTERS

Night of the Living Dead is composed of sweaty close-ups and disorienting handheld action. Establishing shots are rare, which is why the next one, coming at the end of a dissolve of Ben going back to his hammer, is so useful. Romero offers a slow, steady, leftward pan across the whole dining room. What used to be the dining room, anyway. Image Ten has gotten its money out of the $300/month farmhouse fee. Chairs and wooden oddments are scattered willy-nilly. The door and all three windows are boarded up with a slashwork of lumber and table parts.

The shot uncannily resembles the final shot of Francis Ford Coppola's *The Conversation* (1974), in which the camera also pans left across the destroyed remains of a once-ordinary room. Only this time, instead of the camera finding Gene Hackman ignoring the symbolic ruins of his paranoid mind, we find Duane Jones, playing the opposite character. People *are* coming after Ben and always have been.

He notices Barbra, who remains unconscious on the sofa despite the cacophonous gutting of the dining room. (Why the dining room has a sofa is a mystery we'll never solve.) Ben manhandles a detached door into the hallway. In doing so, he hinges the door that connects the hall to the dining room. This reveals (are you ready?) a *secret door*. Ben doesn't notice it but Romero makes sure we do, zooming in on the door's outline while introducing a Stan Livingston track with the Miles Davis–like title of "Danger in the Night, Take 9."

With all this signaling, it's easy to miss the radio man informing us of an emergency presidential conference including "high-ranking scientists from the National Aeronautics and Space Administration." This NASA consultation firms up the sci-fi hints we received from Johnny's car radio and the pulsing telephone.

Barbra's eyes open when Ben begins removing another door. She palms her left cheek. It's bruised. So is her ego. She sits up and the next shot of Ben, in a woozy upward sweep, makes him look ten feet tall, a perspective of dizzy intimidation. An exhausted Ben collapses onto a couch and lights a cigarette.

He manages one drag before getting back up, a wasted smoke in a film that features only six lit cigarettes in the farmhouse and roughly sixteen total in the film—surprisingly few for 1968. And yet Ben's cigarette was important enough for Romero to scribble onto his shooting script *"cigarette,"* while scratching out several references to smoking over the next few pages. Maybe smoking was tough on continuity?

Ben gets up to investigate a closet. *Night*, along with most of Romero's filmography, is largely about men, or at least the world created (and re-created) by men, and his frequent casting of women leads drives this home. His imagery, therefore, tends toward the muscular, militaristic, hubristic, and destructive; men are shown building and dismantling but rarely maintaining. (*Day of the Dead* subverts this with a fake tropical paradise fabricated in an underground bunker by two male companions.)

Night's next shot, therefore, stands out for its femininity. Four pairs of women's shoes lie tossed upon the closet floor: a wearied pair of spectator heels, a bedraggled pair of slip-on flats with plaid interior, classic two-inch white pumps that look to have been only worn on Sundays, and a fourth pair only identifiable as something leather. The horde, so close to the front door, strengthens the notion that a woman, perhaps a widow, is the house's sole resident. Or *was* the sole resident before she bit it at the top of the stairs.

The last time I paused on this shot, the subtitles read: "Misshapen monsters." The phrase comes from the radio broadcaster, ticking through eyewitness accounts of zombies. Descriptions range from "ordinary-looking people" to "things that look like people but act like animals" (a great alternate title to this book) to "murder-happy characters" (even better). As "misshapen monsters" doesn't remotely describe the zombies, I can't help but link the on-screen caption to the women's shoes. They *are* misshapen now, wrinkled and sweat-splotched, direct analogues to the aging woman who wore them, to *all* aging women treated as misshapen monsters, dragged into closets the instant they aren't pretty enough to look at.

Ben picks up the flats (O'Dea reports they were her "old paint slippers," though the rest of the closet contents belonged to co-star Marilyn Eastman) and glances at Barbra. His original plan to flee has been replaced by holing up; the shoes aren't to help Barbra run. Despite their scruffy sweatiness, they are merely a kindness, a post-punch offering.

The closet excursion might have ended at this pair of slip-ons. But another object catches Ben's ever-watchful eye. Perfectly timed to an upward trill of the library cue, Romero's camera zooms in to an upright rifle cradled into the closet corner. All that taxidermy had to have originated with a weapon, after all.

The feminine had its moment. We return to the masculine and are thus damned.

Well, shit. Chekhov's gun and all that. Instantly, the plot trajectory changes. Every combatant will henceforth engage in an arms race to attain the upper hand. It won't ever end, not for any of us. You have a pistol? I'll get a rifle. You got an AK-47? I'll get a fighter jet. You mixed up some napalm? I'll funnel my nation's resources into a nuke.

Unlike most filmmakers introducing a firearm into their work, Romero understands the stakes: Resting against the rifle is a small American flag, possibly the same one we saw flapping over the words DIRECTED BY GEORGE A. ROMERO. (Random note: Romero's dad once designed the world's largest American flag, which covered the entire front wall of Macy's on Thirty-fourth Street in New York.) In Romero's view, a gun is U.S. citizenship, and Ben can only become a true American by accepting it.

The rifle is a Winchester 1894. Picture a rifle in your mind and the 1894 is what you're seeing: walnut finish, steel body, ejection port for .30-30 shells, a twenty-inch barrel, and all at a wraithlike seven pounds. One of the bestselling guns in history, it's scarily easy to use: Pump the bolt-action lever and you're ready to fire seven rounds. By 2006, the gun had sold over seven million units.

Companies don't come more cursed than Winchester. Their rifles were the spear tips of westward progress, clearing Native Americans from their homes and killing hundreds of thousands in the U.S. Civil War. So destructive is the Winchester legacy that it spawned the legend of the twenty-four-thousand-square-foot Winchester Mystery House in San Jose, California. For a scant $48.10, you can tour 110 of the mansion's 160 rooms, built in wayward convolutions (asymmetrical windows, doors and staircases that go nowhere) by Sarah Winchester, widow of gun magnate William Wirt Winchester. Legend has it that Sarah's endless, byzantine designs were to confuse the ghosts of those killed by her husband's rifles.

There's nothing to it: The Winchester brand was revered at the time of Sarah's 1922 death. It still was in 1958, when Chuck Connors hit the small screen (including young Romero's) with his titular Winchester in *The Rifleman*. This and hundreds of other films and shows tried to teach Romero that a man wasn't a man without a firearm. Too much of that linkage lingers today. If you can't see the direct line between the propagandizing of Winchester-toting icons like Connors to the twenty dead children of the Sandy Hook massacre of 2012, you've got manifest destiny gumming up your eyes.

The NRA likes to trot out this quote from journalist and

activist Ida B. Wells, who wrote in her 1892 publication *Southern Horrors: Lynch Law in All Its Phases*, "A Winchester rifle should have a place of honor in every Black home, and it should be used for that protection which the law refuses to give." Hard to argue with that, though it's not like America's Black population had many other good options.

Wells's world is the one Ben lives in. The Winchester appears to confer a pontifical weight. Ben stands as straight as a priest, exhaustion evaporated, and moves with a righteous new energy. He no longer investigates the closet. He raids it. He's a man with a gun: He owns the place now.

He scrounges bullets from the closet. Take a guess where they are kept: a shoebox.

Painful squinting reveals the box brand as Air Step, a product of the Brown Shoe Company of Mattoon, Illinois, which also produced a brand my young feet knew from stiff church loafers: Buster Brown, a line advertised by a horrifying ventriloquist dummy-like child and his maniacal dog. Brown existed from 1878 to 1970, and vintage ads suggest the Air Step women's line had a good run from the 1940s through 1960s. One ad touts "Magic Soles with tiny invisible air spaces to prevent jarring, nerve-jangling shocks and put pleasure into walking, working, and being on your feet." The illustrated shoes, meanwhile, look sourced from of a BDSM dungeon: shiny, leather, exquisitely tortured fetish objects that might comfortably hold a hot dog.

There's no room for beauty in the farmhouse. The Air Step box has been repurposed for killing. Women own nothing, not in the end. They are but receptacles for the domination required from the monsters of men.

00:37:37

PARTIALLY DEVOURED

BARB'S ON THE SOFA TAKING OFF HER COAT. IT'S A big production. Ben strides in and notices. She doesn't acknowledge him. Or anything else. There's no light in her eyes. The dual traumas of death and disrespect have lathed her to a sub-zombie state, unable to groan or shamble.

I'd like to take this catatonic lapse to relay what I just heard from the radio broadcaster, something I'm embarrassed to have never registered before: "This whole ghastly story began developing two days ago with the report of the slaying of a family of seven in their rural home of Gulfport, Louisiana."

Confirmed: ground zero for the zombie uprising.

Ben feels bad about the whole punching thing. He hunkers in front of Barbra and puts the shoes on her feet, manipulating her legs like they are paralyzed. Every time I see it, I'm hit with competing emotions. There's something almost offensive about a strong Black man kneeling before an unhelpful white woman. It's also the tenderest gesture of the film, Ben casting aside societal and interpersonal history in favor of simple mercy.

Leave it to the French to find the visual erotic. A five-by-eight-inch promotional card, circa 1976, produced for *La nuit des morts-vivants* by the TV trivia show *Les fiches de Monsieur Cinéma*, chose to highlight this still among only three others. The French weren't salacious; they were, after all, the first country to embrace *Night* as serious art. Actor Marilyn Eastman reported being beset in Paris airports by autograph hounds. That didn't happen at LaGuardia.

While fondling her feet, Ben gives Barb a pep talk touting his progress (though the unboarded window behind him still bothers me) and anticipating their saviors.

The Zenith 7S363's drone is more discouraging. ". . . suspect an obscure kind of conspiracy . . . creatures from outer space . . ." When the broadcaster warns, "Lock the doors and windows securely," Ben celebrates with joie de vivre: "Hey, that's us! We're doing all right." Barb's vacancy convinces Ben his efforts are useless. If she can hear him, he says, he's going upstairs: "But you'll be all right for now, okay?"

Creeping zoom into Barb's inexpressive face. No, not okay.

Ben leaves and Romero cuts to a wide shot of Barbra on the dining room sofa (let's ignore that her new shoes have vanished), a lamp to her left and Jack Russo's hand-cranked 1930s Victrola record player to her right. Filmed through the slats of a chair, it's as if we're looking at Barb from outside her cage. But it's a feint. The threat comes from within: the radio. In flat monotone, the broadcaster says the worst thing we have heard so far.

"Civil defense officials in Cumberland have told newsmen that murder victims show evidence of having been partially devoured by their murderers."

Every *Night* fanatic can hear this dialogue in their head, the little pause after *been*, the disbelieving emphasis on *partially devoured*. The performance is excellent because the performer is no actor. It's Chuck Craig, an associate of Karl Hardman's whose broadcast résumé reads like a spill of alphabet soup: WWST, WHBC, WJWC, WCKY, WNCO, WRYT, KDKA, and WTAE. He's a pro, even when the topic he's reporting is entirely fabricated.

It's not like cannibalism was absent from movie theaters. This was the era of Herschell Gordon Lewis, whose *Blood Feast* (1963), generally considered the first "gore" film, spawned scads of imitators, some of them a lot of fun, like *The Undertaker and His Pals* (1966), *Spider Baby* (1967), and *The Corpse Grinders* (1971), all three of which involve cannibalism.

Key here is that *Night* bears no resemblance to those bug-eyed cartoons. Hearing Chuck Craig broach flesh-eating is legitimately upsetting. It's also a prophecy. The fictional newscast in *Night* comes less than a year before the real news of eight-and-a-half-month-pregnant actor Sharon Tate being murdered by a hippie death cult, stabbed sixteen times before being hanged from a rope, her blood used to write *PIG* on her front door. How does that make any more sense than what's coming from the farmhouse radio?

A different dead woman awaits Ben upstairs. And guess what? She's barefoot, her Air Steps cordoned off in the downstairs closet. All we have seen of the corpse so far is the gory skull. Now a wider angle provides more info. The severe shadows from previous second-floor forays are gone, revealing a hallway with three doors. The corpse lies curled on its side. Above it on the wall is a fan of blood. It doesn't resemble Sharon Tate's *PIG*, but you'd only know that if you looked at her crime scene photos, which I did and cannot recommend.

Virtually no one who watches *Night* dwells on the death of this woman. But it's a poser. A bite into the jugular wouldn't create such a blood smear. Only a gun to the head would do it (and prevent zombification to boot). But Ben's got the only gun on the premises. Was this woman shot by someone else? If so, they fled the house. The script and novelization tell us these three doors lead to bedrooms, one of them a child's. Good clues, but they go nowhere.

One of Jack Russo's projects, a 2010 eight-issue prequel comic series confusingly titled *Night of the Living Dead*, provides answers that, due to Russo's pedigree, we have to take seriously. The comic isn't essential, but for my money, it's the best thing Russo has been a part of. Cowritten with prolific comic writer

Mike Wolfer and drawn by a slate of talented artists, the nods to *Night* are clever and carefully orchestrated.

The comic details what brought *Night*'s characters to Seven Pines and inserts new characters to up the body count. After a cold open featuring some gobbled randos, the first issue takes us inside the farmhouse, where we meet the woman who becomes the corpse at the top of the stairs. She's a friendly, gray-haired woman named Thelma. Russo's novelization had already ID'd the corpse as "probably an elderly woman" by the name of Miller. (Counterpoint: Handwritten dialogue in Romero's shooting script suggests the house belongs to a "poor old man" named Mr. Fenner.) Thelma lives with her twenty-something granddaughter, Christine, who works at (you guessed it) Beekman's Diner, where soon she will join with Ben to combat zombies. (The name "Thelma" probably has nothing to do with the strangest note in Romero's shooting script, the scrawled-then-crossed-out name of "Thelma Ritter," the six-time Oscar nominee best known for *Rear Window* and *All About Eve*.)

Russo has long been interested in Ben's backstory. Around this point in the novelization, he enters Ben's head for a full page. Per Russo, Ben is a widower with two sons, nine and thirteen. (The Soska Sisters concur: Their 2024 film *Festival of the Living Dead* stars Ben's two grandkids, who still own their grandpop's famous Winchester.) Ben's sons were staying with their grandmother while their dad was working just outside of town. (Counterpoint: Dialogue handwritten into Romero's script identifies Ben as living in Chicago.) After Ben's homebound train failed to show, he hiked into town. There's no Beekman's Diner. Instead, Ben simply climbed into an unoccupied truck and drove until he nearly ran out of gas. There's a chance this isn't solely Russo's invention; in a 1973 *Cinefantastique* interview, Romero references a cut scene that supplied more Ben backstory.

In *Journey of the Living Dead: A Tribute to Fifty Years of Flesh Eaters* (2018), author and academic Dr. Arnold T. Blumberg (a.k.a. Doctor of the Dead) notes an organic but baffling online tendency to apply the surname Huss to Ben. Blumberg's theory is that "Huss" mistakenly grew out of the character Hess that Duane Jones played in *Ganja & Hess*. Weird but probably true. (A 1986 article in the SUNY student paper charmingly mistakes the film as being called *Gwyndeline Hess*.)

Back to Russo's comic: Thelma is visited by gravedigger Eddie, who managed to fend off Zombie #1 before discovering the farmhouse (like Barbra will soon). But the undead get in and kill Eddie, before killing Thelma, too, at the top of the stairs. These deaths, of course, are massively gory, with blood splashed, sinew stretched, and intestines pulled all over the pages. Given where Romero ended up with splatter-fests like *Day of the Dead*, I've got no issue with this.

What sits less well for me is the comic's nudity. Let me re-emphasize that I have zero problems with nudity or sexual content. But the inclusions here are hasty and unearned. The first bared breasts come on page four, Christine flashes her naked ass at her boyfriend as soon as she gets to Beekman's, and on and on. When you see a female zombie, most likely she's at least partially nude, and the zombies have the uncanny ability to instantly shred the dresses and bras of female victims. This tendency persists in Russo's short-story sequel "The Day After," included in the anthology *Nights of the Living Dead* (2017), edited by Jonathan Maberry and Romero. "Her low-cut blouse and hiked-up skirt revealed a terrific figure," Russo writes about a heroine, for no reason at all.

This is Russo reverting to *Scream Queens Illustrated* mode. He was sick of getting grief for it as far back as 1995; in his *SQI* Issue 8 editorial, he writes that his magazine "seems to provoke the sort of women who can't stand seeing other women gaining attention, money, or other forms of success based partially on physical beauty," a misreading of critiques like mine. In an article in the same issue called "Movie Monsters & Sexy Starlets," Russo writes about the decision to have Barbra, and not Johnny, survive Zombie #1's attack: "Females are (stereotypically and often actually) endowed with sweetness and gentleness that noble, honorable males seek to protect. So, when a monster comes after a female, both males and females in the audience tend to cringe." At the risk of being neither noble or honorable, I disagree.

Some of this nudity stuff is just the comics biz. I didn't grow up with comics (with the bizarre exception of issues 10, 11, and 12 of Marvel's *Secret Wars*, which my mom randomly picked up somewhere). But in 2019 I began writing them. While signing at a comics con, the artist beside me told me the key to selling to comic diehards was to always include a sexy female character who could be on the covers. He didn't say this with any relish; he was stating what he felt to be a fact, and several women comic artists I know agree, with most saying they enjoy drawing sexy covers. So I don't know. I feel mixed.

At the same time, I'm spoiled by the complicated, nuanced, fascinating romantic relationships that crop up so regularly in Romero films, nowhere more impressively than *Dawn of the Dead* and *Day of the Dead*. I hold characters in his universe to higher standards. Maybe I shouldn't, but clearly, for me, that ship has long since sailed.

00:39:18 WHAT WOULD HAPPEN TO ME?

Ben, of course, knows nothing about these prequel characters, and that's the way we like it. To the gallant strains of a Spencer Moore cue poorly titled "Somber Emotional (L-33)," Ben sets down the Winchester, grips the rug beneath the corpse (let's not call her Thelma), and drags her away. When Ben makes the sharp turn down the hall, you can see the woman's face for a full second. The woman didn't even *have* a face last time we saw her. It's not even a woman—it's a nine-year-old girl. In fact, it's Kyra Schon, who plays Karen, a character we'll meet soon. It's the film's most puzzling flub. I can't imagine why Romero didn't cut away sooner.

This is quickly forgiven thanks to one of the strongest little sequences Romero ever put together. It's simplicity itself. Barbra's still on the sofa staring into the void. The Zenith 7S363 is still doling out bad news, again using the phrase *partially devoured.* Romero intercuts a zoom into Barb with a zoom into the Zenith (the latter filmed by Streiner, for reasons he can't recall). Two blank faces, closer and closer, a mockery of cinema's typically expressive shot/reverse shot. While Romero has long been lauded for his editing, he's never been known for cinematographic choices. Here, both work in perfect concert.

Then: A little noise and Barbra's head snaps to her left. She's alive after all. The hidden door Romero showed us earlier moves. A hand emerges. A white hand. This isn't Ben.

It flings wide and two men pounce.

In a way, the story ends here. The aggressiveness with which the two men leap into the room tells us, before we're introduced, they are emissaries of the world Ben and Barbra left behind—in some ways for the better. Ben and Barb might have made it through their ordeal if it were just the two of them, their semicouplehood an emblem of hope in terms of both race and class, a hope that Romero (not a super hopeful guy!) doubled down on at the end of *Dawn*, and tripled down on at the end of *Day*. The resolutions of those sequels, and *Land of the Dead* too, act as correctives to *Night*'s despair, before a more embittered Romero circled back to despondency with *Diary of the Dead*, *Survival of the Dead*, our novel *The Living Dead*, and the treatment for *Twilight of the Dead.*

The zombie mayhem outside the farmhouse is gentle compared to the ferocity of these two men dominating a space that, moments ago, belonged to minorities and women. As a kid, I often played in farmhouses, one of which looked enough like *Night*'s house to make me sweat. I never felt at ease there. My friend's father was a glowering figure I never got a good look at, yet who emanated brutality; my friend's older brother was scary, too, either locked in a bedroom with Quiet Riot vibrating the door (papered in disturbing sketches, one depicting a fork serving up an eyeball) or sprawled in the living room blankly watching horror flicks (where I first glimpsed *The Texas Chain Saw Massacre*). Only my friend's mother felt safe; she was incredibly sweet, and yet my friend treated her cruelly. I knew it even then: He was becoming his father.

Atrocities were hidden inside houses all over town. I felt them in my sinuses like ragweed. On Tuesday, October 8, 1991, when I was sixteen, one of these atrocities burst from its hiding place like a zombie through a window. A forty-three-year-old woman named Betty Lou Frieberg, who lived in a farmhouse (of course) in Libertyville (population 274 last I checked), only an eight-minute drive from my house, was arrested for the first-degree murder of her farmer/antiques dealer husband, Harold.

The afternoon before the news broke, I was in the back of a classroom at Fairfield High School working on the school newspaper. I heard a girl scream as she ran full-speed down the hallway. The footsteps echoing off the hallway brick and shivering off lockers haunt me to this day. I cannot be sure, but I believe this was Betty's fourteen-year-old daughter, a high school freshman. She must have just been informed of what happened. Not even she knew the full story yet, but in the coming days and weeks, we'd all learn it.

It was this daughter who pointed out to officers responding to Betty's missing-persons report that the family cats were nibbling something rotten. It was Harold. Part of him, anyway. Detectives began to find pieces of Harold all over the farm. A right arm severed at the shoulder. A left leg stripped of skin and muscle. A heart. A lung. A liver. A penis. A pair of buttocks. A plastic bag full of intestines. Soon it came out that Betty, believing Harold was about to kill her, shot him four times and cut him up with a Black & Decker circular saw using techniques she'd learned butchering his deer. She used a child's wagon to disperse remains over the farm and her car to drop larger chunks along country roads.

Betty's arrest came but ten weeks after the arrest of Jeffrey Dahmer in Milwaukee, a news story still unfolding with revelations of sexual abuse, rape, murder, necrophilia, dismemberment, cannibalism, and bodily keepsakes. But Milwaukee was three hundred miles away, impossible for me to grasp. This was right here in Jefferson County, Iowa.

The county hadn't seen a murder in seventeen years. The act itself intrigued me. As a Stephen King–reading teen who haunted Adventureland Video's horror racks, I imagined Betty Frieberg as Annie Wilkes from King's *Misery*. I scissored out news articles and slipped them into the purple lockbox that held my diary, one more horror story to relish. Betty was becoming Iowa's boogeyman, replacing whoever took Johnny Gosch, a West Des Moines paperboy abducted in 1982 and never seen again. Gosch was the nation's first milk carton kid, and I'd grown up staring at his cheery, haunted face.

But Betty's boogeyman status diminished as details came out in her trial. Harold, a serial abuser on his fifth wife, had spent a year torturing Betty, a past survivor of sexual abuse. He tried to run her down with a combine. He choked her with an electrical cord. He dragged her down the stairs by the hair. He threw her to the ground so hard she spent three days in a wheelchair. He shocked her with an electric fence tool. He poured an agricultural chemical on her stomach and rubbed foot powder into her vagina, telling her he hoped both treatments would boil some fat off her. It was no wonder Betty was on various tranquilizers and antidepressants, and was suffering from blackouts.

I saw Betty's daughter, as well as her children from a previous marriage, all the time. In school. On the bus. It did not compute—and yet it *did* compute, in a deep-down way that fevered my sleep. I had been in so many homes like the Frieberg place. Drafty farmhouses, sagging barns, cornfields receding to the vanishing point. Horrible things were afoot everywhere and none of them had anything to do with risen corpses. I studied newspaper photos of the five-foot, big-eyed, pudgy-cheeked, meek-looking Betty. There was no getting away from it: She looked like my mom. Nearly the same age too.

After three hours of deliberation, a jury acquitted Betty of all charges. I was glad. I still am. I wanted everyone who said Betty would strike again to shut up and, as it turns out, I was right. Betty Frieberg is alive and well, apparently happily married in a town even smaller than Libertyville. Of course she didn't escape scot-free—who could?—but she escaped. So did her daughter, whom I consider a hero. It came out in the trial that she once convinced her mother not to kill herself, asking, "What would happen to me?" Betty listened—Harold, after all, had threatened to cut off the little girl's fingers joint by joint—and for that, Betty is a hero too.

It gave me hope in 1992. It still gives me hope today, even as what Harold did reverberates and, I am sure, replicates. Because most monsters aren't like zombies. They don't break into the house. They already live inside it.

00:40:47

THE SAFEST PLACE

BEN HEARS THE NOISES OF THE BARGING MEN, SNATCHES up the Winchester, and seconds later bursts into the dining room, rifle aimed. The film, which so far has navigated vacant spaces, is suddenly congested: three men in battle poses with a scared woman caught in their triangle. In the aforementioned opera terms, we have evolved into a quartet.

The younger man, whom we'll soon know as Tom, cries out, "Don't shoot! We're from town." If I had a rifle pointed at my chest, I might blurt out a lot of things to save my skin, but this wouldn't be one of them. Maybe Tom means to tell the gun-toting Black man that he's a sympathetic urbanite and not a racist hick? Or perhaps by stating he's "from town," Tom is asserting he's not from that even sketchier place: the grave.

Clad in the shirt and tie ordained by the standing world order, the older man is bald, beady-eyed, and hunched in a reptilian way that recalls the Lizard, a character in those three issues of *Secret Wars* I owned. It's the beaten-dog posture of a man cowed by modern life: a job at which he's forced to stand over some machine all day and a home in which he's unable to express the vexation of a Levittown existence. Like Ben, he wields a weapon, but his is an extension of his rage and emasculation.

Many fans refer to this weapon as a tire iron, same as Ben's.

It's clearly not. Streiner calls it a "bent piece of metal," which it clearly is, though that's too many words to keep writing. What it most resembles is a blunt, hatchet-shaped, fourteenth-century Javan knife called a *kris*. But I'll be damned if I'm going to elevate this hunk of junk to kris status. So I'm going to call it a truncheon, as a truncheon is a police weapon, and there's something about Harry that reminds me of a cop.

The truncheon's owner is named Harry Cooper (Harry Tinsdale in the script). He's the only main character in *Night* to get a last name. Well, his wife and daughter (coming soon) share the surname, but per 1967 rules, they are but tubers of their patriarch. "Mr. Cooper" confers the esteem Harry believes he is owed; see also his refusal to remove his tie. He has followed society's rules in order to be rewarded. How can that all end? Right when he's at the age to benefit most? All he's missing is the darting tongue.

Harry Cooper will spend the rest of the film trying to reassert the social order that has been toppled. He just wants to make America great again. Is that so wrong?

"A radio!" he cries. All sorts of questions here. Why is the radio a surprise? Harry doesn't live here, but it's 1967, man. Homes have radios. Televisions, even. Harry squats before the Zenith, which, incidentally, is next to a table that has a dish full of candy on it. Wasn't Johnny asking if there was any more candy? Maybe Johnny—a different mode of Johnny—will get his candy in the end. (Russ Streiner has opined that Johnny's candy of choice would be M&M's or Good & Plenty. Accessorize your cosplay accordingly.)

Ben takes a seven-second beat to stare in disbelief at Harry before demanding to know how long the two men have been hiding. "That's the cellar," Harry says. "It's the safest place."

Tattoo those words on your arm. They are the whole shebang. In the mid-nineties, MTV had an animation showcase called *Liquid Television*, and my favorite segment was "Stick Figure Theatre," which set the audio of famous movie scenes to crude sketches on three-by-five notecards. The scene they selected to represent *Night* was the Ben-Harry dispute about to unfold. The animators knew it was the film's pivot point: You could replace all of Harry's dialogue with his seven-word insistence, ad nauseam.

The claim's specificity isn't the point. In their power struggle over newly founded Farmhouse Nation, Ben and Harry could have disagreed about anything. Whether it's better to fight zombies with rifle or truncheon. Whether Schlitz or Hamm's was the superior beer. The point is, they have a disagreement and won't back down. Their personal histories won't *let* them back down. And that will be the ruin of them all. Of all of us.

Harry is a spark plug inserted into an already speeding film. The dialogue catches fire. Ben accuses Harry of not coming up to help. Harry claims it sounded like the house was being ripped apart. Ben doesn't believe Harry didn't hear Barbra screaming. Harry says the screams might have meant the joint was crawling with attackers. Ben pounces on Harry's cowardice, and Harry, who knows it's true, springs up into Ben's face.

"We luck into a safe place and you're telling us we've gotta risk our lives just because somebody might need help, huh?" Harry challenges.

"Yeah," Ben says. "Something like that."

Young Tom's willing to hear out Ben about the boarded-up house, but Harry's too far into the argument to visualize world peace. He tells Ben the zombies turned over the family car (efficient storytelling: the Coopers have no vehicle) and demands, "Now you tell me those things can't get through this lousy pile of wood?" Harry gestures his truncheon at the boards over one window, which, I admit, look less impressive with each glance.

Tom offers Ben a weak defense: Harry's wife and kid are downstairs, and the kid's hurt. Doesn't mean shit to Ben. Any five men can turn over a car, he says, and Harry snaps back, "That's my point. Only there's not going to be five, or even ten. There's gonna be twenty, thirty, maybe a hundred of those things. And as soon as they know we're here, this place is gonna be crawling with them."

Ding-ding. Harry wins by decision. But I'll be honest, I could listen to these two spar all day.

The actor going toe-to-toe with Duane Jones is the perfectly named Karl Hardman. Whereas Jones was a trained thespian surgically inserted into the production, Hardman was a part of *Night* from the word go, the latest step along his circuitous path.

Hardman was one of the original Image Ten. His company, Hardman Associates, shows up in the film's fifth title card under MAKE-UP, and then again two credits later: PRODUCED THROUGH THE FACILITIES OF: THE LATENT IMAGE, INC. AND HARDMAN ASSOCIATES, INC. One credit later, Hardman shares the producer card with Russ Streiner. (Though he goes uncredited as the film's still photographer, Hardman took roughly 1,250 photos with his Honeywell Pentax H3v, some of which have become iconic.) In the end credits, Hardman will be the third actor listed and for good reason. Observing Jones's disciplined portrayal, Hardman went the opposite way, and chews the scenery with the vigor of a Joe Pesci, Karl Malden, or George C. Scott. He's fabulous, despite the suggestion by Richard Ricci, in his intro to *The Farmhouse Seven*, that Hardman was only cast "because we needed Karl's sound studio."

Before this renaissance man became a mainstay in the 1960s Pittsburgh media scene, he was a child actor for radio, a budding concert pianist, and a messenger on the RKO Radio Pictures lot in Hollywood, where he became enamored with the makeup department. The wound effects for the 1945 film *The Enchanted Cottage* (molded from Derma Wax, a flesh substitute used by morticians) directly inspired the zombie makeup he and Marilyn Eastman would create twenty-two years later for *Night*.

Like every other studio messenger, Hardman wanted to be an actor. His bio on the Image Ten site says he was an RKO contract player, though I can't find evidence he ever appeared in a Hollywood film. He was serious enough to devise a stage alias for his given name of Karl Hardman Schon. His RKO era seems to have resulted from parents hoping to score their son a draft deferment. It didn't work. Hardman served as a WWII combat photographer—like Tom Savini in Vietnam—before moving back to hometown Pittsburgh, where he became known for voicing characters on a morning variety radio show called *Cordic and Co.* It's almost too quaint to be believed.

Hardman opened his namesake audio production studio in May 1963, the same year the Latent Image opened, and soon made nice with the rabble of young men who, by that point, were doing well enough to have a vehicle emblazoned with their company's name. It was the Hardman Associates conference room where the two entities joined in matrimony to form Image Ten. Hardman even threw his hat into the ring as the film's director.

Though *Night* was shot on 35mm, the gang's editing equipment was all 16mm, so the workprint footage had to be reduced to 16mm and cut by Romero on an eight-track synchronizer, a nightmare to imagine—they didn't even have the sort of Steenbeck flatbed I used in college. The gang had shot fifty-six thousand feet of film and Romero edited it down to ten thousand, a respectable five-to-one shooting ratio. The soundtrack, however, was handled at Hardman Associates, which laboriously ran eight tracks of quarter-inch tape through another exasperating synchronizer, often without any picture for reference.

Hardman's company was stocked with sound effect cues and owned hundreds of Capitol Hi-Q Library "audition discs" from which the film's score was drawn. It was Hardman and Eastman (when they weren't recording foley effects onto 10-inch reels) who took on the numbing task of listening to untold hours of instrumentals (each interrupted by a stentorian voice announcing the next cue) in search of choice cuts to play for Romero. The team then put in their requests for clean production copies to Capitol, and Capitol complied, charging them about $1,500 for quarter-inch tape masters.

In a July 9, 1968, letter to Hardman, Capitol's Ole Georg wrote, "this must be an old old selection that I didn't know existed." He goes on to ask for some of Hardman's LPs to be sent back, as Capitol had no way to pay royalties to composers dead for so long. (The whole thing was a process Romero clearly enjoyed;

for the U.S. release of *Dawn of the Dead,* he ditched several Goblin tracks in favor of music from the De Wolfe library, including the now-immortal "The Gonk.") *Night*'s final mix was done by WRS Motion Picture Laboratory, and for free, after Russ Streiner won a risky double-or-nothing chess match against WRS's Jack Napor.

Hardman's Harry Cooper shook me as a boy. He resembled dads I knew and was, therefore, intimidating. On my block alone was a dad with huge shoulders, some kind of ex-football player, who groped his wife in a way I'd never seen and slapped the crap out of his son after he and I crawled through a culvert pipe; a dad with Xeroxes of *Playboy* pages lining his garage workbench, the quality so poor you couldn't make out nips or pubes until too late; and a dad who got loud, sloppy drunk, and with his loose grin and rangy arms seemed capable of anything.

Harry was even scarier. He was belligerent but also smart, a trait rarely assigned to villains in children's entertainment. Harry's malfunction was his approach. We have all seen it before. We learned it in kindergarten. You may have an important contribution to make (Harry sure does—Ben really wants to draw more zombies with light and noise?) but if you make that contribution like an asshole, it doesn't merit a rat's ass.

00:43:37 TOO EMPTY TO SUFFER

Barbra is the voice of panic. Ben the voice of action. Harry the voice of aggression. Tom, we learn, is the voice of negotiation. After getting Ben to soften by telling him Harry has an injured kid downstairs, Tom tries to broker a peace between the two. After all, neither solution is ideal. While rich in supplies, the upstairs has "a million windows" to protect, while the cellar, should zombies breach its door, is "a death trap" from which they would never know if help came by.

Harry says of the cellar, "There's only one door, right?" but there's evidence to the contrary. If you rewind the film to

00:09:58, when Barbra is looping the farmhouse, she passes a low, slanted wooden doorway alongside the home's foundation. If this place is like the Kraus Road farmhouse, that's the storm door to the cellar, which complicates both men's theories. I know we're not supposed to notice it, but anyway, I noticed it.

What I didn't notice—no one did—until ninety-year-old former zombie extra Ella Mae Smith, who lived next door to the farmhouse until her death on May 21, 2025, let it slip at the 2022 Living Dead Weekend, was that there was a *fourth* entry to the house, a side door that once fed, quite reasonably, to the house's staircase (there were actually two of them). Only after knowing this can you discern a trace outline of mismatched paneling on the house exterior and some shoddily placed drywall on the interior. The takeaway here isn't that there was, gasp, a sealed-up door, but that we're still learning things about *Night* over fifty years later.

Speaking of not noticing things, Tom delivers the line, "I don't know, Mr. Cooper, I think he's right," in front of a fireplace we know is nonfunctional by the radiator placed on the hearth. Atop the mantel, a black paperback lies on its side. You can also see this book in a behind-the-scenes photo in which Streiner and Romero gravely hunch over a script; beside the paperback are two foam coffee cups, one labeled RWS (Russell William Streiner) and the other D.J. (Duane Jones), the latter of which the anxious Jones has halfway shredded, or, if you prefer, partially devoured.

In both the photo and the film, you can see the book's spine and a hint of the cover. The words are unreadable blobs, except for the author's first name, William. To identify the book would take luck. But I got lucky. I identified the book. In fact, I've read it.

William L. Shirer's *The Rise and Fall of the Third Reich.*

It's as startling as the scene in Carl Sagan's *Contact* (1985) when Dr. Ellie Arroway (Jodie Foster in the movie) unscrambles a SETI sequence to reveal a swastika. That's the fuzzy image on the paperback's cover. There's a freaking swastika hidden in *Night of the Living Dead.* Remember that Survinski and company set-dressed an empty farmhouse. That dressing included plenty of books, all tucked between bookends—except this one.

So what the heck? Released on October 17, 1960, Shirer's National Book Award–winning account of the Nazi regime sold millions of copies, two thirds of which came via the middlebrow bellwether of the Book of the Month Club. That put the 1,249-page tome on a lot of shelves, where it generally stayed, making it the 1960s equivalent of Stephen Hawking's *A Brief History of Time* (1988), a bestseller so famously unread that it inspired a principle called the Hawking Index. (For example, the Hawking Index reports people read only 6.4 percent of David Foster Wallace's *Infinite Jest* before bailing.)

Third Reich's placement may be an offhand provocation. But things get interesting when you combine the book's cameo with the framed photo of the clergyman over the fireplace. Was this man of God reading about Hitler? Suddenly we're debating the greatest religious question of all time: Why does God allow evil to befall good people? *Night*'s position is clear. Our superstitious totems, beginning with cemetery markers, have no power in Romero's world. Just look at Farmhouse Nation. There *are* no good people. The only totems workable here are hammers, nails, knives, and guns.

In 1967, *Third Reich* would have been a reminder of what was, and still is, considered a just war fought by united allies. Its cameo in a scene of petty squabbling points a finger at the Vietnam War, which was turning friends, neighbors, and families against one another. Likewise, Ben and Harry's trench-warfare fight over inches of irrelevant territory is a far cry from the Nazi pursuit of Lebensraum. (*Night* remains banned in Germany; as recently as 2019, German Netflix was forced to remove the film under the German Interstate Treaty on the Protection of Minors in the Media.)

It seems unlikely Romero read Shirer's book. While he was politically minded, his heart was in the movies. But someone on set might have read it. I bet Duane Jones did. Any who did would have learned about Heinrich Himmler, the SS Reichsführer on the hunt for holy relics he believed could bring the dead back to life. We're not talking dead nobodies like Johnny. We're talking dead Nazi leaders—including, one day, Adolf Hitler. Both Hitler and Himmler were sniveling, unattractive, bitter men whose failures ulcerated into power complexes. A type of man not so different from Harry Cooper.

Seen through a swastika, zombies themselves conjure up comparisons to the so-called Muselmänner, the wasted, starving "living dead" of Nazi concentration camps. In his memoir *Survival in Auschwitz* (1947), Primo Levi describes the Muselmänner as "an anonymous mass, continually renewed and always identical, of non-men who march and labour in silence, the divine spark dead within them, already too empty to really suffer. One hesitates to call them living: One hesitates to call their death death, in the face of which they have no fear, as they are too tired to understand."

The description ought to unnerve any viewer of *Night*. I get a bad taste in my mouth from the booming subgenre of Nazi zombies, films like *Dead Snow*, *Overlord*, and *Outpost*, and video game franchises like *Call of Duty* and *Wolfenstein*. No judgment if you like these things, but I, for one, am out.

00:44:27 THE TERRIBLE PLACE

Tom pleads the rational case. "We can make it to the cellar *if* we have to. And if we do decide to stay down there, we'll need some things from up here." We can tell Harry knows Tom is right by how he white-knuckles his truncheon. It's progress from a few seconds ago, when Harry was threatening to lock the cellar door behind him for good.

Thus is a tense, temporary armistice reached in Farmhouse Nation. Between the three, anyway—Barbra has retaken her place on the Sofa of No Opinions. I'm struck at this point by how each man, despite the running around, has his shirt tucked into his belted pants. It encapsulates the buttoned-up mores trying to hold fast in 1967. Take a gander at Woodstock photos from two years later and see if you can find a tucked shirt.

Tom peeks beneath a window board and sees seven zombies beside Ben's truck, which he relays as "eight or ten" to Ben. This compels Ben to hasten into the kitchen to see how many more are out back.

Arms shoot from gaps in a boarded window and grab Ben.

It's what most people think when they think *Night of the Living Dead*: arms exploding from an untamed outdoors to infringe upon a secure interior. Nature versus civilization is a tension inherent to horror, especially slashers. *Night* has never been called a slasher, but it kind of is, except with a whole army of Michael Myerses.

The farmhouse is what film theorist Carol J. Clover calls the "Terrible Place," a location that seems safe but is vulnerable to penetration. Honestly, I can't believe I got this far without mentioning Clover. While buying my textbooks from the University of Iowa bookstore as a freshman, I stumbled across a book Clover had just put out, *Men, Women, and Chain Saws* (1992). It picked up where *Fangoria* left off for me, conferring a legitimacy to my interest in horror. (Clover also originated the concept of a "final girl," which, obviously, had legs beyond academia.) As W. Scott Poole writes in *Dark Carnivals: Modern Horror and the Origins of American Empire* (2022), the terrible place of the farmhouse is "the dead West, the Spahn ranch, the Texas cannibals' homestead, the last house on the left."

Jack's ax splintering the bathroom door in *The Shining*. The knife into Meg through the shower stall in *Sleepaway Camp*. The killer chainsawing a shower stall in *Pieces* (or *Terrifier 3*). The drill through the ceiling in *Body Double*. The knife through the canvas convertible roof in *Killer Workout*. Charred-to-hell Chucky stabbing Karen through a door in *Child's Play*. A blade impaling Phil's cheek through a restroom stall in *Scream 2*. Carmen clawing through the movie screen in *Demons*, across which capers a scene of a knife slashing through a tent—a penetration twofer. And on and on and on.

All owe a debt to the grasping arms of *Night*.

This scene is worse for being the first time imperturbable Ben is caught off-guard. Thankfully, Tom is affixed as our new right hand. While Ben tries to wrench the Winchester from the attacker's grip (in reality, the hands of Regis Survinski), Tom snatches the knife Barbra left atop the fridge and goes after the zombie hands.

He does it weirdly. Instead of stabbing, Tom clubs the knife like it's a mallet. (If you look fast during Tom's close-up, you'll find Duane Jones chilling in the background with his hand on his hip.) The foley effects are weird too: no squishing or squelching, only heavy thumps. The visual effects are the weirdest of all: The zombie hand dents and crumbles like it has no bone structure. (It hasn't: Romero sculpted it from clay filled with fake blood.) Though biologically ridiculous, it's got an eerie grotesqueness that stays with you.

Tom looks confounded as we hear one of *Night*'s signature tracks, "Shock/Stormy" by Ib Glindemann, a heartbeat-like double-bass strum in three-four time that John Vullo adroitly describes as "a zombie shuffling: step, step-*step*, step-*step*." (Vullo is the reigning MVP of the Official George A. Romero's *Night of the Living Dead* Facebook group—a bottomless well of *Night* knowledge and enthusiasm, and the most positive thing Mark Zuckerberg ever had a hand in creating.)

Ben sneers and gets a shot off. From outside, we see the bullet plume the back of the zombie's shirt. The zombie backpedals, then straightens back up, no worse for wear. Though 1959's *The Mummy* is rarely mentioned as an influence on *Night*, Romero loved it (he drafted a two-part *Mummy* project in the 1980s, and in 1994 was attached to direct a Hollywood remake after Universal rejected takes by Clive Barker and Joe Dante). Christopher Lee's reaction to being shot in *The Mummy* is identical to the reaction of this zombie, and all zombies thereafter.

This ghoul is Richard Ricci. Not to be confused with his cousin, Rudy Ricci, originally cast as "Truckdriver." For clarity, we'll call Richard "the Rev," a nickname some say was given to him in the 1960s for his wise counsel, though it seems likelier the alias was applied in 1980 on the *Knightriders* set due to his resemblance to Christopher Lloyd's Rev. Jim Ignatowski on *Taxi*.

Like Rudy, the Rev was an original Image Tenner, and his influence on Romero was the most formative of all. It was the Rev who nearly decamped to the Bahamas with Romero to build a sound studio at the behest of the Rev's father. Who gave Romero a copy of *I Am Legend*. Who cofounded the Latent Image. Who, after he'd moved to the Ketchum agency (which today handles clients like Mastercard, IBM, and Pfizer, and, troublingly, has done PR for the Russian Federation), hipped his Latent Image pals to the Calgon ad that made it possible to make *Night*. Who had roomed with Duane Jones at Pitt and suggested (along with *Night* crewperson/zombie Betty Ellen Haughey, who had dated both the Rev and Romero) that they get him to read for Ben while he was home for Easter—the same apocryphal Easter break during which Romero wrote the first forty pages of *Night* (a rather fitting time to hatch a tale of resurrection).

And what did the Rev get for his trouble? A bullet! Harry's wife asks from the cellar what's happening. But Harry's caught up in the drama. He and Tom watch as Ben shoots the Rev in the chest again—and again, the Rev recovers in seconds. Ben mutters a line so buried in the soundtrack that it has become my own private mini-mystery; I have seen it transcribed or captioned as "You take it," "Damn thing," "God damn you," and "Up tight" (the most baffling option). Only Ben's third shot, a forehead bull's-eye, downs the Rev.

It's smart storytelling: We intuit the importance of a headshot without having to be told. It would be another fifty years until Dr. Arnold T. Blumberg would translate the life-death cycle of the Romero-Russo zombie to a mathematic formula. You're not going to understand it unless you read *Journey of the Living Dead* (and even then, maybe not) but, for posterity, here it is:

$$S' = \Pi - \beta SZ - \delta S$$
$$Z' = \beta SZ + \zeta R - \alpha SZ$$
$$R' = \delta S + \alpha(1 - p)SZ - \zeta R$$

Per this math, the Rev's zombie is dead for good. Four days before the Rev died in real life (and a long, strange life it was, including an extended stint in Mexico doing psychedelic mushrooms with members of the Hopi Tribe), he wrote a poem meant to be read aloud and paired with the aforementioned rediscovered Romero short *Elegy*, in which the Rev costars. *Elegy* is beautiful, and so is the Rev's poem. One could hardly ask for a finer send-off.

00:46:07 GREAT CAESAR'S GHOST

Romero takes advantage of being beside the Rev's body to segue to what the hell's going on out there. The next shot contains the largest zombie horde we'll see in the film. Sixteen, by my count, slowly advancing beneath a black canopy of Norway spruce to a soundtrack of cricket chirping that gradually cedes to the murky quaver of a Livingston cue titled "Acoustic Space Station, Take 11." I can't imagine what an acoustic space station is, but I like it.

The next five shots break new ground in the (very) nascent subgenre of zombie films. So far, zombies have been forces of nebulous antagonism. Now, in quick succession, we are introduced to what I'm going to call Neighbor Zombies.

I borrow the phrase from the new version of the *Night* script Romero wrote half of in 2016. In this script—quite remarkably given fifty years of semantic parsing—Romero does not refer to his dead as "zombies" or even "ghouls." Or any of the other terms that show up in the Russo-Romero script, as logged by Jeff Moreno: *creep, attacker, bohopper, dead things, creatures, behoppers, beings, aggressors, humanoid beings, flesh-eaters*, and *bojobbers*. Romero refers to them throughout his new fifty-two pages as "neighbors." The term links to comment Romero made in a 1997 episode of the BBC's *Clive Barker's A-Z of Horror*: "The most frightening thing to me is the neighbors." Neighbors are, first and foremost, recognizable, as we are meant to recognize the Neighbor Zombies that follow.

Early in the shoot, the makeup applied by Karl Hardman and Marilyn Eastman aped the ghost makeup from the marvelous *Carnival of Souls* (1962): white face paint with black around the eyes. *Carnival*, by the way, is the only 1960s American horror flick that approaches the miracle of *Night* (and the curse—it, too, suffered from a missing copyright bug). Shot by another industrial filmmaker, Herk Harvey of Lawrence, Kansas, for the even smaller budget of $33,000 (Harvey didn't have to pay the type of fees Image Ten did—$9,500 for the right to shoot in Evans City Cemetery, for example), *Carnival* features similar Bergman-inspired visuals and a female lead even more idiosyncratic than Judith O'Dea—Candace Hilligoss, giving one of my favorite performances of all time. (My friend Sara once took me to the corroded ruins of the film's central location, the Saltair Pavilion, on the edge of the Great Salt Lake, a site that feels more haunted than anything connected to *Night*.)

As *Night*'s production progressed, the zombie makeup made leaps, and here is their finest showcase. The first and arguably most famous Neighbor Zombie is the so-called Nude Ghoul. She is, well, nude (but painted greenish-gray so she wouldn't look too nubile). Image Ten's excuse was that naked cadavers would be among the first wave to come back to life. True, but shouldn't the first wave also include a lot of old people? A more likely reason for the Nude Ghoul was the shock and transgression. She is first seen from behind, buttocks sliding from shadows, then from the side, bare-breasted. (She was snipped from the versions I saw with my mom as a kid.)

It's a far cry from sexy, but anyway, sex sells. Of the fifty-one VHS covers of *Night* collected in Geoff Turner's *Night of the Living Tapes*, thirty-one feature Nude Ghoul. (Newspaper ads, more chaste, often inked underwear onto the figure or hid the cleft of her buttocks under another piece of art.) The body tag tied to Nude Ghoul's wrist reads "Smythe Carole 40916," and, in fact, the actor's name is Carol—Carol Wayne, an artist's model in Pittsburgh. I don't know much about her but feel certain she didn't think taking her clothes off in rural Pennsylvania for a couple hours in 1967 would land her on sixty years' worth of merch. (Carol wasn't really such an outlier: a "nudist park" called Camp Halcyon was a mere seven-minute drive from the farmhouse.)

Carol Wayne made her first and only convention appearance in 2019 at Living Dead Weekend in Evans City. She was older and wiser: She did not allow photos.

The third shot of this sequence features the film's most oft-seen Neighbor Zombie, a thick, bare-chested man with a ragged wound near his left shoulder. This is John Simpson, best known for gnawing on a human bone later in the film, an image that, like Carol Wayne's backside, ended up on a lot of posters. I'm more interested in the zombie behind Simpson, played by a guy named David Barbour. Barbour's in the background of the two shots before this, and in two of the three he makes the most curious gesture, touching his left index finger to his bottom lip as if reflecting upon a memory. I don't really have an insight here. It's just odd.

The fourth shot highlights a Neighbor Zombie played by Roger McGovern, a local ad man best known for coining "Beat 'em, Bucs," a ubiquitous 1960s Pittsburgh Brewing Company catchphrase that was on everything from billboards to diapers to novelty 45s. PBC's flagship product is Iron City Beer—"the Beer Drinker's Beer" and the unofficial brewski of Romero-ites. Romero used to direct Iron City commercials. Per the 2024 doc *Chasing Zombies: A George Romero Tribute*, Jeannie Jeffries, who played "Blonde Zombie" in *Dawn*, was a model known as the "Iron City Beer Girl." In the 1990 *Night* remake, one character wears an Iron City shirt. When I visited Romero's grave in Toronto, an unopened can of Iron City sat on the headstone.

McGovern (father of Terence, who voiced Launchpad McQuack on *DuckTales* and invented the word "Wookiee" for pal George Lucas) came to my attention after I introduced my friend Matt to *Night of the Living Dead* in the summer of 1994. Matt didn't like horror; in 1989, we'd gone to see *Pet Sematary* together and halfway through he hightailed it from the theater. I had to convince him *Night* was camp, and to sustain that illusion, we cut up through the whole film, and then, as was our habit, recycled our best jokes for future viewings and casual repartee.

We weren't the first. With its sharp characterizations and motivations, *Night* has always lent itself to parody. Some are in title only, like the "Night of the Living Bed" episode of *St. Elsewhere* (1987), the "Night Court of the Living Dead" episode of *Night Court* (1988), and "The Night of the Dead Living" episode of *Homicide: Life on the Street* (1993).

The first full parody I saw was *Night of the Living Bread*, an eight-minute short Kevin S. O'Brien made at Ohio University in 1990 that somehow made it onto a two-tape VHS set put out by Anchor Bay in 1995. It's terrifically literal: A quartet of farmhouse strangers are besieged by flying slices of white bread. I doubt O'Brien was overthinking the whole "white bread" thing, but considering that his Ben remains Black, it's amusing to consider. The second parody I saw was the (fairly disturbing) "Attack of the Street Pimps" segment of Robert Townsend's *Hollywood Shuffle* (1987).

More (in)famous than these is *Night of the Day of the Dawn of the Son of the Bride of the Return of the Revenge of the Terror of the Attack of the Evil, Mutant, Alien, Flesh Eating, Hellbound, Zombified Living Dead*, a 1991 cult item created by James Riffel, who dubbed a public-domain copy of *Night* into a comedy haphazardly spliced with music videos and short films. It's the kind of thing a '90s tape-head could order from underground zines, which is how I first got my grubby hands on *Begotten*, *Cannibal Holocaust*, and *Meet the Feebles*.

It's easy to disdain Riffel's curio. Johnny's obsessed with sex dolls. Zombie #1 is a "fag." Ben's a jive-talking horn-dog. But it also demolishes taboos in a way that recalls, well, *Night of the Living Dead*. The zombie horde, largely coded as gay, can be read as taking revenge on a population that let them die (at least two tasteless AIDS jokes tell us the topic was at least on Riffel's mind). And it's just plain cathartic to hear Ben tell Barb, "Listen up, baby. I got a bunch of cracker-ass white zombie honky motherfuckers jacking up my fresh ride, and if I don't waste their white asses, they're gonna come in here in the house, so take a chill pill."

Proof that Riffel had a genuine knack for this stuff is provided by two lousier copycats. Anthony Rudd's 2022 redub, *Night of the British Dead,* is exasperating despite its clever tagline, "They're coming to get you, Barbawa!" Gen Xers will better recall *Mad Movies,* a Nick at Nite show offering reedited films dubbed by improv group the L.A. Connection. Aired in 1985, their tedious, laugh-tracked, half-hour *Night* follows ghouls, cops, and survivors as they throw a farmhouse party.

We're not even close to finished. There's *Night of the Living Babes, Night of the Living Carrots, Night of the Living Deb, Night of the Living Dicks, Night of the Living Doo* (Scooby, that is), *Night of the Living Dorks, Night of the Living Duck* (Daffy, that is), *Night of the Living Jews, Night of the Living Heads, Night of the Living Karens, Night of the Giving Head* (porn), *Night of the Living Pepperoni, Night of the Living Trekkies, Flight of the Living Dead, Diet of the Living Dead, The Mennonite of the Living Dead,* and much, much more. Surely such homages reach a zenith in the "Night of the Living Pharmacists" episode of the kids' show *Phineas and Ferb* (2014), and a nadir in *Killer Poop 3: Night of the Living Poop* (2022).

The only *Night* joke Matt originated that I still remember is crying "Great Caesar's ghost!" every time we saw Roger McGovern's zombie. He's outfitted in a white sheet—a toga, basically, though the Image Ten site insists it's a hospital gown. McGovern also sports the film's most extravagant makeup, a fleshy fissure through his forehead, a goopy abscess in his jaw, and a right ear that looks like it's melting off his face. In his introductory shot, McGovern swats at the air as if seeing prey that isn't really there. There's something sad about an old man (McGovern was fifty-one but made to look older) acting on survival instinct and failing. It brings to mind nursing homes, hospice, the slow crumbling of one's faculties.

Great Caesar's ghost! Try it. Not a bad way to ward off the willies.

Our last Neighbor Zombie comes in an eleven-second shot of

a woman picking a centipede from a tree and eating it (with some juicy sound effects). Lots of questions raised here. Zombies eat bugs? Romero never makes this mistake again. In fact, it's key to his ethos that zombies only hunt humans. And that's not even the strangest thing in this shot! Bug-Eating Zombie is played by Marilyn Eastman, who, in just two minutes and twenty-two seconds, is going to show up as an entirely different character. Sure, she's wearing a wig here and half her face is obscured by oatmealy makeup—but it's clearly her! I have yet to read a good explanation for why Eastman doubles up here instead of drafting an extra. (Unless the bug was real? Was she the only one willing to eat a bug? One issue of a Jack Russo–written comic called *Night of the Living Dead: Hunger* actually provides an origin story for the bug-eater. The dude leaves no stone unturned.)

If Hardman and Eastman hadn't gotten so creative in the makeup chair, it's possible Romero's zombie hexology might have taken a different route. You can draw a straight line from *Night*'s Neighbor Zombies to the highly specified zombies of *Dawn of the Dead* (Hare Krishna Zombie, Machete Zombie, Screwdriver Zombie, Chopper Zombie), and then to Bub, the fully realized zombie from *Day of the Dead*. This through line is critical to understanding Romero's view of zombies as the good guys, the antibodies to the human plague—an idea worked through extensively in *The Living Dead*.

The timing of the Neighbor Zombie scene is a chef's kiss. It lets us see the zombies through the lenses of our characters. They all see the threat differently, and this, in short, is why zombies became such a force in horror. What they represent is in the eye of the beholder. For Tom, they might be high school buddies who died in a war he shouldn't have supported. For Harry, they might be young radicals seeking to topple the old guard. For Ben, they might be the opposite, the white establishment trying to defend the good life they refuse to share. If the film were made today, they could be the Covid dead coming back to haunt anti-vax conspiracy theorists. As long as we find new things to fear, zombies will never die.

00:46:39

IT AIN'T NECESSARILY SO

BACK TO BEN AND HARRY: WINDOWS, CELLAR, DEATH trap, et cetera. Romero had no choice but to shoot these dialogue scenes stiffly. The farmhouse's cramped quarters and the eighty-pound soundproofing blimp inhibited dollying or tracking. Romero had but three lenses in his arsenal—10mm, 35mm, and 70mm—and it was the 10mm most often used in the house to imbue the quarters with a bit more space.

Cordoned off in one of these tripod shots, Harry tries a new tactic, pointing at Barbra: "I'm taking the girl with me!" Ben lays the smack down. No Barbra for Harry and nothing else either: "Because if I stay up here, I'm fighting for everything up here!" To them, Barbra is a claimable object as much as the radio, though she *is* acting a bit object-like. Harry complains he can't bring his injured daughter upstairs, to which Duane Jones gives one of the best line deliveries in history.

"It is tough for the kid that her old man is so stupid. Now, get the hell down in the cellar. You can be the boss down there. I'm boss up here."

Ben's no longer fighting for survival. He's fighting for totalitarian control of Farmhouse Nation. Ben's likely never been boss of anything despite clearly having the goods, and here's his run at the throne. There's little commonality between the film's Ben and the script's Truckdriver, but one line of description transcends: "He exudes an air of resentment, as though the strangers have intruded on his private little fortress." Ben climbed on this teeter-totter first and has no intention of sharing it—despite that a one-man teeter-totter doesn't move.

Harry's face is lit parchment: It curls with loathing. He calls Ben and Tom "bastards," as close as *Night* gets to cursing. He backs toward the cellar door, throttling his truncheon, until Tom stops him by shouting, "Wait a minute!" The demand is delivered in a tight close-up that provides an unadulterated study of the acting stylings of Keith Wayne.

The stylings, it must be admitted, are middling. Of all actors with speaking roles in *Night*, Wayne is the least natural. You can see him rehearse his next line in his head before saying it. He's never *listening* to other actors, only awaiting his cue. The Tom in the script is an older cemetery caretaker who is "big and powerful looking." Keith Wayne is twenty-two and about a foot shorter than Duane Jones, though compactly muscled. But his perpetual slackness—feet planted, arms dangled—can't compete with the full-body commitment of Duane Jones, Karl Hardman, or Judith O'Dea.

It's a good face, ruggedly handsome, if a bit bland. This is an odd comp, but he reminds me of Eddie Mekka, who played Carmine Ragusa—"the Big Ragoo"—on *Laverne & Shirley*. Neither were obvious heartthrobs, but what they lacked in physical appeal they made up for in sweat equity, singing and dancing their ways into our affection. Eddie Mekka, however, had a self-awareness Wayne did not. Every time Tom refers to Ben's boarded-up windows, he says "windas," blissfully unselfconscious of his rural pronunciation.

Keith Wayne was not, in fact, trying to make a career as an actor. But he was very much a performer. His story is a strange one.

Legend has it, the Rev was patronizing a local music club in 1967 (possibly the Las Vegas Club on Route 51) when he noticed the lead singer of a band called Ronnie and the Jesters. They weren't nobodies. The Jesters spent three summers touring the Midwest, and the year before had shared a bill with the Beatles in Milwaukee. Wayne had scored more than one club residency, including an ill-timed weekend gig at the Gaiety Follies in Myrtle Beach smack in the middle of *Night*'s shoot, obliging four weeks of Sunday and Wednesday redeye flights to and from Pittsburgh, where he roomed with Duane Jones. No wonder he always looks dazed. Once you notice Wayne's excessive blinking in *Night*, you can't unsee it. "Eyeblinking every other word" is how *Variety* put it in their glib pan.

The Rev chatted up Wayne and learned the kid had performed in musical theater all through college (the tell is how Wayne cheats his body too much to Romero's camera) before focusing on music. A native of Houston, Pennsylvania (population 1,865 in 1960), Wayne had been performing since age five, and for seven years was part of the Betty Dugan Starlets on Parade, a youth group that sang on KDKA radio for sixteen years and put out a few seven-inches on Pittsburgh's Dix Records. For what it's worth, the Dugan name remains prominent in Steel City and is these days most associated with personal injury attorney Mitch Dugan, who in commercials spells out his name on each curling finger, *D-U-G-A-N*, until he's got a fist. A fist that will fight for *you*, I imagine.

On the LaserDisc commentary, Romero recalls Wayne having a nickname, but it evades him: "The Male Go-go? Mr. Go-go?" (Romero was adamant Wayne was a go-go dancer, but that's news to me.)

Wayne was, for sure, a man of many names. He'd left behind his birth name of Ronald Keith Hartman by 1966 ("Wayne" was an homage to a brother who died at eighteen months old), when he cut two solo tracks for J. J. Jules, manager of the Marcels (famous for their doo-wop cover of "Blue Moon"). This two-song 45 put out by the St. Clair label is hard to find nowadays. I have yet to hear the A-side track "Say Hey, Hey, Hey," but I found his B-side cover of the Gershwins' free-thinker anthem "It Ain't Necessarily So" from *Porgy and Bess*. It's a sinuous creeper that replaces the original's scatting with a Doors-like organ interlude. Wayne's tense vibrato is sexy, if a bit forgettable, but it was enough to get him touring.

My hunch is that "sexy" and "forgettable" were the adjectives that ultimately doomed him. Instead of taking the 2 percent of the gross offered on *Night*, Wayne went for a straight $1,500 payout ("I asked my father the millworker and he said, 'Take the money, son'"), with which he bought the brand-new Lincoln convertible he used to drive to set like a proper superstar. It tells us where his headspace was: He was chasing the limelight at a pace the others weren't.

Night was the closest he ever came to catching it. Even when the film found its foothold, Wayne rated scant attention. He pushed on as a musician through 1974, when the Washington, Pennsylvania, *Observer-Reporter*, in an article heartbreakingly titled "Former Houston Man Heading for Stardom," noted Wayne for scoring a "major nightclub engagement" at Harrah's in Reno, Nevada. Elsewhere, Jack Russo reported Wayne singing in South American countries for the State Department.

Only three years later, he quit the biz at age thirty-two, reverted to the surname Hartman, went to chiropractic school in St. Louis, moved to Cary, North Carolina, and opened Cary Chiropractic Center in 1984 (specializing in athletes, said Marilyn Eastman). But the restlessness didn't die. In 1989, at age forty-four, he became a powerlifter, and in 1990 won his weight class at the National Masters Powerlifting Championship and came in seventh in a worldwide Australian competition, with personal bests of 578.7 pounds squatted, 303.1 pounds benched, and 600 pounds deadlifted. Combining these areas of expertise (when he wasn't waking up at 3:30 a.m. four days a week to pump iron at the Powerhouse Gym), he began writing the Chiropractic Forum column in a strange little powerlifting zine called *Hardgainer*.

I started buying vintage copies of *Hardgainer* and came across his final column, published in the January–February 1996 issue. After subhead sections on "Knee Care" and "Neck Care" comes an alarming and emphatic subhead penned by publisher and editor Stuart McRobert: "Dr. Hartman, *dead!*"

A single paragraph tells the sad tale: "With great regret I inform you that Dr. Keith Hartman died on September 8, 1995, from what police believe was a self-inflicted gunshot wound. He was fifty years old. Keith had had a very traumatic last couple of years and apparently succumbed to depression." Russo has added to the record that Wayne was going through a divorce, and *The Cary News* confirmed he and his wife, Brenda, were living apart.

McRobert mentions a biographic feature on Wayne from Issue #36, roughly eighteen months earlier. I searched out the issue. I wanted to know what might have driven Wayne to take his life, and this one-page, self-written bio is the closest we have to a final statement. It features a small black-and-white photo, taken by Brenda, of a grinning Wayne and his two teenage children, both of whom, twenty-four years later, would speak at *Night*'s fiftieth anniversary screening (held in the same theater as the film's 1968 premiere). As I should have anticipated by this point, Wayne's life story, as related in *Hardgainer*, was bent with hard lefts: a childhood airplane accident, youth training in vaudeville, the youngest member of the Guild of Variety Artists, and a more extensive touring career than I expected.

Around the same time I was snapping up *Hardgainers*, a deep eBay search led me to a mysterious factory-sealed 8-track cartridge apparently recorded at Sundance Recording Studio at the Cardinal Shopping Center in Winston-Salem, North Carolina. Titled *The First Time*, it is by a band called the Keith Wayne Show and even sports a funky "KW" logo. In small type on the front, it reads, "Produced by: Ronald K. Hartman for Keith Wayne and L.A. Tymes." This was my guy, all right.

As reluctant as I was to sunder the fifty-year-old cellophane, I did anyway, then passed it off to the University of Pittsburgh Library System's Ben Rubin, who had a bead on a working 8-track player. The tape still worked. Heard for the first time in half a century, Wayne's thirty-three-minute opus is a batch of upbeat, gospel-influenced R&B covers of songs by Barry White, Barry Manilow, Gladys Knight, Grand Funk Railroad, and more. Wayne never fully lets loose, as if too cognizant that *The First Time* was, in fact, his last time: The release dates of the songs he covers suggest he cut the record in 1974, while the last piece of evidence we have of Wayne performing is a flyer for a three-week engagement, starting February 17, 1975, of "Keith Wayne & Company" at a Knoxville hotel called the Inn-ter-section Lounge. Wayne is hyped as "Another Tom Jones."

At his best—namely, the Neil Diamond medley that kicks off *The First Time*—Wayne wins me over through sheer perspiration. When he hits the chorus of "Brother Love's Travelling Salvation Show," you feel him forget his shortcomings, his failures, his regrets, all of it.

Briefly, he's a star.

The most telling thing about Wayne's *Hardgainer* bio is what it *doesn't* say. There's nary a mention of *Night of the Living Dead*. This is despite Wayne having recently been drawn into what other *Night* longtimers had discovered was a lucrative convention circuit, starting with the warmly remembered Zombie Jamboree, held August 27–29, 1993, at the Pittsburgh Expo Mart in Monroeville, advertised as "24,000 square feet of horror, movie, comics, toys, cards, and collectable dealers" including a "zombie swimsuit/beauty pageant" and a "zombie breakfast," whatever that was. It could all be yours for the wistful ticket price of $10 for ages six to twelve, $15 for adults—just call (toll free!) 800-926-NOLD. (The flip side of the tickets sported a free Pepsi offer from Pittsburgh's Original Oyster House, one floor down from Russo's Market Square Productions office. Businesses were always offering free Pepsis in the nineties.)

The Zombie Jamboree—surely named after Harry Belafonte's 1962 calypso classic of the same name ("Back to back, belly to belly / Don't give a damn, I done dead already")—was the first *Night*-focused fan event, and to most attendees, the best, and was successful enough to beget events still happening today. Per a meandering documentary called *Zombie Jamboree '93* (directed by

Russo, which you can tell by the relentless promotion of Russo projects), auxiliary guest stars like Adam West (Batman), Gunnar Hansen (Leatherface), and David Prowse (Darth Vader) paled next to Romero's mythic eight-hour, bathroom-break-free sign-a-thon.

In 1994, the same year Wayne attended his second and final horror convention (Creature Features in Durham, North Carolina), he participated in the aforesaid LaserDisc commentary. He starts shy but warms up. When O'Dea innocently asks him, "You still do any band singing?" Wayne replies, "No," and then repeats, sadder and softer, "No."

His melancholy echoes my own feelings about conventions. The first one I attended was in summer 1996, a Star Trek convention in Des Moines along with my college buddy Marcus Dunstan, who went on to cowrite scads of *Saw* sequels with Patrick Melton and direct films like *The Collector* (2009). We were shooting 16mm and 8mm film for a documentary I was making, but I recall little of that. What stays with me is turning around and finding Keir Dullea, star of *2001: A Space Odyssey*, alone at a table, unbought headshots fanned before him. He'd worked with *Kubrick*. And here he was in *Des Moines*.

News of the Cary, North Carolina, chiropractor's past had begun to spread like the undead. In 1992, after Wayne's past was more or less outed by film writer Joe Bob Briggs, Raleigh's *News & Observer* published an article on Wayne titled "A Zombie in His Closet." The forty-seven-year-old Wayne, whose laugh looks manic in the story's photo, admits, "I should have taken this film and I should have marshaled it into a career. But I didn't. Because I didn't know how to do it." Instead, the article explains, Wayne did a weight-training TV show for the religious network Victory Television.

The snarky tone of the article goes sober in the final column. "I left that person," Wayne says of his youthful alter ego. "I divorced that person. I buried that person, and now that person is being resurrected . . . He wants to be noticed. He wants to be admired. He wants to be respected for that ability he had. It is difficult . . . Because unless I deal with that, I'm really not going to be happy."

Russo confirms this on the LaserDisc commentary: "I think the Zombie Jamboree kind of got it back in his blood, because he was starting to talk about scripts and projects. And I said, 'Well, does it get you thinking that maybe you should have stayed in the business?' And he said, 'Yes, it definitely does.'" On a January 14, 1995, *Night* cast reunion episode of *MonsterVision,* Briggs asks Wayne, "How could you do it to us? How could you be the most famous person blown up in a George Romero movie and choose to be a chiropractor instead of an actor?" Wayne's wounded expression, before he covers it with a chuckle, haunts me.

It brings me no joy to draw the following conclusion. By reopening the door to *Night* (and, by extension, the stardom he'd chased for twenty-five years), Wayne reopened the door to depression—the equivalent of a reformed alcoholic picking up a bottle again. Everyone involved in the magnificent crash of *Night of the Living Dead* staggered away with injuries, but none more so than the young man who looked so strong and capable on-screen. Keith Wayne could have told his truth had anyone had the insight to ask: It ain't necessarily so.

00:48:04 HEY, KID

Tom ducks his head through the cellar door and gently calls down for Judy.

Judy? Tom mentioned Harry's wife and injured child a few minutes ago, but this is the first we have heard of any Judy.

Our operatic group becomes a quintet as a young woman of Tom's age cautiously emerges from the cellar. Judy, played by and named for Judith Ridley, has long blonde hair, a mock turtleneck, denim jacket with sleeves rolled back, clamdigger pants, and thong sandals.

Judy greets the first floor with feline caution, aiming wary looks at Harry and Ben before sitting next to Barbra. The Sofa of No Opinions is where the film is going to park its females. Harry makes good on his threat by lizarding through the cellar door and closing it. And for only the third time in the movie, we find ourselves in a new location.

Fandoms make temples out of film sites. It's more logical to me than grafting significance onto some church that happens to be near your home. (The most moved I ever felt at church was in 1987, at age twelve, when I hid the *Re-Animator* novelization inside my hymnal and got to *that scene* while the minister droned.) By making pilgrimages to Luke Skywalker's igloo house in Tunisia, or the Hobbiton Peter Jackson left in New Zealand, fans are able to see bracing new facets, touch the walls or the soil, and breathe the same air as the people who inspired them, and honestly changed them. Supranatural notions are physicalized into reality, which is, after all, what churches purport to do.

This pursuit frustrates the *Night of the Living Dead* faithful in a way it doesn't the *Dawn of the Dead* faithful—Monroeville Mall remains open. Inside the mall, by the way, is the Living Dead Museum, which includes relics like the actual production lights used on the film. Pretty cool, but imagine if the Living Dead Museum were inside the actual farmhouse! Not impossible: Look at the similarly dilapidated white-paneled farmhouse from *The Texas Chain Saw Massacre*. In 1998, it was sliced into six pieces and transported to Kingsland, Texas, where it's now a restaurant called, naturally, Hooper's, festooned with memorabilia. (Writer C. Robert Cargill took me there in July 2025, and yes, I ordered the BBQ.)

But the Gass house on Ash Stop Road, per plan, was demolished in 1969. For most, the house's precise location is a mystery, and there's an appeal to that, even a relief. It reminds me of another farmhouse, the one owned by Ed Gein, "the Butcher of Plainfield," whose necrophilic exploits inspired *Psycho*, *The Texas Chain Saw Massacre*, *Depraved*, and *The Silence of the Lambs* (shot in Pittsburgh, by the way, with a Romero cameo). Upon rumors that Gein's house might be purchased as a tourist attraction, an arsonist burnt the place to the ground in 1958.

The Seven Pines fields that were once ground zero for the encroaching undead today grow eighty-five acres of Evans City Sweetcorn (slogan: "So good, even the butter gets excited!"), readily available at nearby Deener's Farm Market. In 1994, a new house was built on the foundations of the old—single story, brown paneled wood—though the towering pine trees in the film (from which Marilyn Eastman plucked her delicious bug) still stand.

Peons like yours truly have to view the house from eight hundred feet away. It's private land, though the owners have made exceptions for select guests of more than one Living Dead Weekend (quite nice of them, as they are deluged by requests). Photos from one event reveal a trampoline on the house's lawn, a detail that makes me smile. On my only visit (escorted by Matt Blazi, who shooed me from poison ivy), I noticed railroad tracks not a hundred feet from the driveway; how the crew kept train noise from their Arrivox Tandberg audio recorder is the kind of quiet accomplishment that makes me appreciate Image Ten all the more.

While Blazi and I were ogling the property (like creeps), a truck on its way to the house paused beside us. Laura, a horticulturist and daughter of the property's owners, engaged us in pleasant conversation, in which she admitted she'd watched *Night* but once, and only to peep the scenery. When her parents bought the property, they sold some of the foundational house stones to collectors. This was the first either of us had heard of such a thing; I wonder who has them. Purportedly, the remains of the house were buried on-site, but please don't start digging. Instead, try to track down one of the fifteen authorized "wooden siding fragments" that exist. Good luck.

While the farmhouse might frustrate fans, the cellar site holds the title of Most Inaccessible. Because the Gass house had only a crawl space beneath it (the way in was through the kitchen door Ben removes in his lumber raid), the gang took advantage of 247 Fort Pitt Boulevard, the home of the Latent Image (a twenty-minute drive from Romero's place at 245 Amber Street). Today, as then, it's a five-story structure separated from the Monongahela River by the Penn-Lincoln Parkway and within sight of the Steelers-yellow Fort Pitt Bridge. It's the coolest-looking thing on the block, built of green-accented gray brick in the Italian Renaissance Revival style, except for the ground floor, which was updated, probably in the 1940s, to a rounded and recessed Moderne facade. The cellar doubled as the Latent Image's prop room.

It's virtually impossible to get into the cellar today. If you peek through 247's sidewalk doors (like creeps), you can make out the elevator to the basement on the left. (Romero was once mugged outside this elevator by a man wielding a glass shard from the front door he'd just shattered.) On the right is a door that still has an old sticker pasted on it. LAUREL, it reads—the shingle Romero and producer Richard Rubinstein created to produce *Martin*, *Creepshow*, *Day of the Dead*, and *Tales from the Darkside*. A board inside the lobby suggests the office may be available for lease (in case you're in the market). On the top floor, meanwhile, are the offices of personal injury attorneys Goldsmith & Ogrodowski. Not *D-U-G-A-N*, but close.

There are five ways to get contemporary glimpses of the cellar. The first comes via *Fan of the Dead* (2007), what I'd charitably call a "video diary" by a French horror fan named Nicolas Garreau. It tracks his three-day visit to the 2003 Pittsburgh Comic Con, where Karl Hardman appears to reply to Garreau in fluent French. (Sadly, the con's "Celebrity Roast" of George Romero to benefit the Make-a-Wish Foundation fell apart.) What Garreau lacks in journalistic technique he makes up for with a willingness to trespass, which does not make me especially like him but does result in footage of the guy simply walking his way into the cellar, which is cluttered but otherwise looks exactly as it did in 1967. The visit is brief, probably because Garreau got chased out. (I suspect his farmhouse visit lasts only five seconds for the same reason.)

A year after *Fan of the Dead*, directors Robert L. Lucas and Chris Roe got into the cellar under Image Ten's imprimatur for

One for the Fire. Russ Streiner and Jack Russo provide bittersweet commentary on being back down there, particularly a side room in which Latent Image film reels were stored, and where a Monongahela flood ruined all known *Night* outtakes, deleted scenes, and more. Including, hauntingly, the *Night of the Flesh Eaters* title screen. The copyright bug was literally washed away.

In 2009 came *Autopsy of the Dead*. While not for beginners, the doc is a marvelous resource for diehards, as it skirts the usual suspects to interview those who performed smaller roles. When possible, director Jeff Carney films interviews in the location each person is most identified with. The delightfully droll Kyra Schon, who played Karen, is interviewed in the cellar, at that point filled with stuff like outdated computers. Just like yours and mine.

The all-time best view of the cellar comes in "Night of the Living Steelers," a 2016 episode of the TV series *The Timeline* shot for the NFL Network. The forty-four-minute doc is an odd duck, only occasionally succeeding in drawing parallels between the history of the Pittsburgh Steelers and Romero's career. Because it was funded by the NFL—and not, for example, a Frenchman with a camcorder—the production values are superior to anything else involving *Night*. It's also possibly Romero's last on-film appearance and for that reason is to be cherished. The NFL hauls Romero out to Evans City Cemetery one last time (Monroeville Mall too) and ends the episode with Romero being introduced to roughly seventy thousand fans at Heinz Field on October 1, 2015. He looks giddy. In fact, my favorite photo of Romero was taken at this event. It reminds me of a time before gambling sites made people watch football like AI bots, when you rooted for teams because they embodied your home—and Pittsburgh, for Romero, was home. In this photo, he's not the Godfather of Zombies, not a cult director carrying the weight of a whole subgenre on his back. He's just a sports fan, just a yinzer.

The NFL also gets Romero down to the cellar, which has, perhaps in deference to the maestro, been tidied up. It remains breathtakingly unchanged, as if the space had been hermetically sealed like a pharaoh's tomb. (The place looks the same in the fifth and most recent trip into the cellar, a January 2025 episode of YouTube's *Horror's Hallowed Grounds*.) It's all there down to the last divot—including the staircase Harry now stands atop to bolt the door with a board that does, in fact, look capable of holding back a zombie horde.

This won't be the last time we're forced to consider it: What if Harry's right?

Tom, bless his heart, makes a final plea through the locked door to the morose violin strains of the cutely titled Glindemann cue "Weird Suspense." Ben kneels in front of Barbra again (no shoe stuff this time) while Judy turns a sympathetic eye to the soporose woman. In the script, Truckdriver encourages Barb with a "Hey . . . hey, honey," but I far prefer Ben's approach. In a chummy high pitch, he says, "Hey . . . hey, kid." It's heartwarming, but he gets nothing back, and Judy fluffs her hair and looks away as if thinking, *Yee-ikes*.

00:49:01 DYING TOGETHER

The second Harry's feet hit the floor, Romero gives us the lay of the land. It's a cellar, all right, chaotic with crates, boxes, and bags; a sink draped with drying rags; and a table built from a door laid across sawhorses. On the door, between a blanket and sheet, lies an unconscious nine-year-old girl named Karen. Sitting next to her is Harry's wife, Helen.

Instantly, the farmhouse bisects into an upstairs/downstairs melodrama like *Downton Abbey* or *Gosford Park*, except in this case, the privileged nuclear family dwells below, while the upper floor houses a scrappier cohort—different ages, races, and genders all trying to make it work.

The cultural risks *Night* takes are easy to enumerate: the shock, the gore, the sundered mores. Structurally, though, the biggest risk is following a long dialogue scene upstairs with another long one downstairs. Remember, though the film rolled out in theaters, it seemed destined for drive-in crowds (a November 1, 1967, piece in the *Pittsburgh Post-Gazette* is literally titled "Pittsburghers Make Chiller for Drive-Ins"), and was voted "Greatest Drive-In Movie in the History of the World" in a poll conducted by Joe Bob Briggs.

Romero himself said it was only when he, Hardman, and Eastman watched *Night* at a drive-in during its opening week that they felt they had truly made it. Actor Matthew Modine felt the same. In an episode of Criterion's famous Criterion Closet videos (at least six of which include film luminaries gushing over *Night*), Modine says, "My father was a drive-in theater manager and I watched this movie in the projection booth of the drive-in—it was called the Highland—in Salt Lake City, Utah. And I was much, much too young to have seen this film, and it damaged at least ten years of my childhood."

What's important here is that drive-in crowds chiefly consisted of randy young people packed into vehicles (drive-ins often charged per "carload") with only one ear tuned to the grinding, treble-heavy speakers clipped to car windows. A lot of dialogue got gobbled by those contraptions, making long, talky scenes risky. *Night* gets away with it mostly because it's hardly *Waiting for Godot*. Not quite *The Connection* either. *Night*'s emotions are big and the acting bigger; Hardman understands that playing to drive-in crowds is like playing to a theater's farthest balcony. While Harry groundhogs for cigarettes, he mutters to Helen that there's two new people upstairs and Tom and Judy are with them. When he gets Helen's report that Karen is feverish, his response is to blow a big cloud of smoke in his daughter's face. Ah, the sixties.

The cellar sure feels like the death trap Ben said it was. The black-and-white photography turns Harry into a dungeon dweller, skulking between harsh, bare bulbs and ink-black shadow. Harry's only hope of improving his mood is to mock the upstairs strivers: "We'll see who's right. We'll see when they come begging me to let them in down here."

Helen doesn't let him get away with it. "That's important, isn't it? To be right, everybody else to be wrong." When Harry asks what she means, she gives a dismissive flap of her hand that tells Harry he isn't worth arguing with. Harry hurls his cigarette (which he'd worked so hard for!) to the floor, and Helen shuts up and takes a seat.

It's a brilliant spot of acting. It's so good I watched it in slo-mo to enjoy each subtle shift. Helen cleanses her emotions, a mechanical return to the obedience with which she's forged her union with Harry. Her mouth closes and she looks to the side, like you do when you are worried you might explode at someone. Her eyes go downcast, a decision of docility for whatever reason—the comfort of her daughter, an unwillingness to increase the stress, an embedded belief that her insubordination may be found out and neighbors will start avoiding her at the grocery. Finally, there's a little sniff, her mouth twitching briefly in the manner of a boxer reprimanding themselves for letting a punch get through. All in six seconds.

I can only compare these six seconds to an equally fleet expression Julia Roberts gives in *My Best Friend's Wedding* (1997). (I bet that title wasn't on your Bingo card.) There's a moment when Roberts first lays eyes on her crush's fiancée, played by Cameron Diaz, and with a single dip of her eyeline, Roberts imparts wariness, defensiveness, exhaustion, pride, and self-loathing. It's a shame Roberts never caught on.

Helen sits. And softly utters her famous line: "We may not enjoy living together, but dying together isn't going to solve anything."

Marilyn Eastman, ladies and gentlemen!

Picking my favorite actor in *Night* makes me feel like a kid ranking the Super Friends. Realistically, Duane Jones is my favorite. There's a rascally part of me that periodically prefers Karl Hardman, that son-of-a-bitch. I have a set of *Night of the Living Dead* lapel pins and the thought of sporting the Harry one makes me laugh. Who'd wear a Harry Cooper pin?! (Me.)

These days, I often favor Marilyn Eastman. It's hard to

imagine anyone matching Hardman's energy as well as Jones, but Eastman does, eschewing traded punches for the strikes of a ninja who never appears to move at all. A big reason she's killing this scene is that she wrote it. That famous line I quoted a minute ago? That's all Marilyn Eastman.

Russo and Romero infused their script with legendary ideas. But as a literary work it's eccentric and ungainly and hardly hints at the greatness it would inspire. It weighs in at ninety pages, normal enough, but doesn't resemble any other screenplay I've seen. There are no scene headings, no INT. FARMHOUSE - NIGHT. Character dialogue is not only all-caps—a nightmare to parse—but, for some reason, enclosed in quotation marks. Action is delivered in lovely but longwinded prose (making Russo's novelization a simpler translation than you'd think). "Beyond the distant trees, the last receding gray of dusk is surrendering to the black." "The mood relaxes in intensity, becomes calmer, more analytical." These impressionistic descriptions are bricked into walls of unbroken, justified text, even harder to read than the dialogue.

The cellar scene is the flattest writing in the script, and credit goes to the gang for acknowledging it and taking Eastman up on her offer to rewrite the Harry-Helen dialogue. You can see her changes written right onto her copy of the script if you have the *Night of the Living Dead Scrapbook*, which you don't, because Eastman and Hardman only made twenty-four for the Zombie Jamboree. (Technically there were two volumes of this scrapbook, but the weeds here are already too thick.)

The scrapbook is truly bespoke: a three-ring binder containing eighty-six pages of ephemera amended with handwritten notes and slipped into forty-three plastic sleeves. The book meant a lot to Eastman; she clutches it proudly all through the episode of Joe Bob Briggs's *MonsterVision*. To this day, the *Scrapbook* contains material that can't be found elsewhere, like an October 2, 1967, letter from Keith Wayne to Eastman that kicks off with "Hey Baby" and is signed "the Big Bopper."

Eastman had the chops to write new dialogue. She had, in

fact, *all* the chops—of the many Image Tenners who raised their hands to direct *Night*, Eastman's absence is the most conspicuous. Gender politics, no question.

It's thanks to Eastman's ambidextrousness that the Criterion edition was able to include eighteen minutes of rarer-than-rare raw footage (or "dailies" as they are called in the biz). This random collection of takes, printed so Eastman could practice film editing—therefore sparing it from the 247 Fort Pitt flood—answers the prayers of super-fans hungry to see those last-second adjustments before action is called. Subtle little reframings. Focus checks. The tongue gymnastics of actors. Clapboards emblazoned with FLESH EATERS / ROMERO. Zombies standing still until they go into motion like marionettes lifted by their master.

I'm sure Eastman made use of this reel. She was loaded with moxie. Born Marilyn Marie Johnson, she grew up in Davenport, Iowa, a two-hour drive from my hometown. En route to a Des Moines *Pay the Piper* event in October 2024, I impulsively took the Davenport exit from Interstate 80. It's a charming place despite the rusty surfaces and beleaguered unhoused of so many post-industrial Mississippi River towns.

Eastman once said she grew up in a railroad apartment that looked straight at the ten-story Capitol Theatre, a sumptuous movie house that opened in 1920, was reduced to pornos in the seventies, and shuttered in 2010, only to be refurbished and reopened in 2023. I stood beneath the theater's marquee (Bad Religion had just canceled a show there—bummer) and considered the buildings across the street. Until age six, Eastman lived at the Dorothea Apartments at 319 W. Third Street. From which window had the striking dark-haired girl gazed out at the coruscating theater lights? Or at the neon sign of Mac's Tavern, an Irish pub with a forty-foot bar that opened in 1934? The two businesses must have seemed to her like a choice of fates.

Fate, in this case, worked out. Eastman dreamed of her name on the Capitol marquee, and there's little doubt in my mind that *Night* played there more than once.

Eastman was a single mother raising two sons when she joined up with Hardman Associates in 1963 and soon attained the title of vice president and creative director. She was every bit as multitalented as her boss. She was a writer and producer, but foremost she was an actor. A Pittsburgh mainstay of stage, TV, and radio, Eastman performed in hundreds of commercials.

This is probably the place to mention that Eastman was a knockout. Though Judy Ridley was the one inserted as eye candy, it's Eastman no red-blooded viewer can keep their eyes off. She's like Ava Gardner with flatter eyebrows—stormy eyes, a defiant underbite, and a bone structure that didn't quit until her 2021 death. Hers was the kind of beauty that the film's hairstylist (Bruce Capristo, a salon owner who made O'Dea's wig and was the spitting image of Paulie Walnuts from *The Sopranos*) couldn't nullify with a harried bouffant, nor could the film's costume designer (Marilyn Eastman!) conceal with a plaid, going-to-church overcoat and orange-striped dress that resembles salmon nigiri.

Only Duane Jones and Marilyn Eastman had the talent and looks to make it in Hollywood. (I know there's *Night* fanfic out there, and I hope some lusty author is shipping Helen and Ben.) The internet insists Eastman notched two Hollywood gigs. One was as Society Woman in the Pittsburgh-set Sinbad vehicle *Houseguest* (1995). It's a ten-second, five-word appearance, but, you know what? She nails it.

The other is the role of Secretary in a 1960 episode of *Perry Mason* entitled "The Case of the Ominous Outcast." I've watched the damn thing twice, and while it's lousy with secretaries, none of them are Eastman. The root of the untruth lies in the closing credits, which assigns a "Secretary" role to a *Mary* Eastman. A simple instance of sloppy data entry, one that has been repeated now a thousand times. Take your pick of Marilyn Eastman obituaries, and it will mention this nonexistent role.

Of all things *Night of the Living Dead*, Marilyn Eastman and Karl Hardman's relationship is the most tenderly tiptoed around. In 1947, Hardman married Evamarie Scheufler, who'd fled the

German town of Stettin (now Szczecin in Poland) during WWII to Switzerland, where she met serviceman Karl Hardman. They divorced in 1984, and Evamarie died in 2005, two years before Hardman was taken by pancreatic cancer. Prior to the divorce, Hardman took up with Eastman. To this day, everywhere you look, Hardman and Eastman are referred to with the hazy catch-all "partners." The furthest anyone has officially gone is Eastman's son, John, who upon her death, called Eastman and Hardman "life partners."

It was a romantic relationship that began around 1965, though Hardman's daughter, Kyra Schon, is careful to point out on her website that the couple never married, despite what many claim. Even Romero got that wrong sometimes, as in a 1972 *Filmmakers Newsletter* interview in which he refers to Eastman as Hardman's wife. In the Felsher tapes, Romero gets it right, admitting, "I never met Karl's real wife. It was always Karl and Marilyn. It was like Tracy-Hepburn."

As pioneer Image Tenners, the life partners carried their share of bitterness. In *Memories of the Living Dead* (2013) by Bob Michelucci (chairman of the Zombie Jamboree), a collection of interviews with Romero colleagues, the couple vents defeat and self-incrimination. Hardman: "I have been continually embarrassed by people thinking that I'm on easy street because of the success of the film. They really don't believe that I could be so stupid as to let the rewards slip through my fingers." Eastman: "The film was a success. We were not. That was our fault."

The result of all this was humility. On the final episode (October 27, 1989) of the British TV program *Son of the Incredibly Strange Film Show*, Eastman, balancing herself on a cane, introduces herself like someone who still can't believe anyone has seen her little movie: "I played Helen Cooper—the lady in the basement."

The lady in the basement!

On the upside—and it's a big upside—all photos and videos I have seen of Hardman and Eastman together seem to depict two people deeply in love. Hardman renamed his company Hardman

Eastman Associates. In 1978, Hardman directed Eastman in a local production of Edward Albee's *Who's Afraid of Virginia Woolf?*, a 1962 play that had to have inspired the Harry-Helen dynamic. The duo appeared at countless horror conventions, handing out Dead Fly Productions business cards printed with the email address of easthard@aol.com, Hardman applying Harry's forehead bruise for photos, Eastman signing glossies of her younger self while wearing a T-shirt with Helen Cooper's image on it.

The vitality and believability of the cellar scene comes from the actors' shared trust. Ironically, the cellar, where their characters spew hatred at each other, is where we best see the actors' mutual devotion.

That devotion is even more strongly evidenced on one of the rarest pieces of *Night* ephemera: a cassette tape Eastman and Hardman produced in 1992 to sell at the Zombie Jamboree. The hand-styled black ink on the yellow label (applied to white cassettes) reads: NIGHT OF THE LIVING DEAD! SOUND EFFECTS. NARRATION: HARDMAN & EASTMAN. © HARDMAN EASTMAN STUDIOS INC. PGH. PA. That doesn't answer the question of what's on the tape. Surely it's not just a series of *Night* noises?

That's exactly what it is. Thus, it's hard to imagine a satisfied audience. Even I, cozy among the zealot fringe, don't foresee listening to it a second time. Like an album of John Coltrane studio cuts, the forty-five-minute program treats us to multiple takes of sound effects like automobile engines, creaking floors, hammer noises, and all-purpose grunts. Things get a bit more interesting with takes 54A and 54B, a group of O'Dea utility screams, gasps, and heavy breathing. Emotion this convincing is hard to manage in a studio setting; I'm reminded of once killing time at an editing studio by watching an hour of raw auditions for a pizza commercial. It was the most depressing thing I've ever seen, and I've seen *The Plague Dogs*.

The cassette's real value lies elsewhere. First, the impulse to have put it together in the first place. It ain't fair, but no one cares about sound recording, editing, and mixing. Those are the Oscars folks skip to refill their plates. But Eastman and Hardman had worked extremely hard on *Night*'s sound. They wanted that documented. Celebrated, even.

The main reason to listen to the tape (once) is the short introduction to each set of sounds. Though the couple's dialogue is obviously scripted, their repartee is affectionate and their banter infectious. "Hello! I'm Harry Cooper, better known as Karl Hardman," he begins, followed by "And I'm Helen Cooper, better known as Marilyn Eastman." Side Two's closing is left to Hardman to intone, "The hot kiss of the bonfire caresses the bodies of good and evil alike, and the saga of *Night of the Living Dead* comes to an end. Ashes to ashes, dust to dust."

The tape was listened to by few, of course, and you'll probably never find it. Those longing for a Hardman–Eastman coda have a couple to choose from. In 2004, Thomas Brown wrote, directed, shot, and edited a half-hour anti-bullying educational short on S-VHS called *Empty Shadows*, in which the duo star as an old married couple amazingly named Harry and Helen, thereby providing us with a placid alternate fate for the Coopers. Unfortunately, this, too, is a curio you'll never track down.

That's why I'm happy to offer you another option. Certain Blu-ray editions of *The Mothman Prophecies* (2002) feature a two-minute, twenty-second deleted scene shot at the Allegheny County Airport south of Pittsburgh. This scene, which has no sound, features Richard Gere gazing with satisfaction at all the people (presumably saved from the Mothman bridge disaster?). The crowd includes none other than Hardman and Eastman, ages seventy-three and sixty-seven, the former tenderly helping the latter down some stairs. It's haunting and heartbreaking, and represents the best possible timeline, one in which Harry and Helen Cooper happily grew old together. I suppose it's fitting the scene was cut. Their relationship had always been kept to the shadows.

00:51:32

DON'T BE AFRAID OF ME

TOM'S MUFFLED VOICE CALLS FROM UPSTAIRS WITH a trump card: Ben has found a television. Helen races to Harry's side, grabbing his arm, and her face flashes a smile—the only genuine smile she'll give in the film—and we glimpse the Helen of yesteryear, the young woman who used to delight in dragging her grumpy hubby to movies or dances or carnivals. "Let's go up," she says in breathless excitement, and Harry is struck silent, a rare thing, perhaps recalling the animated voice of the woman he once loved.

Eastman calls up, "Tom?" and then there's a jump cut—the "famous jump cut" to *Night* obsessives. At 51:43, Eastman is facing the stairs, giving us the back of her bouffant. At 51:44, Eastman is suddenly in profile as she negotiates with Tom. (A scrawl in Romero's shooting script notes the need to record "Kieth"—always misspelled—giving such sophisticated replies as "Yeah!" and "OK, yeah!"). Can Tom send Judy down to watch Karen so Helen and Harry can come up?

As I'm sure you're sick of hearing, editing was Romero's superpower. No way he would have artlessly hacked these moments together, especially given the abundance of available cutaways—Tom by the basement door, Karen on the makeshift table, et cetera.

And he didn't. This is one of two cuts Romero didn't make. Once the Walter Reade Organization was on board with *Night,* they wanted their nifty new acquisition to push the envelope as far as possible, while also keeping the pace snappy. At their insistence, Russ Streiner, in New York with them, snipped about six minutes of Harry-Helen bickering by simply eyeballing the film strip as best as he could. I can't say it was the wrong call, though I miss this line of Harry's dialogue from the script: "All right . . . this is your decision . . . we'll go up . . . but don't blame me if we all get killed." The notion of Harry and Helen continuing to argue as undead zombies is perfection, and predicts the final shot of Romero's final film, *Survival of the Dead,* in which two zombies fire empty pistols at one another, presumably for eternity.

I'm getting ahead of myself here, but the other Walter Reade edit was a single shot of zombies in a field. Romero mourned this loss, recalling it as "the best photographic image in the film." In 2015, as Criterion was preparing their definitive edition, the *Night* faithful lost their shit when Romero said (or was at least *quoted* as saying) that all the material cut by Walter Reade had been rediscovered on an old work print. It was a false alarm. (But keep looking, folks. The improbable recent rediscoveries of both *The Amusement Park* and the three-hour black-and-white cut of *Martin* tells us anything is possible.)

Criterion did find a low-res 16mm workprint with the title card *Night of Anubis.* While it doesn't have the missing cellar dialogue, it does have Romero's ballyhooed lost zombie shot, which includes at least fifteen zombies (some of which may have been the apocryphal mannequins with halved ping-pong balls for eyes, some of which were stolen off the set by meddling teens). Romero's memory, though, is rose-tinted. The shot is too distant from the zombies to make an impression, and is oddly bordered, as if shot through a keyhole.

Back to Tom, who pressures girlfriend Judy to comply with Helen Cooper's request. Judy's first words in the film are a whispered "Do I have to?" She does, apparently, have to, in order to keep the two teams tenuously united. Harry unbolts the door and Judy steps in—the two have a nervy little moment on the landing—before Judy heads downstairs, right in front of a huge array of transformer boxes, which surely tipped off to any electricians in the audience that this was actually the cellar of a five-story office building.

Judy glides to where Helen holds her sick daughter's hand. It's our first all-female interaction. "I'll take good care of her, Helen," Judy says, and Helen's reply stabs the corpse of her marriage: "She's all I have." She doesn't have to get any more explicit. Judy's deference to Tom shows she is trundling into the same cage as Helen. There is a resignation to Judy that suggests she sees her fate coming but knows no way of dodging it.

So Harry returns to the dining room only five minutes after saying he'd never do it. His squeezing fists pestle his humiliation into more anger. Helen emerges next and looks at ol' Barb, sprawled across the sofa to examine the doily on the armrest. Of all of Barbra's shenanigans, this is my favorite. She looks dreamy, and why not? The doily's pattern is an emblem of the decorum she left behind the second she got into Johnny's LeMans, same as the ring on the finger she trails along the lace.

I always found the lace an unexpectedly fancy flourish for the farmhouse, but closer inspection—Barb's level of inspection—reveals the doily as being a mass-market product from the 1940s or '50s that had its pattern machine-burned into cotton. This particular pattern looks like flowers as interpreted by an 8-bit Atari, so boxy they become abstract. These doilies are as disposable as napkins, which leads me to think Barb's life back in Pittsburgh is similarly disposable, a mass-produced matrimony with no human touch behind it.

Tom tells Helen that Barbra's brother was killed, then leaves to answer Ben's call for help with the TV. Here, on page 68 of the script, the name "Truckdriver" finally switches over to "Ben." Had Duane Jones been cast at this point? Had the writers suddenly named him? No idea.

Romero then cuts to the most perfect composition in the film. It's a triptych with Harry directly in front of the camera, the wide lens elongating his nose and making his head too large for his body—an exaggeration of an already exaggerated character. The kitchen's two walls slant toward a corner behind him, accentuating his centrality. Over his right shoulder, Barb and her doily. Over his left shoulder, Helen clutching her lapels. Both women are out of focus, obscured in the after-burn of Harry's runaway vehicle. When Harry darts from the frame like the Lizard, the lens rack-focuses to the women, alone in a room that is suddenly, shockingly empty. Nothing awry. A sofa, a piano, a couple chairs. The men have vamoosed and with them their big ideas and pugilistic inclinations.

Here we are again: women only. But having two X chromosomes doesn't mean a woman is used to speaking freely to another woman. Helen takes one step toward the sofa before giving an impotent hand gesture that conveys befuddlement over how to handle the interaction. Instead she takes a seat in a chair, cracks her knuckles, and—importantly—plays with her wedding ring. Barb keeps doing important doily research. Helen sighs and strikes a King Edward match to light a Herbert Tareyton cigarette.

At the fiery hiss, Barbra snaps her head around. Her look is that of a startled animal, both surprised to see the person there and angry that her reverie has been broken. (I have this close-up of Barb on a custom-made coaster, a gift from someone who knows me all too well.) Romero lets the Barb-Helen contemplation stretch out for forty-four seconds, silent apart from the creaks of Helen's chair. It's a well-needed counterpoint to all the talking.

"Don't be afraid of me," Helen says sweetly before contradicting herself by association. "I'm Helen Cooper. Harry's wife."

Barbra looks plenty afraid, though, and Helen glances at her match flame before flapping it out. An interesting moment: Helen's interpretation is that Barbra is afraid of fire. Certainly possible, as Barb was around when Ben torched an easy chair.

Her fear, I deduce, is that Helen might pull a Ben and set her on fire too. Barbra and Helen's helpless/helpful dynamic bizarrely echoes O'Dea's first screen appearance, a fourteen-minute 1954 industrial short about sloppiness called *Habit Patterns*, in which she plays a blond Goofus named Barbara opposite a dark-haired Gallant named Helen. I shit you not.

When Harry stomps back into the room, Romero cuts to an angle that reminds us how shattered the house is. Tabletops nailed over windows, scrap wood across the floor: the men carry destruction wherever they go. Harry snatches the cigs from Helen, bulldozing whatever connection the women were building toward. To Helen's explanation that Barbra's brother was killed, Harry nods bitterly, as if to say, of course. That's what happens to women who venture out without husbands. It's another stellar composition, Helen stewing in the foreground while Harry sharks the waters behind her, back on his old saw about the shoddiness of Ben's stockades and the potential millions of zombies beyond them.

At last, Ben and Tom shuffle in carrying a television between them. It's been too long (five minutes, fifty-four seconds) since we have seen Ben. He's the steel pole that turns our flabby tarp into a sharp-angled tent. Each time I witness his return, I'm optimistic anew. Maybe we can survive the mess this night has become. Not only inside the farmhouse, but inside us too.

00:54:58 IT HAS BEEN ESTABLISHED

Where the farmhouse's Zenith 7S363 is handsome, the TV is downright goofy with a brittle Bakelite chassis, retro space-age design, and rabbit ears that look like Elroy Jetson's hat. I'm pretty sure it's a 1952 Motorola Model 17T5E. A yellowed manual I dug up boasts how the 17T5E contains fifteen tubes and a tuning range of "Channels 2 through 13," and has a "Bilt-in-Tenna," which is the most 1950s thing I have ever read. Though it's but

18 inches high, 18.5 inches wide, and 20 inches deep (televisions used to be *deep*), one online auction seller warns the 17T5E is "very heavy," hence the requirement for *Night*'s two strongest men to lug it.

The introduction of a TV makes *Night*'s ad hoc dysfunctional American family complete. After another quick spate of arguing—Harry demanding that Barbra pay attention, Ben reasserting his dominance ("If you stay up here, you take orders from *me*!"), and Tom paving over the argument by finding a live broadcast—the characters jostle for position around the tube. It's remarkable how much it resembles a family hunkering down to watch *The Andy Griffith Show.* Everyday routines flipped upside down is what *Night* does best.

My childhood viewings of *Night* came amid just this sort of tableau: Mom watching from the sofa, a sister or two dorking around on the furniture, Dad doing something else at the periphery, me generating static with corduroyed knees, inches from the screen so I didn't miss a beat. Nearness to the tube helped me decipher whichever grainy, scratched, copyright-free version of *Night* the station decided to play.

A number of my early viewings were of colorized versions, a process devised by Hal Roach Studios that used an "electronic palette" to add color to black-and-white films to cater to (per their original press release) "generations of audiences that are oriented to color." The first high-profile film to undergo this plastic surgery was *It's a Wonderful Life* in 1985 (my diary dutifully notes my mom recorded it off TV on Thanksgiving Day 1989). *Night*'s first colorized version had its TV debut on October 31, 1986; I remember the hype from the *TV Guide* I studied religiously. "They Scream Louder in Color!" promised the ads.

Some sources report it was authorized by Image Ten and Romero. But we need to contend with a chilly September 18, 1988, letter from Romero to Jack Russo, in which Romero comes in hot: "Dear Jack, This is to assure you that I have made no plans whatsoever with Hal Roach, with LBS, or with any other party, to help in the sale or promotion of the colorized version of NIGHT OF THE LIVING DEAD . . . Of course I would support a colorized version that was authorized by Image Ten, but I will in no way support or endorse the current activity which I consider to be piracy."

Colorization was a weird-ass effect (colors were washed out, zombie skin was green), but not without charm. At least three such versions have been produced. The latest (and, I guess, greatest) is the 2004 version put out by Legend Films in 2004 (and converted to 3D in 2010), which comes with RiffTrax commentary from *Mystery Science Theater 3000* star Mike Nelson. (It strikes me that RiffTrax and *MST3K* both evolved from Mad Libs. A few years back, my pal Tara gifted me a used copy of 1993's horror-themed *Night of the Living Mad Libs*. Several pages already filled out by kids gave me LOLs: "It is believed that psychics can predict such things as the name of the ass you are going to marry or what your mom is peeing for dinner.") Colorization also brings unnoticed details to the fore, like flowers on a cemetery tree. The downside? The movie is as pastel as a basket of Easter eggs. Nothing drains tension faster. (Probably more successful was a St. Patrick's Day version a Chicago station once aired that tinted the whole dang movie green.)

Regardless of which versions of which films I watched, it was a delicate dance. The primary MO of my adolescent years was watching verboten movies on a TV situated in a living room bustling with spoilsports, most notably a dad who would quash anything he deemed too mature. My diary records me fuming over canceled viewings of *Creepshow 2* and *The Shining*, but the over-policing reached its absurd zenith when, on July 18, 1988—a day of infamy—he made me eject *Adventures in Babysitting* during the opening credits, mistaking it for *Porky's*-era sexcapades.

I combatted this conservatism with a fine-tuned repertoire of sleight-of-hand tactics; my mastery of the VCR remote included being able to switch to network TV in a blink. It required exhausting vigilance, but these stop-and-starts were how I got through stuff like *From Beyond* and *Hellraiser*. Half my fear was the film itself; the other half was getting through it unspotted.

One helpful ruse I concocted was convincing my parents that "Unrated" films were a level more innocent than G-rated films, so squeaky clean they didn't even require a rating! That's how I got my hands on *Demons*, *Re-Animator*, and *Bloodsucking Freaks*. (Honestly, no one should be allowed to see *Bloodsucking Freaks*, but that's a different book.)

Night of the Living Dead never required such chicanery. It had the huge advantage of being black-and-white. Anything black-and-white was presumed toothless. I took subversive delight in how wrong that was. Once I stumbled upon this invulnerability cloak, I prioritized black-and-white films when the Movie Police were around. *Freaks*, *Psycho*, *Eraserhead*—those were the days, right?

Only *Night* offered the experience of watching a TV on which characters watched *another* TV. It mixed me up. Do two levels of fiction cancel themselves out and become fact? That's how it felt: Nothing in *Night* has more verisimilitude than the TV news segments. If aired in isolation in 1967, they would have had an impact on par with Orson Welles's *War of the Worlds* radiocast. In fact, early broadcasts of *Night* had to run disclaimers assuring viewers dead folks weren't really coming to get them.

At the time of filming, CBS's Walter Cronkite was "the most trusted man in America." Only four years had passed since Cronkite imprinted himself onto the national heart by relaying JFK's death with brave professionalism. Seven months before *Night* premiered, just after the Tet Offensive, Cronkite trash-canned what remained of America's support for the Vietnam War by throwing in the towel on-air. It's easy to feel nostalgic for an era in which we broadly trusted fact-givers.

Local newspeople surely fantasized about breaking news of equal weight. Among their numbers was Chuck Craig, whose voice we heard earlier coming from the radio. It's Craig's narrow, bespectacled face we see now on the farmhouse TV. (Even in colorized versions, this footage is left black-and-white.) It looks like Craig's in a bustling newsroom, but it's actually the A-Deck master control room of Hardman Associates. It looks better than live TV did in 1967, of course, because it was shot on 16mm film and matted onto the Motorola's exterior. To further sell it, the first shot of Craig is matted into what's actually a still photo of a hunkered Ben.

In his steady, unruffled clip, Craig repeats what we know: "Medical examinations of some of the victims bore out the fact that they had been partially devoured." It's the third time we have heard the phrase *partially devoured*—it's beginning to feel important. Low-angle shots of Harry and Helen, then Ben and Tom, swap the set-dressed walls behind them with the empty ceiling above them, symbolically pulling out the rug. This is no longer the world we thought we lived in. Creature comforts no longer mean shit.

Craig is handed a piece of paper with the confirmation: "It has been established that persons who have recently died have been returning to life and committing acts of murder." I have a hunch Romero forgot to shoot his characters reacting to this. The next shots find them still staring blankly, which somehow is even better. I think back on how I watched the World Trade Center fall. I wasn't screaming. I was quiet and still—a defense mechanism aided by the psychological separation of a TV.

The plot of the final half hour of *Night* is sparked by Craig's next statement: Civil defense organizations have scrambled all over the Pittsburgh area to form rescue stations equipped with food, shelter, and medical help. They are staffed by National Guardsmen, and everyone watching better get to the nearest one. So begins a series of supers listing rescue locations—what today would appear in one of the omnipresent scrolls that launched after 9/11 and have yet to quit. (These supers, too, were originally blacked out for local screenings to prevent Pittsburgh-area panic.)

It's help. It's hope. Ben is jazzed. But Craig's not done blowing minds. He reports on a meeting of the president, cabinet, FBI, joint chiefs of staff, CIA, and space experts, which compels him to editorialize that this whole thing might be connected to an explorer satellite that orbited Venus but was destroyed by NASA because it carried mysterious radiation. "Could that radiation," Craig asks, "be somehow responsible for the wholesale murders we're now suffering?"

00:58:29 EVERYTHING IS BEING DONE THAT CAN BE DONE

You think? This ain't our first rodeo. You don't mention a detail as bonkers as the Venus probe if it's not germane. But Romero and Russo were adamant the Venus probe was one of several explanations they worked into dialogue. They insist it's happenstance the other explanations got cut, leaving only the Venus probe for future nerds to obsess upon. (Hi, Mom.)

I don't buy it. Yes, the lack of Venus material in the script opens the door to on-set improvisation. But the oft-mentioned Venus probe (an idea Bill Hinzman believes he hatched) must have been inspired by the Mariner 5 Venus Probe that launched the same month *Night* began filming. (Creepily, it remains in heliocentric orbit, fifty-nine years after launch.) On the *MonsterVision* episode, Marilyn Eastman is insistent about the zombie origins: "The Venus Probe. It's very clear." It's only for the Venus scenario that the crew trucked their butts to Washington, D.C., to film the complex and risky sequence that comes next.

Craig segues to a film clip from "newsman Don Quinn," played by Romero in a turtleneck and blazer, tall as hell and jabbing a microphone into the faces of three walking gentlemen, two in suits, one in military garb. There are two other reporters with mics: One is Regis Survinski, Vince's brother, a *Night* investor who doubled as a zombie and handled the film's gunshots and explosions, and the other is Jack Givens, an audio engineer at Hardman Associates who also appears as a zombie. Quinn establishes that the trio of stiff shirts have just left a meeting on the Venus probe. The professor insists there is a connection. The general disputes this. The scientist gets the best line, the kind of pap officials dispense when there's nothing to say: "Everything is being done that can be done."

This verité snippet is executed in a single eighty-second take that moves from a sidewalk in front of the Library of Congress's Thomas Jefferson Building, across a First Street SE crosswalk, to a car parked illegally right outside the U.S. Capitol. While I dislike the snarky zom-com *Zombieland* (2009), I appreciate that its first shot is framed from this exact spot by the Capitol.

Everything about the shot astonishes. The backward-walking 16mm cinematography is a high-wire act, shot on the Latent Image's 16mm Eclair (a lightweight camera that helped launch the era's cinema verité movement) by Russ Streiner (while brother Gary appears as Don Quinn's sound guy, though in reality he's simply recording *Night*'s sound). The Latent Image loved their Eclair (for a while, it was the only major piece of gear they owned, along with a Nagra recorder). In the 1979 film *Effects*—a grimy but affecting piece of regional filmmaking involving scads of Romero associates—lead actor Joe Pilato (best known to Romeroites as Captain Rhodes in *Day of the Dead*) sports a bright red *Eclair* shirt.

The acting in the D.C. sequence is unbelievably believable. The professor is played by yet another Ricci, Mark, who worked in statistical analysis at Bettis Lab. The general is A. C. MacDonald, a Pittsburgh ad man so natural in the role that Romero cast him as a different general five years later in *The Crazies*. The scientist is Samuel R. Solito, who one could argue had more pro acting roles than anyone in *Night*, peaking with a character on Norman Lear's syndicated 1976–1977 soap opera spoof *Mary Hartman, Mary Hartman*. Together, they generate another *Night* miracle. They are perfection. (A loose page in Romero's archives collating names for the end credits expends a lot of ink confirming the spelling of Solito's name, which makes the misspelling of "Barbra" and "Heinzman" all the more egregious.)

Attempting this shot today would land your ass in the clink. The military flags Marilyn Eastman made for the hood of Karl Hardman's Lincoln Continental (from whence Hardman sourced Ben's tire iron), combined with the car's saluting driver (Russo in his army duds), were convincing enough to let them slide by without permits. Eastman recalled a capitol guard finally ordering them to move the car, saying, "If we let one general park here, they'll all want to park here." (The Latent Image returned to D.C. three years later to shoot *Lenore*, which was not, in fact, a Poe adaptation, but a paid campaign film for senatorial candidate Lenore Romney, mother of Mitt. Not much there worth discussing, except that it gave Romero a chance to interview both Bob Hope and Gerald Ford.)

In sum, so much work went into firming up the Venus probe narrative that it must be taken seriously. To get *really* into the weeds (why stop now?), one of the many characters Karl Hardman voiced on the radio show *Cordic and Co.* was Omicron, a tiny man from—you guessed it—Venus. It doesn't seem preposterous that Hardman, a confirmed rascal, might support an Easter egg like that. (Bizarre sidenote: Hughes Aircraft, where Judith O'Dea ended up working, had an aerospace division that built things just like the Venus Probe.)

Though Romero's subsequent zombie films never mentioned outer space, that wasn't the case for the 1979 Japanese release of *Dawn of the Dead*. Recently surfaced camcorder footage shot inside a Japanese theater reveals a surprise opening title card: "In 19XX, an exploding planet in a far-off galaxy beamed strange rays across space to earth. It caused the transformation of the dead one after another into resurrected zombies seeking the flesh of the living." Not quite the Venus Probe, but similar vibe.

In the end, of course, it matters not. Romero used *Dawn* to jettison all the zombie stuff that hadn't sat well with him over the intervening decade, including their genesis. *Dawn*, by the way, begins inside a TV studio where employees squabble over rescue stations, which included some of the same towns listed in *Night*. Half the stations, we learn in *Dawn*, are overrun, which means the supers are sending survivors to their deaths. Who plays the switchboard operator rolling the supers anyway? George Fucking Romero, that's who. The intimation is devastating: Muckraking young truth-teller Don Quinn has grown up to become part of the crooked, lying establishment.

The whole TV interlude, largely scripted by Craig based on filmmaker notes, gives *Night* the scope of something larger than the budget could aim for. We're forced to view a collapsing world through a crack, which is often scarier than staring at it straight on. Genre filmmakers have used this technique ever since and I'm a sucker for it: *Ghostwatch, The McPherson Tape, Pontypool, Signs, The Mist, Monsters, 10 Cloverfield Lane, A Quiet Place, The Head Hunter, We Need to Do Something.*

In total, twenty cities appear on the TV supers throughout *Night of the Living Dead*. Nineteen are real. For the record, and so that no one has to repeat my work: Youngstown, Sharon, Mercer, Butler, Ford City, Indiana, Blairsville, Latrobe, Greensburg, Beaver Falls, Foxburg, East Brady, Harrisville, Pittsburgh, McKeesport, New Castle, Clairton, Canonsburg, and Connellsville. (After I transcribed this, I found Russ Streiner's handwritten list of these supers in Romero's archive, which includes a few not listed in the film: Uniontown, Masontown, Bentleyville, Aliquippa, and Evans City.)

Plus one more, the only fabricated town on the whole list: Willard.

00:59:54 DUBIOUS COMFORTS

I can't say why the filmmakers chose to invent Willard, a town the characters will never reach. I do, however, have a theory on where the name came from. Costar Judy Ridley lived at 534

Willard Street in Crafton, Pennsylvania. She was a Latent Image employee and a pretty girl. No doubt Romero knew her coordinates.

The offhand detail of Willard has ended up in endless *Night* homages. In college, circa 1997, my honors thesis was a screenplay called *He Was a Hunter,* a sort of art-film quasi-sequel to *Night* (before it was cool!) that took place in Willard. (Some of the ideas got blended into *The Living Dead.*) As zombie fever enveloped the 2000s, I kept seeing Willard, Pennsylvania, pop up, most importantly in the works of John Russo, including his *Night of the Living Dead* comic and the *Night of the Living Dead: 30th Anniversary Edition.*

After Helen seizes on the idea of getting Karen to a rescue center for help, Ben notices the Willard super and recalls seeing it on a road sign. Tom says, "It's only about seventeen miles from here." (The "about" is funny, as seventeen is pretty specific. Indeed, a Latent Image press binder lists the setting of the film as "17 miles outside Willard, Pennsylvania.") They converse in the film's ugliest composition. It looks as if the camera has been knocked six inches to the right, upsetting every principle of properly weighted framing. Both Ben and Tom are too far to the left, and half of Ben's head is cut off. Barbra is squished way over by Ben.

By accident, the focus of the shot becomes a framed print of a woodsy mountain scene. It's a painting (possibly a paint-by-numbers kit) done by Vince Survinski's sister Margie—the same woman whose Roundelay got filched.

The farmhouse, actually, is rife with framed art prints. Before Ben raided the shoe closet, he sat beneath a 1940 painting by Louis Claude called *Saut au brook,* depicting a steeplechase. At least three prints are by Maurice Utrillo (1883–1955). The Frenchman must have been a popular choice at the time; one eagle-eyed *Night* fan noticed one of *Night*'s prints, *La rue du Mont Cenis,* also on the wall of the Ricardo apartment in *I Love Lucy.* On the very week I'm writing this, the framed print of Utrillo's

Rural France used in *Night* has been posted to Propstore Auction with a starting bid of $1,500 and an estimated final price of $3,000 to $6,000. All the farmhouse prints hit me with the poignancy of the Air Steps—the longing for anything beyond this hopeless home.

Tom woodenly explains that he and Judy are from the area and had been en route to go swimming when they heard about the crisis on Judy's handheld radio, whereupon they found the Seven Pines farmhouse and the dead woman on the stairs. It's not a well-thought-out backstory. No vehicles are mentioned, so Tom and Judy must have been headed to the swimming hole (in April?) on foot. But from where? They must live nearby. But if they live nearby, why wouldn't they just go home? And why wouldn't there be a vehicle at home? Rural Pennsylvania is car country.

Professional naysayer Harry insists there's no way to get to a shelter: "We've got a sick child, two women, one woman out of her head, three men, and the place is surrounded with these things." It's an entertaining if misogynistic synopsis of the state of affairs. He's not entirely wrong. Think about how hard it is to walk to a *restaurant* with seven people.

Back to the TV. Chuck Craig says something that ends with "for NASA," which suggests the slick-haired, horned-rim-glasses-wearing, church-deacon-looking fellow to Craig's right works for the space agency, which is all kinds of confusing. The Pittsburgh-area supers assure us Craig is a local broadcaster, so how the heck did he land an in-person NASA interview at 11:42 p.m.? (The four time-zone clocks behind Craig give us the exact time. Few props from *Night* still exist, but collector Jack Geller owns one of these metallic Sessions clocks, signed by cast and crew.)

Ah, who cares? The interview that follows is one of the best parts of the film. The guest, identified only as "Dr. Grimes," is played by the dryly hilarious Frank Doak, who worked as VP in charge of sales and marketing for Hardman Associates. It's been speculated that Rick Grimes from *The Walking Dead* was named for the good doctor, though I can't think of two characters more opposite. Doak was fifty-two at the time of filming, but as we all know, fifty-two in 1967 years comes off like seventy-two today. Dr. Grimes is the kind of guy who drinks his coffee black, wears sock suspenders, watched a stag film or two in his day, and speaks like a mortician—resolutely calm no matter what atrocities pass his lips.

Grimes, who semi-improvised like Craig, kicks off by saying people who have been injured by the undead need to seek medical help; Ben reacts by requesting a Helen-for-Judy swap, so worried mother can reunite with chomped kid. Grimes then spins an anecdote about a morgue cadaver that had all four limbs amputated: "Sometime early this morning, it opened its eyes and began to move its trunk." Sheesh, that's *dark*, yet Grimes sounds like he's explaining how to change a tire.

Downstairs, Helen taps Judy for caretaker duty. We get our first close-up on Karen, who conveniently wakes up to utter her only line: "I hurt." It always struck me as odd syntax for a kid, and in *Autopsy of the Dead*, Kyra Schon concurs that, even at age nine, she balked: "'*I* hurt?' What? Why not, like, '*It* hurts?'" (RiffTrax's Mike Nelson doesn't let it slide either: "Kid thought she was in a Tarzan film for a minute: 'Me hurt.'") Still, two-word proclamations have a particular power. I've thought so since doing a felting project in Sunday School and choosing the shortest Bible verse I could find: *Jesus wept.* Creepy then, creepy now.

The pages Eastman neatly typed up for the cellar scenes (black ink for dialogue, red for screen direction) are not housed in Romero's shooting script yet are pristinely preserved in his archive. The pages place one more word, a poignant one, into Karen's mouth: "Daddy."

Back to Dr. Good Times telling Chuck Craig, with zero perturbation, that all dead bodies need to be carried to the street and burned. Craig doesn't care for that, but Grimes doesn't have time for his snowflake bullshit: "The bereaved will have to forgo the dubious comforts that a funeral service will give." Calling a Christian funeral "dubious" is radical stuff for 1968 and this assault on Main Street values probably shocked viewers as much as anything. (So far, anyway.)

It might seem strange this bitter pill is doled out by a man representing NASA, the most beloved American institution of the time (Neil Armstrong's One Giant Leap was only two years off). But six months before *Night* started filming, NASA had suffered its worst disaster, the January 27, 1967, launch pad incinerations of astronauts Roger Chaffee, Gus Grissom, and Ed White. Human lives were the accepted price of space-race progress, and now, after the Venus probe, that price has risen considerably.

That *all* comforts are dubious is the overriding message of *Night*. The overriding message of the sixties too. It's really the same lesson we learned growing up, year by bewildering year. Mommy can't make everything better. Not all neighbors can be trusted. Your teachers don't always know what they are talking about. Companies are lying about their products. The government isn't looking out for you.

"They're just dead flesh," Grimes concludes. The dead flesh in question: the relationships we wanted, the dreams we were promised. Both dot the land like carrion. We chased them and will die chasing them, and in our last hours we will wonder why we bothered.

01:02:39

A WIND PASSING THROUGH

BEN RESUMES HIS SELF-APPOINTED BOSS ROLE BY doling out duties. Judy: Find bedsheets and tear them into strips. Tom: Scrounge up some canning jars. The aim is to create Molotov cocktails someone can hurl at zombies from the upstairs window while someone else gets the truck to the gas pump. I wouldn't say Harry is swept away by the youngsters' can-do attitude, but he begrudgingly mentions a key ring he saw in the cellar.

Harry's logical concern is that a door will have to be opened. Ben is characteristically matter-of-fact: "Yeah, that's right. It better be this door." He indicates the front door, closest to the truck. Romero emphasizes how efficiently things get done when bickering subsides: a mere twenty seconds after going to the cellar, Tom emerges with jars, kerosene, and the holy grail of the pump key. All dialogue in this scene and the next is sourced directly from Romero's shooting script, neatly penciled onto the backs of pages 74–75. It's the first and only draft.

Ben's next moment trips me up. With all the tools he needs in place, he (the purported truck driver!) quails a bit. "I'm not really used to the truck," he says. "I found it abandoned." Gumptious Tom responds as Ben hopes he might, enthusing that he "can handle the truck, no sweat." It's not like the truck is a refrigerated eighteen-wheeler or jerry-rigged dune buggy. Ben, you might recall, mowed down a flock of zombies outside Beekman's with the truck before driving it here without trouble. I interpret this as it begs to be interpreted: Ben is scared, doesn't want to go out there alone, and is too proud to ask for help.

"You're it, then," Ben tells Tom, with the finality of a death sentence.

Ben describes what will happen, which should be superfluous seeing how we are about to watch it happen. (It goes without saying the women get no input.) But Romero focuses on Harry as Ben goes through his instructions, a canny choice. We see in Hardman's twitchy face every nuance of his evolving reaction. Anxiety and fear mix with shame for having stood in Ben's way, then pride for being enlisted as the scheme's fireballer. An entire struggle between courage and cowardice inside a thirteen-second microcosm.

What we expect to see next is action: Harry building the cocktails as Ben and Tom unboard the door. Instead, Romero cuts to a loving close-up of Judy to the strains of a maudlin Loose-Seely violin ditty called "Serene Heart (TC-306)." She's cutting up bedsheets with scissors. Actually, the scissors are just sort of pressed ruminatively to her chin as Tom slides into the adjacent chair with a jar of kerosene. The boar head over his shoulder informs us we're in the den.

"You've always got a smile for me," he says.

If this sounds like a tonal shift, affirmative. The scene doesn't exist in the screenplay, appearing only as a four-page handwritten addendum at the back of Romero's personal script. Feeling the need to boost audience investment in the young couple before, well, stuff happens, Romero whipped up the scene on two hours of sleep to capitalize on a spurt of Keith Wayne availability.

The result is generally pooh-poohed as the film's weakest scene. Russo has called it "sappy." Suffice it to say, my interest in sap is low, yet I find this scene not only effective, but subversive. First, Tom undercuts his compliment, asking Judy, "How can you smile at a time like this?" Tom has been a model male so far, but this statement shows that he, too, can be cruel to a woman doing everything she can to advance the menfolk's plot. When Judy asks about the phone, Tom impatiently tells her it's dead.

Unlike the teen relationships displayed in most genre movies of the day, Tom's umbrage is sharply realistic. When the scene bends more lovey-dovey, it feels indicative of the immature, stop-and-start paroxysms of young love, that floundering for grown-up cues. Judy asks if Tom thinks they're doing the right thing by leaving Seven Pines. He replies, "Well, the television said that's the right thing to do." It's a fine enough excuse for the Cronkite age, but less so when future Toms migrate to Facebook, Reddit, and 4chan.

High on responsibility, Tom crows, "I know how to handle that truck," and reminds Judy how hard she'd resisted taking refuge in Willard during "the big flood." I like the flood reference; it's the rare bit of dialogue that hints at a character's external life.

Of all people, you don't expect Tom to be the poet, but the way he refers to the zombie uprising is more abstruse than anything else in the film, and I love it. "It's not like a wind passing through," he says. Floods, winds—the natural disasters native to local folk now pale alongside *unnatural* disasters. I'm not saying Romero's predicting climate change. He's noting changes in American life and who gets to live them. While they coo, Tom and Judy are making Molotov cocktails! They might well be members of the Weather Underground preparing to bomb the Pentagon. Unnatural, for sure, but a coherent approach to straighten a contorted world order.

The zombies are part of that straightening. Romero never called his zombies a "plague." To him, it was always an "uprising," a wave of discontents trying to topple the scaffolds of power. It is a classic young person's perspective, one that aligns *Night*'s young couple with the dead, who are also young, if you consider they were only just "reborn."

Sidenote: The filmmakers often carp on this scene being out of sync. Their camera that day didn't have "crystal sync"—something I dealt with when shooting 16mm but never really understood—and instead relied upon a sync cable. Which, of course, was tetchy. They had to resync in the lab with a resolver, which then threw the voice pitches off. A whole lotta woe, yet I *still* can't sense anything wrong.

The weakness of the Tom-Judy scene isn't in its sync or content, which ends with the de rigueur kiss. (The film's only acknowledgment of sexual desire, unless you count the omnisexual carnality of zombies ready to ravage anyone at any time.) The weakness lies in the limitations of its performers. As discussed, Keith Wayne's stage training translated unevenly to the screen. Left to pick up the slack is Judith Ridley, whose acting career radiated reluctance, or at least (by her own admission) under-qualification.

As far as I can tell, Ridley's first media appearance was in the background of the Latent Image's Calgon commercial. Fresh from the Art Institute of Pittsburgh (she was a talented caricaturist, an abstract painter, and an amateur blues harpist), Ridley became a receptionist first at Hardman Associates, and then at the Latent Image. Instead of one of them marrying her (as went the 1960s cliché), the Image Ten folk cast her. (Actually, one of them *did* marry her in 1969, Russ Streiner, with whom she opened a small Pittsburgh boutique and had two kids before they divorced.)

Ridley was lovely. There's no debating that. With her big brown eyes, long blonde hair, and show-stopping smile, she exuded hippie energy with an edge of despair; her performance channels the Woodstock-era exhaustion of flower-power girls realizing that even free-love choices lead to a relinquishing of power. The nineteen-year-old Ridley was first eyed for Barbra but didn't have the skills. Russo confirmed that's why the role of Judy was Sharpied wholesale into Romero's shooting script. They all knew the market value of a pretty girl. In fact, Ridley graces *Night*'s very first VHS release, put out in 1978 by MEDA.

Today, it's the most valuable physical release, despite blown-out visuals that make it unwatchable.

To get out of having to hire a makeup person, the gang asked Ridley to take a makeup course at Earl Wheeler Modeling and Finishing School, where her final project was completing a full face of makeup, right down to false eyelashes, on a subject, who ended up being the perennially game Jack Russo.

No other major cast member has more willfully spurned the spotlight. Ridley agreed to attend the 1993 Zombie Jamboree, but pulled out for what Russo's *Jamboree* doc says was a "family commitment," but is now understood to have been a response to a threatening letter from an obsessed fan. That sent Ridley packing: She was the only major cast member to not partake in the 1994 LaserDisc commentary. She did not involve herself with the Living Dead Festival until 2009 (as evidenced in Joe Barbarisi's thirteen-minute *2nd Living Dead Festival 2009*, a charmingly lo-fi documentary shot on Minolta Autopak Super 8 Ektachrome 64T). Even today, the enjoyment Ridley finds in *Night* events is predicated on safety. At the 2023 Living Dead Weekend, she complimented fans as being "not someone who is going to stalk you, or embarrass you, or ask you questions that maybe you don't want to answer. No, they're very respectful."

This is in character. Ridley never seemed to have a passion for acting. (In *The Living Dead Reunion*, she admits she never read the *Night* script, instead relying on Romero's direction.) She makes me think of a guy from high school who was awkward and shy, but physically a giant. The football coach succeeded in getting him onto the gridiron, and I'm sure he worked hard to do what was asked. But it didn't last. His body was what it was, but his heart was somewhere else.

Same deal with Ridley. She was attractive, sweet, often in the vicinity of actors, and ended up drafted. It had to be flattering. Ridley still lived with her parents and would drive a half hour back home each night only to collapse on the porch glider. Set photos reveal a girl who is having a ball. One of the most famous behind-the-scenes photos depicts five of the cast and crew posing amid a gory display. Ridley steals the shot with an expression of humored disgust, while yuckily holding a sloppy jar of chocolate syrup (which reads as nice, thick blood on film).

The most famous image of Ridley comes from the left side of the classic *Night of the Living Dead* poster—and it's only half her. It's Ridley's head, all right, but it's clearly been pasted onto Marilyn Eastman's body (Russo suggests the distributor didn't find Ridley's jeans sexy enough). That means, crazily, of the five living characters featured on the poster, Eastman is four of them. (Bonus: She's one of the zombies pictured too.)

The Latent Image was bullish on Ridley despite her watery portrayal. Convinced they had a starlet, they cast her as the female lead in their second feature, a 1972 romantic drama shot under the title *At Play with the Angels*, released as *The Affair*, and known today as *There's Always Vanilla*. (Tip: Never put the word *Vanilla* in your title.) A very early *Vanilla* document in Romero's archives—a loose page of budget scribbles—lists "Duane" as one of the lead actors. Duane Jones? It had to be, though there's no evidence the gang ever reached out to their disenchanted former star.

An attempt to keep the filmmakers from being pigeonholed, *Vanilla* is the sort of pessimistic, counterculture, Godard-or-Cassavetes-influenced drama that *The Graduate* (1967) had brought into vogue. The film is nearly good, replete with the rapid visual and sonic editing Romero would employ more successfully in *Season of the Witch*, *The Amusement Park*, and *The Crazies*. As the Latent Image's attempt to go mainstream, however, it's an outrageous failure, a far more difficult film to enjoy than *Night*.

It's a story about settling, something Romero and the gang were fighting not to do—so desperately, in fact, that the milieu *Vanilla* skewers is the same commercial industry putting food on the filmmakers' tables. (The Latent Image charged $125 per day for a director.) Ridley's abilities remain limited, but her Sharon Tate–like openness makes her character, Lynn, beguiling and a good counterweight to insufferable guitarist Chris (Ray Laine), who refers to Lynn as "the chick" and mumbles beatnik hooey like "Playing the guitar is fish."

My interest in *Vanilla* grew when I reconsidered it as Romero's take on Keith Wayne. After all, Judy Ridley *was* paired with Wayne on Romero's previous film. I enter into evidence the following. Like Wayne, Chris is a musician; like Wayne, Chris can no longer stand living on the cusp of success; like Wayne, after Chris meets a girl, he starts changing careers, first as a prospective ad man and then as a novelist. Chris ends up as he started—unhappy—which is the most Keith Wayne quality of all.

After *Vanilla,* Ridley hung it up and eventually moved to Arizona. "Russ and I were about to be married and my priorities changed; I was interested in being a wife," she said in a rare interview. Again, it's astonishing how precisely this mirrors the end of *Vanilla,* which skips ahead to a *Lolita/Splendor in the Grass*-type coda. We find Lynn settled into comfortable if wistful domesticity. "Maybe I'm just cut out to be a wife and mother," she sighs.

Ridley became, at different points, a hand model, a librarian, and a food stylist for ads and commercials, just like those depicted in *Vanilla.* Her claim to fame was an ice cream that didn't melt under film lights. A pretty cool thing to be remembered for. As noted earlier, in life you don't get to choose.

01:06:45 FUCK YOU, SIR!

The close-up of Judy's face dissolves to reveal, well, Judy, back on the couch alongside the immobile Barbra. Probably a happenstance edit, but I like it: After a single moment of being central to her boyfriend (and the film), Judy is demoted to the Sofa of No Opinions. Ben and Harry, meanwhile, are fully human, fully mobile. The former hands a box of Molotov cocktails to the latter. Judy tries to get Barbra to come downstairs. No dice. Ben has to revert to his "Hey, kid" tone to tell Barb that, if she goes down, they can leave soon.

"Oh, I'd like to leave, yes," Barb replies, as if being picked up from kindergarten.

Ben leads her by the small of the back to the cellar door.

I'm on record as pro-catatonia. As director John Landis says in *Reflections on the Living Dead*, "Similar to the way Hitchcock killed off Janet Leigh, I think even bolder is to have your lead go catatonic!" But for naysayers, this is where Barbra's rag-doll manner starts cheese-grating their patience, a feeling exemplified by the *Night* episode of Hulu's *13 Nights of Elvira* (2014), in which our curvaceous hostess bounces up on-screen during Barb's sprint away from Zombie #1 to say, "Now, if this were a schlocky movie, she would fall right about now—oh."

Romero himself led the naysayers. If O'Dea had been an actor of different strengths, he might have hewed closer to the script, which has Barbra fully coherent at this point ("I don't know what to think about my brother . . . Maybe we'll find him in Willard"). Romero obliquely addressed Barb's flaw in *Dawn of the Dead* by having heroine Fran tell her male cohorts, "I don't want any of you to treat me differently than you'd treat another guy . . . I'm not gonna be den mother for you guys . . . And I want to know what's going on. And I want something to say about the plans." Stephen, Roger, and Peter squirm at having been called out for treating Fran like the men of *Night* treated Barbra. Sarah, protagonist of *Day of the Dead*, goes even further against her sexually threatening coworkers; she leaves the lecherous Captain Rhodes with the words, "Yes, sir! Fuck you, sir!"

Even these sequel correctives weren't enough for Romero. His final word on Barbra came in 1990 with the first and only official remake of *Night of the Living Dead*. The film was the feature directing debut of the "Sultan of Splatter," special-effects master Tom Savini, whose fame, in part, had come from his work on Romero flicks. What had really impressed Romero (and me) was Savini's direction of three episodes of the Romero-produced anthology TV series *Tales from the Darkside*. Savini's "Inside the Closet" is often considered the best of the series, and I agree it's up there, though I have a special relationship to the episode that debuted two weeks later on December 2, 1984, "A Case of the Stubborns," which had a final shot so horrifying to nine-year-old me that I used to actively fret I might stumble across it while channel surfing. (Six years later, on September 8, 1990, it happened. To quote my diary entry: "Didn't watch it!")

It feels out of character for Romero to participate in a remake, but two things convinced him. The first was a rumor that 21st Century Film Corporation was eyeing a remake, for which Romero and company would make zilch. The second was the grievances of Image Ten, who, twenty-two years on, were still fighting legal battles brought on by the copyright bug and Walter Reade's failure to pony up.

In September 1979, Richard Rubinstein of the Laurel Group posted an ad in trade journals proclaiming, "The Laurel Group, Inc., announces that it is now the exclusive agent for worldwide rights to George A. Romero's horror classic 'Night of the Living Dead.' These Rights were granted to Laurel by Image Ten, Inc., the owner of the film." Romero's archive contains an official United States Copyright Office form filed on October 3, 1979. But even these efforts failed to stanch the piracy. Romero's ongoing trauma over *Night*'s copyright snafu is evidenced all over his Laurel projects, which are slathered in © and TM symbols.

Bringing together the original gang for a remake would bolster their copyright claims, or so went a legal theory best spelled out in a January 20, 1995, letter written by Romero's lawyer, Barry Gutterman. It's worth excerpting:

> Because of the complex and convoluted history of the rights to "Night of the Living Dead" when Twenty-First Century was interested in making a remake of the original movie, in order to satisfy their concerns about the rights, we had everyone associated with the original film convey whatever

> rights they may have had (if they did in fact have any) to George's company Sanibel Films Inc. and then Sanibel conveyed over to Twenty-First Century the right to make one remake and the allied rights pertinent to said remake only.

A draft of the May 3, 1989, Sanibel agreement, found in the Romero archive, details the Purchaser (Sanibel) paying the Seller (Image Ten) $250,000, with the first portion arriving with the remake's preproduction. The gang would finally make some money! The budget of Savini's remake was $4.2 million, which was about $4.2 million more than Image Ten was used to seeing.

The remake debuted on October 19, 1990, to terrible reviews. Roger Ebert (a critic whose chaotic thoughts on horror have given me the fantods my whole life) stamped it with a dreaded one-star review, while the ever-glib Owen Gleiberman gave it a D+ in *Entertainment Weekly*, lazily quipping the decision to make the film "has to rank right up there with New Coke."

Owen can suck an egg, as my mom used to say. I loved *Night of the Living Dead 1990* (as fans refer to it) as a teen and I'm here to tell you that teen me was correct. Viewed thirty years after the garish goings-on of late-eighties horror, *Night 90* is not only good, it borders on *very* good. Savini approaches the affair with admirable sincerity, and Tony Todd as Ben and Patricia Tallman as Barbara (spelled correctly this time) are both fantastic. Bill Moseley as Johnnie (he insisted on the new spelling in deference to OG Johnny) is fine, with the juvenile exception of following up the "They're coming to get you, Barbara" with "They're horny, Barbara." (Todd and Moseley reprised their roles in 2015's *Night of the Living Dead: Darkest Dawn*, a motion-cap feature that has the ugliest, jankiest animation I've seen outside a PS2 game.)

If you'd like to see all the non–Image Ten remakes of *Night*, I wish you luck on your odyssey. A check of only the post-2000 era reveals versions released in 2006, 2007, 2009, 2011, 2012, 2013, 2014, 2015, and 2021. Because I hate myself, I've seen them all.

A few deserve mention. *Night of the Living Dead: Reanimated* is more a gallery of artist responses to the film with 125 different artists (cartoon, Claymation, puppets, you name it) each animating a small slice of the film set to the original soundtrack. It's fascinating, frenetic, and exhausting. But it towers over *Night of the Animated Dead*, a 2021 remake that pairs recognizable voices (like Josh Duhamel and Nancy Travis) with the original film's script, then adds rudimentary animation. It has no reason to exist. It was distributed by Warner Bros., a company with deep pockets, and yet the Bros. give no, and I mean *no*, credit to Image Ten.

The highest-profile unofficial remake is the Sid Haig–headlined *Night of the Living Dead 3D* (2006), which, while I didn't see it in 3D, has a shockingly good first ten minutes, in which Barb and Johnny show up late to their aunt's funeral only to hear thumping from her casket. The text Barb later receives from Johnny—*COMING 4 U BARB*—gave me the chills. Is Johnny alive, coming to save her? Or does zombie Johnny simply recall how his gadget works? Unfortunately, the rest of the film is redundant (save one character who believes they are cursed by watching the Romero film) and commits the ne plus ultra of *Night* trespasses by casting the luckless Joshua Desroches as Ben. In the words of one Letterboxd user, "Recasting Ben with a white dude may be the single most offensive thing that has ever happened." (There's a 2012 sequel, *Night of the Living Dead 3D: Re-Animation*, but I only have so many years left in my life.)

Oddly enough, Haig also appears in *Mimesis: Night of the Living Dead* (2011), less a remake than a meta manipulation of the IP, in which a number of party people with boringly predictable names (Duane, Judith, Karl, et al.) are roofied and wake up in a sort of live-action game, forced to re-create *Night* against other people playing zombies.

Rebirth (2020), originally called *Night of the Living Dead: Rebirth* before director Roger Conners graciously retitled it at Image Ten's request, is a decent redo featuring one inspired alteration: Barbra is swapped for a gay man named Adam (they wear the same coat, though). Conners (who also plays Adam) refuses to "fix" the character, letting Adam be as hysterical and comatose as his female counterpart, which, to me, only emphasizes O'Dea's strong choices. *Rebirth* is also notable for being the only version of *Night* to include full-frontal male zombies, which were honestly overdue.

Just as *Rebirth* may have the best Barbra (in a fashion) since the original, the sober British take *Night of the Living Dead: Resurrection*, features the best Ben since Duane Jones, played by Sule Rimi. While he lasts, anyway: Ben's shock death happens only twenty minutes into the film. (The film is otherwise only notable for its sickening final lines: "Stick her in the rape van. Let's get out of here.")

Finally, I'll mention Joe Barbarisi's *Flowers for the Dead* (2013), which posits the question: What if Barbra (here named Linda) never even made it out of the cemetery? Nearly the entirety of this forty-minute, practically dialogue-free homage follows Linda trying to get back to her car through a zombie-filled graveyard, mostly filmed in New Jersey but with some key shots done at Evans City Cemetery. That's pretty much it—but the vibe is ace. Shot on jittery black-and-white 8mm film (my favorite format) and boasting a bevy of cheap but effective ghouls, this just *feels* right, the same kind of no-budget labor of love that came from Image Ten.

Rare bright spots aside, the main effect of this bushel of remakes is making Savini's effort seem all the nobler. *Night 1990* features the best-looking zombies I've ever seen in an American film, designed after photos of actual corpses. The conceit, while unpleasant, works: Human brains react instinctively to what looks (or better yet, smells) legitimately dead. Death feels *real* in this film and therefore bears no resemblance to all the undead shoot-'em-ups birthed by *Night*.

Stories told by those involved suggest the gang, Romero included, liked Savini's movie and were optimistic about its blockbuster potential. But no production company in history is more luckless than Image Ten. The going theory is that Columbia

Pictures was so pleased by advance surveys regarding the film's name recognition that they pulled back on advertising, thereby dooming it. I believe it. It happened to me too. At age fifteen, I convinced my boss at Fairfield's Co-Ed Theater to program the theater's first—and, to my knowledge, last—midnight movie right around Halloween: *Night 1990*. I went with my friend Jami. We were two of four people who showed.

Cue the bitterness of the Image Ten group. As usual, you can't blame them. Savini has not been shy in calling the production "the worst nightmare of my life," one that, for a time, removed Savini and Romero from speaking terms. (Savini has since admitted part of the trauma was finding out, one week into filming, his wife wanted a divorce, which left his involvement with his daughter in the lurch.) Savini went so far as to release a 2019 book called *Night of the Living Dead '90: The Version You've Never Seen*, populated by annotated storyboards for ambitious sequences he wasn't allowed to shoot. (Savini's version actually *was* finally released by Sony in 2025.) Nonetheless, the film is filled with clever subtleties. One example: The name on the farmhouse reads M. CELESTE, surely a reference to the famous ship that was discovered in 1872, entirely missing its crew.

The film's failure isn't surprising in hindsight. The film was bankrolled by Menahem Golan, known to film geeks as co-owner of the Cannon Group, who filled VHS shelves with quickie action flicks like Charles Bronson's *Death Wish 4: The Crackdown* (1987) and Chuck Norris's *Braddock: Missing in Action III* (1988). Savini's book rails against a "sleazy scumbag of a producer who constantly lied." I could name this person, but what's the point? He went on to an illustrious career while the talented Pittsburgh gang once again got ground beneath the Hollywood heel.

What's important is the remake's screenplay. Because it was written by Romero—not Romero and Russo—it provides an undiluted look into what Romero wanted updated from the original. The biggest change is Barbara. While she begins as shocked and numb as her predecessor, her spine gradually and believably turns to steel, and by the end, she's navigating the new world better than anyone. This time, Ben doesn't slide Air Step shoes on Barb. She finds her *own* pair of boots.

The predominant read of nu-Barb is that she is a "modern" woman, and therefore tougher. But as Romero told Tony Williams in *Quarterly Review of Film and Videos,* his intent was more nuanced: "Well, my idea was that all along she's becoming a guy!" This isn't a positive development in Romero's eyes. Whereas 1968 Barb was neutralized by males, 1990 Barb is contaminated by them.

The two Barbras converge in Mark Kidwell's radioactively unofficial three-issue comic series *Night of the Living Dead: Barbara's Zombie Chronicles* (2004), which catches up with Barb some twelve years after the collapse of Farmhouse Nation. Barb 1968 has, in essence, become Barb 1990, a lean, muscled zombie slayer sporting a six pack, semiautomatic handguns, and suddenly huge boobs. (Same hot-rollered flip, though.) *Chronicles* gets points for being the most batshit *Night* takeoff I've encountered, attributing the undead uprising to a sick alien that crashed its UFO in Roswell, and managing to get Barb all the way to the White House, where she meets self-declared president Charles Manson.

To be fair, Romero wrote something similar into the fifteen-issue *Empire of the Dead* comic series put out by Marvel in 2014–2015 (with art by Alex Maleev, Dalibor Talajic, and Andrea Mutti). The series, which involves a struggle between zombies and vampires, follows Penny Jones, who, in the first issue, tells the tale of her sister, Barbra, who managed to evade her apparent fate at the end of *Night*. For what it's worth, two people close to Romero have told me he hated this comic series. (Marvel's first nod to Romero came back in 1988, with *Spectacular Spider-Man* Issue #148, titled "Night of the Living Ned!")

Back to *Night 1990*. Romero's script includes a line that resonated with fifteen-year-old me. "They're so slow," nu-Barb says of the zombies. "We could just walk right past them." Eventually, she does just that. Romero was emphasizing how simple it should have been to quell the zombies. All we had to do was stay calm and work together. Romero didn't live quite long enough to see America bear out his pessimism during the Covid-19 pandemic, when millions died as people refused to wear simple masks and stay inside their respective farmhouses.

01:07:19 GOOD LUCK

Tom holds out a hammer to Ben as one might offer giant scissors to a ribbon-cutting mayor. Ben takes it, tells Tom "good luck," and the two of them, buddy cops now, start prying lumber off the door. If you pause at 1:07:39, you'll see UPPER RIGHT CORNER markered on a board—instructions for the crew to reset the door for future takes. Though the farmhouse scenes were filmed mostly in order, resets were common enough that poor Vince Survinski had to devote time to straightening nails so they could reuse them.

It's disconcerting to watch Ben and Tom undo the barricades that took so long to put into place. The wasted labor seems to confess that boarding up was a bad idea. The sheer noise of the operation feels foolhardy.

Right before the door is clear, Tom's attention is snagged by Judy—she has resurfaced from the women's prison of the cellar. She gives the tiniest of smiles and he returns an even tinier one. It's the best moment for both Ridley and Wayne, so genuine it's possible the naysayers are right and the previous Tom-Judy scene is gratuitous. The hormonal certainty of their union is right there in this look.

Romero's rapid-fire editing engages like a geared machine. Abruptly we are with Harry upstairs, our first look inside a second-story room. It doesn't look like Survinski had the energy to set-dress it: a bare wall, a draped window, and a table with a lackluster flower vase. Harry opens the window and readies cocktail one. Outside: zombies, milling, growling. At least ten of them, fronted by Roger McGovern (*Great Caesar's ghost!*). First floor: Ben, a fresh table-leg torch wielded, calling for Harry to start tossing bombs, while Tom and Judy trade anxious looks. Upstairs: Harry lights a bottle and chucks it. (Hardman aimed for a particular rock, as the sod was too soft to break glass.)

As upset as I was about the flaming chair, I'm twice as disapproving of the seven-foot ring of fire that whooshes to life beside Ben's truck and two zombies. What were these maniacs thinking? Either zombie could have gone up. The truck could have caught fire. It was the middle of the night in the middle of nowhere.

Harry chucks a second Molotov cocktail, then a third and fourth. Like the first, each lands beside the truck, timed to the brass blurts of Loose-Seely's "Sting 44 (TC-344)." The fourth explosion sets a zombie on fire. *Really* on fire, all up his back. The man who volunteered for this—for three consecutive takes of this—is Jack Russo. If you need a reason to love Russo, here you go. No one, Romero included, believed in *Night* as wholly as Russo. As he writes with understated humility, "When I felt myself getting hot, I'd fall to the ground, and people were ready with blankets to smother the flames."

Harry runs downstairs to tell the men to go, setting forth a flurry of kinetic edits. Ben and Tom rush outside. We haven't seen anyone run since Barbra's initial getaway and it's cathartic. We, too, are breaking free of the claustrophobic house.

Tom rips the shirt off a zombie played by Rudy Ricci (insert joke about his *Night* investment taking the shirt off his back) and gets into the truck just ahead of a zombie played by William Mogush, another guy who'd invested in *Night*. Mogush, an artist and ardent Catholic, would find infamy in 1973 when he participated in the Three Rivers Art Festival with a piece called "America Betrayed"—an upside-down American flag painted with a swastika and featuring photos of aborted babies—a protest against the recent legalization of abortion. A jury later judged him innocent on grounds of political dissent, and he went on to collaborate with Marty Warhola (nephew of Pittsburgher Andy Warhol) on silkscreens they set aflame and bulldozed—a statement on art's commercial disposability.

Ben wards off ghouls with his gun, torch, and steely look. So far, so good, until we cut back inside and Judy squeaks, "I'm going with him!" Harry tries to stop her, but she's a girl in love. She dashes outdoors only to see her beau inside the truck—and with a thunk Harry locks the door behind her. (This is where we get the image of Ridley's head spliced onto Eastman's body on the *Night* movie poster.)

Ben speaks for everyone when he yells at Judy to come on already. She slides into the passenger seat while Ben shoots an advancing zombie. Cast and crew consistently report that Duane Jones's only weakness was his unfamiliarity with stereotypically masculine activities. No good at using hammers, taking apart furniture, that kind of thing, though you'd never know it from the finished film.

Jones was also a dedicated pacifist. He despised guns. The second after any take involving the Winchester (originally owned by the production's George Kosana, the gun sold for $7,000 in a 2007 auction), he wanted someone, anyone, to take it off his hands. Obviously, he had no idea how to shoot it. Lee Hartman, a zombie in this very scene (he worked at the animation studio The Animators, which did *Night*'s credits and had offices in 247 Fort Pitt), happened to be a Navy vet. He handed Jones his .30-30 rifle and had him shoot live ammo at a farmhouse tree so he could understand, and emulate, the recoil. I find this image strangely comforting: a white military man teaching a Black aesthete how to shoot.

It worked. Jones shoots like a pro. It's the first real gunshot effect since the Rev got plugged twenty-four minutes ago, and frankly, it's perfect. The spark from the Winchester's barrel is in perfect sync with the spark that blows open the back of a zombie's coat. These squibs (movie talk for small explosives used to replicate gunshots) were created and set by a two-man team of Korean War vets: Regis Survinski, who did pyrotechnics for the fireworks outfit the Zambelli Brothers, and Tony Pantanello, who worked with the Lisbon Fireworks Company. I'm especially enamored with Pantanello. In every behind-the-scenes shot, he's got a wee stogie mashed between his lips—Christian Stavrakis described it to me as "Pantanello's panatela"—and exudes an aura of being a quiet man (he was a postal carrier for over thirty years) who doesn't fully get what these young fellers are up to but likes to blow shit up. (A 2009 convention photo shows Pantanello signing autographs with the wee stogie still in place.)

In production photos, the duo's squib rigs are terrifying to behold: swaths of leather taped to the back of extras (the filmmakers refused to do head squibs, a sign of sanity) centered with a teeny fused bomb and an ink-filled blood bag. (Anytime *Night* folks mention these "blood bags," it feels like they're avoiding the word "condom.") How these squibs didn't catch fire is another *Night* miracle. It's actually Pantanello, under heavy makeup, playing the zombie closest to the first Molotov cocktail explosion. Makes sense, as he's probably the one who set the flame by dropping a match to the gas-soaked grass.

The squib victim backpedals, but by now we know a torso shot isn't going to do much good. In the background behind Ben, the two people in the truck are clearly not Keith Wayne and Judy Ridley. The man is taller than Wayne and the woman has a short black hairdo instead of Ridley's long blonde locks. Romero gambled we'd be too thrilled by the gunplay to notice, and he was right. You don't catch it till your one-hundred-and-seventy-third watch, trust me.

Two shots later comes a detail I never noticed until Jim Cirronella pointed it out on an episode of *Night Talk*: a zombie visible behind Tom for only a couple frames of film. Pause the movie at exactly 1:09:49 and you'll see the face of Rudy Ricci, whose frown somehow evokes the deformed doctors of *Twilight Zone*'s "Eye of the Beholder." It's arguably the film's creepiest image, hidden like the subliminal Captain Howdy of *The Exorcist*. (In an April 8, 1976, interview with the *Pittsburgh New Sun*, Romero ranked *Night* as "superior" to *The Exorcist*. I agree but, still, it's a cocky stance to take.)

The scene so thoroughly captures the implicit terror of a mob trying to breach your vehicle that it was invoked in a tense scene from the documentary *Ramones: Raw* (2004), in which the punk band's van slowly shoulders through a rabid crowd of Ramoniacs beating at their windows. Director John Cafiero turns the footage black-and-white, adds *Night*'s music, and intercuts shots of Zombie #1 trying to get into Barbra's car.

Tom finally gets the truck into motion. Ben climbs into the bed. (Is he really sure the whole gang couldn't simply drive away now?) Four zombies approach in a spooky low-angle shot (replicated in a Christmas card Adam Hart sent me, each zombie topped with a Santa hat under the words *SILENT NIGHT OF THE LIVING DEAD*). Ben reaches down with his torch to set Zombie #1 on fire. The courageous Hinzman looks none too worried as he bats out the flame. Next we get a shot of Harry, but it's from outdoors through the boarded gap of a window. Romero thereby keeps our eyes, attention, and heart outside, with Ben.

The truck is actually a dupe of the first one, with headlights magically repaired—it's easy to ID the two different trucks by the painted-over versus untouched *CHEVROLET* on the hatch. Tom makes a basic two-point turn (is this what he meant by "I know how to handle that truck"?) and heads off the right side of the frame. Stepping from behind a zombie played by Jeannie Anderson is a male zombie, who grips the truck's bumper and is dragged for a couple seconds.

This is Rudy Ricci again. There's a bit of Mozart/Salieri to the Romero/Ricci relationship. They were friends—but friendly rivals too. In the documentary *Birth of the Living Dead* (2013), Romero cops to envying Ricci for being cooler and more popular with girls. (My favorite part of *Birth*, by the way, is when Romero uses the past-tense verb "bullshat.") According to Russo, Rudy Ricci showed up to the *Night* set exactly once during production (photos suggest it was twice), which Russo chalks up to Ricci's general disdain for horror.

There's something to this. Ricci, the first friend Romero made on his first day of college, probably felt Romero had abandoned their art-film aspirations. The two had cowritten the ambitious *Whine of the Fawn*, and after *Night*, Ricci felt it was his turn to shine. On the DVD bonus feature documentary *Affair of the Heart: The Making of "There's Always Vanilla,"* the Rev says this about Rudy, who, if you recall, was originally slated to play Ben: "George owed Rudy a favor. And Rudy was going to collect."

The first project the gang tried to get going was a Rudy Ricci script called *Beauty Sleeping*, a drama about a loveless marriage that we might today call a "prestige drama." When that failed to attract investors (surprise), the gang pivoted to another Rudy Ricci project, *There's Always Vanilla*, and we know how that turned out. Paul Gagne quotes Ricci as saying of those times, "If I saw George coming down the street, I'd walk the other way."

Ultimately Ricci lowered his standards to cowrite, codirect, and costar (all with Jack Russo) in 1976's *The Booby Hatch* (a.k.a. *The Liberation of Cherry Jankowski*), a distasteful $20,000 screwball sex farce that features no fewer than four slapstick rape scenes. Its only accomplishment is managing to cast, in a bit part, *Mr. Rogers' Neighborhood* star Betty Aberlin, long ago eyed to play Barbra. (Continuing this bizarre preschool pipeline, Romero later cast Molly McCloskey—Miss Molly in *Romper Room*—in *Knightriders* and *Dawn of the Dead*.)

In the 2024 documentary *My Life with the Living Dead: The Man Who Created Flesh-Eating Zombies!* (adapted by Russo from his own autobiography), Russo offers a partial excuse: The new company he and Ricci had just founded with the Streiners was $50,000 in debt.

The January 1975 *Cinefantastique* interview tells us where the heads of this splinter group were in regards to *Night*:

CFQ: George Romero has called his original story for the film an "allegory." Do you agree with him?

RUSSO: I don't agree with him.

HARDMAN: I don't either.

STREINER: No, I don't.

RUSSO: I think the film is an attempt to make money . . . I think George wants to encourage that kind of thinking on the part of some critics. But I'd rather tell them they're full of shit.

It's a minor tragedy that Ricci turned up his nose at *Night* only to wade willingly into *The Booby Hatch*. But let's be real. After *Night*'s runaway success, the gang went all in, and when you go all in and things don't pan out, you get desperate. Triple-X films enjoyed a spate of respectability in the 1970s. "For that brief moment in time, adult cinema was a golden ticket and a lot of young, ambitious filmmakers got in on the action," Joseph Maddrey writes in *The Soul of Wes Craven* (2024), his biography of Romero's peer, who got his start in sex films. Dredged from Romero's own archives is a twenty-two-page treatment by Romero and Bill Hinzman for *Peterstein*, a tasteless X-rated Frankenstein parody in which the patchwork monster is bestowed with a donkey dick (literally) that drives sexual assault victims mad with lust. Mistakes were made all around.

All that said, Ricci was plenty interested in *Night* back when he was in the running to direct it and slated to star. As Romero summarized, "He went from directing, to the lead, to complete disinterest." It's understandable, and rational, for Ricci to have felt bitterness. Ricci's loosening grip on *Night* is perfectly visualized by his loosening grip on the truck's fender. Years of bad blood might have been avoided if Ricci could have realized that everyone on that shoot was hanging on to that fender too. In a lot of ways, they still are.

1:10:27

MY JACKET'S CAUGHT

BEFORE IMPROVED FILM STOCKS AND SENSITIVE DIGital cameras made it unnecessary, "day for night" photography was commonplace in low-budget films, where lighting a night scene could be cumbersome, expensive, and dangerous. By underexposing daylight shots, you could get a not-great-but-good-enough nighttime facsimile. *Night* largely gets around this by blasting farmhouse lights right into zombie faces, but purportedly the film includes a few day-for-night shots. They must be good, because I can't tell you where they are.

The exception is here—the biggest action shot of the film. The framing is unremarkable as Romero compositions go, but I'll give him a pass due to the hundred other things going on. The truck is fifty feet away, turning toward the camera along a tire-trodden path through the lawn. (The 2018 *Box Office Bargain Bin* edit of *Night* speeds up the truck and adds comedic silent-film music.) Ben stands in the truck bed waving his torch at eleven zombies, one of whom falls against the truck, another risky stunt. The trees are black against a sky silver enough to take you out of the drama for the shot's five-second duration. It looks like dawn, which makes me think, oh, morning is here and our team is going to be okay.

Sadly, no. It's night again when the truck pulls up to the pump.

A metal tag identifies the pump as a product of the Wayne Pump Company of Salisbury, Maryland, specifically the 202 model, which was sold in the 1950s in red, white, and blue models. (There's no telling which color this is, though *Night*'s most recent colorization makes the bold claim of blue.)

Right next to the pump is a barn. This is interesting. When Barbra paused at these pumps when spotting Seven Pines, we didn't see any barn. (There is, in fact, a barn on the property today. It's hard to believe it's the same one, though it looks pretty old on Google Maps.) Here, the barn door is wide open. If it's anything like the barns I played in as a kid, it's chockablock with weapons—pitchforks, especially. (Harry wields a pitchfork in the script.)

Ben doesn't explore. He hops from the truck and faces the oncoming shamblers, an action star with his torch and rifle. Tom races to the pump with the keys. This shot actually tells us when it was filmed. Though no shooting schedules survive, John Vullo used the position of the moon over Ben's shoulder (newly visible on the Criterion edition) to isolate the shooting date as Sunday, June 18, 1967 (accurate to within a day or two). The science is beyond me, but if we take Vullo at his word, at the same moment Romero was filming Duane Jones waving his torch, Jimi Hendrix was lighting his own fire—on his guitar in front of 90,000 fans at the Monterey Pop Festival.

Tom's key doesn't work. This really impacted me as a kid. All the searching, all the planning—and it's the wrong key? Ben pushes Tom aside and *shoots the lock off with the rifle*. That's right: He fires a fucking gun at a fucking gas pump. Romero atoned for this reckless behavior in his script for *Night 1990*, in which Tom does the ill-advised shooting, causing the pump to explode and burn him alive.

When OG Tom drags the nozzle to the truck, gas (in real life only water) spills over both the truck and Ben's torch, which Ben had set on the ground. Like that, things go up in flame, including the truck's back left fender. Few who watch *Night* assign this disaster to Ben. But the script makes clear what common sense should tell us. After Ben shoots the pump lock, "gas spurts all over the place . . . creatures advance . . . gas still spurting, Tom crams the nozzle into the mouth of the gas-tank." Russo's novelization makes the cause-and-effect even clearer, with Ben's bullet fracturing the pump's nozzle.

In short, it's Ben's fault. Rarely in cinema do we see capable heroes make mistakes this catastrophic.

Whether it's your first time viewing *Night* (if so, wow, you bought this book?) or your four-hundredth (I'll meet you there soon), your stomach drops to the floor when the fire begins. Until now, there have been arguments about the best way to handle the zombie crisis. But there hasn't been a full-on debacle. It's like seeing a rescue helicopter crash into a mountain—few things are more horrifying than the downfall of those who are supposed to save you.

The handheld camera whips around a lot here, but slo-mo viewing reveals no trickery—Jones and Wayne are dealing with a truck that is actually on fire, while Ridley sits inside it. (One DVD commentary track assures us "legions of firemen and hose trucks" were on hand, but still.) "We've gotta get away from the pump!" Tom cries, and I couldn't agree more. But what he evidently means is get the *truck* away from the pump. So while Ben starts stamping out fiery grass with a rug, Tom takes off in a truck on fire.

After a few seconds of this idiocy, Tom hits the brakes. In reality, the truck's not moving, but there's a sound effect of screeching tires (on grass?). Tom leaps from the truck but Judy doesn't. She looks at Tom and clenches her teeth. It seems she's contracted Barbra's paralysis. After four seconds of this odd but edgy inertia—the Harry Bluestone–Emil Cadkin cue "Heavy Dramatic (CB-16B)" does a lot of work here—Judy utters a line that Romero, in 1972, said was the only dubbed line in the whole film (while Judy's mouth is covered by her hair): "My jacket's caught."

I have studied Judy's jean jacket to see if it had any troublesome frayed edges. It looks brand new. I guess I'm searching for sense in the senseless. I like Tom and Judy, all the more for the earnest efforts of the actors who portrayed them. To have them both die, not because of zombies but by a stupid mistake, is every bit the gut-punch the filmmakers intended.

Indulge, if you will, an idea I have for a slight alteration of the film, what I would have suggested had I been on location that night. Judy realizes what is about to happen. She stops struggling with her jacket and smiles at Tom, a sweet, apologetic goodbye that pays off their earlier conversation, all of that stuff about Judy always having a smile for Tom. *How can you smile at a time like this?*

Romero smash cuts to white leader (a white film strip usually used to add projector buffer at the starts and ends of film reels) for about a third of a second to create a nuclear flash. Maybe it's not how explosions look, but it's how explosions *feel*, particularly when set off in the dark of night.

Throughout the escape attempt, Romero has intercut to Harry watching through the window in mounting dismay. Now Harry covers his eyes as he's blasted with light. This is followed by a similar shot of Ben, pulling back in naked shock as his skin glows bright.

Here at last is Regis Survinski and Tony Pantanello's finest hour. Even after practice blowing shit up at a rock quarry, the gang's first attempt to explode the truck fizzled. Nothing would drain the juice out of this crucial moment like a limp flare-up, so the firebugs tried again. Around two in the morning, they loaded the truck (which cost the production all of $45) with the ingredients for a proper extravaganza: a TNT bomb brewed with Survinski's secret sauce, bottles filled with gas and oil, and a pile of junk (carpet, wood, timber) that could catch fire and fly through the air. Pantanello smoked his trademark stogie the whole time, taunting fate.

Three cameras were scrounged up, Romero on the Latent Image's 35mm and Streiner and Russo providing redundancy, one on the company's Eclair and the other on a rented 35mm. This was not a shot to fool around with.

Having no clue how big the blast would be, Image Ten arranged themselves (and the sizable Evans City crowd that had gathered to gawk) pretty far away, and yet still ended up dodging shrapnel. The effect, however, is marvelous, one of cinema's quintessential vehicle explosions. I like to imagine everyone involved with *Night*—the cast, the crew, the extras—basking in it, exhausted faces warmed with incandescence, each of them allowed, for a few seconds, to dream of a future that suddenly felt graspable.

Jones: a long road of film roles he'd instill with enough pathos to offset spectacle.

Wayne: a spotlight brighter and more enduring than any explosion.

Ridley: an adulthood of excitement, of being valued, of being seen and seeing.

O'Dea: the esteem of meaty roles, Tennessee Williams, Shakespeare, you name it.

Eastman and Hardman: their hard work rewarded, the rest of their lives to capitalize.

Russo: just being in the game, his post-Army gamble paying off.

Romero: a career steadily serving up bigger effects on projects at a *Ben-Hur* scale.

In not a single case would such dreams come to pass.

01:11:54 THE SOFTEST VOICE YOU COULD IMAGINE

Romero did dream of *Ben-Hur*. Rudy Ricci recalled sketching a nude (could it have been Carol Wayne, our Nude Ghoul?) in a 1957 art class at Carnegie Institute of Technology (since renamed Carnegie Mellon University), one of the only colleges that accepted the academically struggling Romero. (One of Romero's student paintings resurfaced in 2025, a lovely, naturalist bodegón—a.k.a.

still life with fruit.) When Ricci glanced at his pal George's paper, no nude. Romero was drawing a movie poster for *Ben-Hur*. Later, he'd lavish attention on a portrait of Yul Brenner from *The Ten Commandments*. It was the dichotomy that existed inside—and tortured—George Romero. Part of him longed for experimental, art-film intimacy. The other part longed for spectacle.

The first time I met Romero's wife, Suzanne, in 2017, to prep for work on *The Living Dead*, I asked her what George's favorite movies were. I had a theory that if I studied his dearest works of art, I could be inspired by what inspired him, thereby closing the gap with a cowriter who wasn't there. Little had changed in sixty years: *Ben-Hur*, she said. *The Ten Commandments*.

Blowing up the truck in *Night* was a first step in that direction.

George Andrew Romero, an only child, was born on February 4, 1940. His father, Jorge (Americanized as "George"), worked three jobs—the Navy Reserve when needed, the post office at night, and commercial art during the day, the last of which provided son George the fallback career he'd study in college. Jorge was born in A Coruña, Spain, but emigrated to Cuba with his parents when he was two. Like many of his generation, Jorge was prejudiced against America's Puerto Ricans, something George found distasteful. Still, his father's Hispanic heritage meant something to him. Beginning with *Day of the Dead*, nearly all of Romero's films involve a major Latino character, and the main character of the pages he left for *The Living Dead*, Luis Acocella, was Mexican. In September 2020, I attended (in Romero's stead) the Latino Comic Con to discuss *The Living Dead*, and I don't know that I've ever felt stronger adoration from Romero fans. In Mexican American actor and playwright Raúl Castillo's episode of Criterion Closet, he picks up *Night* and says, with reverence, "It wasn't lost on me that it was a guy named George Romero. As a kid, you didn't see a lot of Spanish-sounding names."

In 2025, Xabier Fole, an assistant professor at Rockford University, published *George A. Romero: Zombis, política y cine independiente* (George A. Romero: Zombies, Politics, and

Independent Cinema), partially a study of Romero's Latino heritage, influences, and outputs. Fole read over two hundred Spanish-language letters from Romero's forebears, and definitively identified the Romero homeland as the Galicia region of Spain on the northwest Iberian Peninsula.

Fole's biggest bombshell is the revelation (from an interview Romero gave to a Spanish magazine from the Sitges Film Festival in Barcelona) that his concept of zombies might have roots in tales his Spanish aunts (who also put money into *Night*, he said) spun for little George—"Jorgito," they called him. Santa Compaña was a mystical local belief about a procession of the dead through the world of the living. Now consider the Haitian influence—Haiti is just across the Windward Passage strait from Romero's heritage home of Cuba. One of Romero's last pieces of published writing was an intro to a 2016 edition of William Seabrook's infamous *The Magic Island* (1929), the book that first brought crooked interpretations of Vodou zombis to the western world. It all adds up to an exciting transnational spark behind Romero's global phenomenon.

Meanwhile, George's mother, Ann, was of Lithuanian descent, a background he'd plumb in his most personal (and favorite) film, *Martin*. George loved, but didn't like, his mother, whom he saw as overly reliant on her husband for everything. For a time, Ann's immigrant father, Vincent Dvorsky, lived with them in the Parkchester neighborhood of the Bronx. (On October 12, 2024, a stretch of nearby Metropolitan Avenue was dedicated as George A. Romero Way.) Vincent, who worked sweeping subway tracks, shared a room with George and laid down the future filmmaker's horror foundations by telling him about body parts and corpses he came upon in subway tunnels. Vincent made up for this by later getting a job at Nabisco and bringing home Social Tea cookies instead of dismemberment reports.

When it comes to the macabre, my own family history can compete. Thanks to detective work done by my sister, Jenny, in 2021, I can report on my mother Susan's side of the family, which began, for little Susan, in poverty, accepting food from friends and living in an unfinished shack so cold she slept in winter coats. Her extended family included a grandfather who had molested his daughters, a grandmother who believed she was haunted by the ghost of her stillborn child before perishing in a nursing home fire (I only knew her as a dementia-riddled octogenarian babbling cuss words), aunt-and-uncle hoarders who moved each time their house became unlivable, one uncle who was a schizophrenic recluse, another uncle whose mob dealings were laundered by video rental stores (and who won half of a $6.5 million lottery in 1984, with which he bought a mansion with a basement movie theater), an ex-con brother-in-law with a murder rap, a sister pushed down the stairs to her death (we saw her bruised inside her open casket), a cousin married first to an alcoholic and second to a guy she caught in bed with another man, a brother who ran away from his illegitimate children to join the circus only to die eight years later from a heart attack while driving a car filled with luckless family members, one nephew beaten so severely he couldn't thereafter work, and another nephew threatened at gunpoint (and, I suspect, ultimately executed) by his drug dealer. Raging unchecked through this Midwest telenovela was unchecked smoking and calamitous heart disease. Even limiting the pool to my mother's generation and younger, she's the only one who lived past the age of fifty. So far. This year, I'm set to break her record.

The last time my mother saw anyone in her family was at the funeral for her own mother, Dorothy. Afterward, she walked into the trailer where Dorothy had been living, took four or five pictures to remember her by, then closed the door on all of it. Not a bad idea, really, though my father's haunting speculation is that closing that door is what killed her. In refuting her past life, my mother also refuted the heart disease picking them off. She simply pretended it didn't exist. She stopped taking her heart pills. She died.

There's not much to report on my dad's side of the family:

salt-of-the-earth types who were, and are, decent people living understated American lives, with the exception of my first cousin once removed Arlo Landolt (1935–2022), the son of a hog farmer—typical Kraus—who embarked upon perilous Arctic expeditions before becoming renowned in astronomy for his photometric standards. I suppose I edge him out in the fame game (it's easier to get people to read my novel *Bent Heavens* than it is Arlo's article "Two Short-Period Eclipsing Binary Stars in the Field of PG 1047+003"), though I'll never achieve honors half as cool: An Antarctic mountain, an LSU observatory, and an asteroid are all named after Arlo. In short, he was just the sort of chap Don Quinn would have interrogated about the Venus Probe.

My father's ancestors (spelled Krauss or Krauz) moved from Bavaria to the United States way back in 1861, which effectively ends worries about Nazi sympathies. Not that I wondered about any of that as a kid. I didn't wonder about *any* of this as a kid. But there are things you know, and there are things that float in the air you breathe, that fold into your DNA. Things that turn you into Daniel Kraus, or, if you're really lucky, into George A. Romero.

Little George was smart. Romero (a name that means "a person on a religious journey") skipped two grades at Saint Helena's, a Catholic grade school in the Bronx, but at St. Joseph's high school, his ancestry landed him in the Sharks-Jets crossfires of gangs like the Golden Guineas. He got beat up regularly. His schoolwork cratered. He took a pass on milestone events—for example, skipping his senior prom to go to the movies. He emerged from the parochial system as an outcast with a slew of Catholic fears and guilts (which, again, he'd mine in *Martin* by portraying a priest). Cue Uncle Harold, who picked Romero's ass up in the Bronx and dropped it off in the Ivy League: Connecticut's Suffield Academy prep school, where at age sixteen Romero won a 1957 Science Achievement Award, to the tune of a $75 savings bond and a gold pin, for an 8mm geology short film he recalled as titled *Earthbottom*, though the May 19, 1957, *Hartford Courant* reports it as being called *A Study of the Earth.* (I don't trust the *Courant* either: They call our young pin-winner "George A. Romano.") It was due to this short that Romero got into Carnegie.

In discussing Romero's formative years, two things always pop up. The first is Michael Powell's 1951 filmed opera *The Tales of Hoffmann.* Local TV station WOR-TV chose *Hoffmann* as a Million Dollar Movie, which meant multiple airings—and twelve-year-old Romero caught several. He credited it as sparking his interest in film and was such a vocal fan that he got his own special feature on the *Hoffmann* Criterion release. Powell's influence wasn't even new. Powell's *The Thief of Bagdad* (1940) was the first thing Romero ever saw on a TV (a rented TV, no less). On the Felsher tapes, Romero confesses—"between you, me, and the lamppost"—his dream project was to remake the film that ended Powell's career, *Peeping Tom* (1960).

The second thing is a name: Monroe Yudell, another Romero uncle. As a doctor, Yudell had disposable cash, but he and his wife had no kids on whom to dispose it. Romero became a periodic beneficiary. When Romero nosed around the Revere 8mm camera Yudell owned but wasn't using, Yudell told him to take it (and later gave Romero the same directive with a 16mm Bell & Howell). Romero was fourteen.

It's uncanny how much it mirrors what happened when I was fifteen—my dad bringing home the mini-VHS camera and me making my claim on it. I made my first short films (*The Geek, Doll House, 4-D*) just as, thirty-five years earlier, Romero made his own (*Gorilla, The Man from the Meteor, Death in Small Doses*). Romero premiered his movies in his uncle's basement; I premiered mine in my living room.

Neither of us had any inkling you could do this for a living. That changed for Romero in 1958 and me in 1996. For Romero, it was doing gopher jobs on *Peyton Place*; *Bell, Book, and Candle*; and *It Happened to Jane*; and working as a second-unit assistant on *North by Northwest.* For me, it was serving as a production assistant on a $500,000 indie film in Chicago called *Err on the*

Side of Caution. *North* is an immortal classic; *Err* is a forgotten vanity project. But both left the same taste in our mouths. We felt disrespected, underestimated, patronized, and bored. Both crews included narcissists who didn't give a shit about the movie they were on, yet appeared to believe their jobs were among the world's most important. If either Romero or I were to pursue filmmaking, it would need to be in scenarios where all parties were emotionally engaged.

For me, that meant working mostly alone. I directed five moderately successful documentaries (also handling cinematography, sound, and editing) before turning to novels, which gave me even more control. It was the same reason Romero turned to novels, albeit unfinished ones. For Romero the filmmaker, control meant taking on co-op projects like *Expostulations* (partially funded by Uncle Yudell) and *Night of the Living Dead*.

As a young director he suffered the same shortcoming I did when I directed my sole narrative feature, *Ball of Wax* (equally forgotten as *Err on the Side of Caution*, though I'd like to think it clears that low bar). I, like Romero, was nonconfrontational to a fault. The instinct came from a good place: We'd both observed moviemaking assholes and wanted to be different. In the case of *Ball of Wax*, the downside was misbehavior I didn't nip in the bud. Romero had a similar reticence to wrest control: "Because there were ten of us, it was getting so fucking democratic that it got sort of crazy." I don't love it, but it may be true that nonconfrontational folk don't make the best generals. (I can't believe I have just spent a paragraph comparing *Ball of Wax* to *Night of the Living Dead*. I am duly ashamed and will never do so again.)

A potential upside to this approach is artistic sensitivity. Judy Ridley recalls Romero sitting cross-legged on the floor with her to talk through scenes "in the softest voice you could imagine." (This quote comes from a video shot at the 2018 Monsterpalooza in which Ridley is interviewed by a hand puppet named Flick.)

Still Romero longed for spectacle. For that, he needed, as he would have put it, "bread." And with more bread came more problems. He shot *Dawn of the Dead* for $640,000. *Day of the Dead* for $3.5 million. *Monkey Shines* for $7 million. *Creepshow* for $8 million. *The Dark Half* for $15 million. And, finally, *Land of the Dead* for just shy of $19 million, the biggest budget he'd ever have. While *Land* is a handsome production, it's not a set-piece spectacle on par with the $26 million *Dawn* remake, the success of which helped *Land* get made. Presumably, most of *Land*'s cash went to star Dennis Hopper and all those zombie extras.

It would be Romero's last stab at big-budget filmmaking. The epic dream projects Suz told me about—most notably *Tarzan of the Apes*—would never happen. It hurts to think about. But it's evident the movie-biz disdain he built up on *North by Northwest* never left. It's also evident Romero was at his best when working independently—he was a "maverick" or "trouble," depending on which side of the studio fence you stood. *The Dark Half* proves this. It's a miracle the movie is good given Romero's friction with his star Timothy Hutton, who is excellent in Jekyll-and-Hyde roles but kicked off the shoot by demanding separate trailers for both personalities, and a production company, Orion Pictures, in the throes of bankruptcy. Romero wouldn't direct again for seven years.

By all accounts—and I mean *all* accounts—Romero was a joy to be around. He was a grizzly bear, six foot four, big and gregarious. He hoarsened his voice to a growl to take the piss out of himself anytime he said something borderline pretentious. When he grinned, which was often, his mouth revealed the roller-coaster swoop of his upper row of teeth. He valued friends over experts, often choosing to work with people he liked even if they weren't the most prestigious option. His open heart extended to his romantic life. He married Ketchum, MacLeod, and Grove ad exec Nancy "Jeannie" McKim in 1971 and brought her into the Latent Image as VP of Marketing. The couple had a son, Cameron (who, as of this writing, runs a Kentucky restaurant called Romero's). Romero and McKim parted ways (the oddest thing in Romero's *Night* shooting script is a half-finished, never-sent letter breaking the divorce news to his Uncle Harold and Aunt Helen—Harry and Helen, sound familiar?), and in 1980, Romero married Christine Forrest, whose family owned the house in which he shot his third feature, *Season of the Witch.* Forrest would go on to serve critical duties on Romero films, but is best loved for her entertaining acting turns in *Martin, Knightriders, Monkey Shines,* and *Two Evil Eyes.* They had a daughter, Tina (a DJ known as DJ TRx, who has, as of this writing, just premiered her directorial debut, the queer zombie flick *Queens of the Dead*), and an adopted son, Andrew, whom I know nothing about except that he made a cameo in Romero's *Bruiser* (2000). In 2005, while shooting *Land of the Dead* in Toronto, Romero met Suzanne Desrocher, who was bartending at a local hotel. He left Christine, and he and Suzanne married six years later, and were together until his death. Though no horror fan (she'd never heard of George Romero), Suz, in my biased but emphatic opinion, has been an exemplary steward of Romero's legacy, always with an eye toward education, inspiration, and access. She has presided over a fruitful nine years of refocusing attention to Romero's artistic breadth, kicking off on October 25, 2017, (three months after his death) with Romero getting a star on the Hollywood Walk of Fame (6604 Hollywood Boulevard, one block west of Musso & Frank) before establishing the George A. Romero Foundation and spearheading the creation of his archive.

My point is that Romero *lived a life,* he really did, even if it wasn't precisely the life he'd hoped to live, and probably still hoped for until his last year, writing in maniacal bursts on his laptop from his Toronto home, the TV screen to his left playing Turner Classic Movies, all the thunderous cattle drives, globe-trotting romances, fantastical journeys, battle charges, chariot races, pirate ships, and space chases he was never allowed to make, his own Million Dollar Movie, his own *Tales of Hoffmann.* (Romero's archive includes material on a project so unlikely to happen it breaks my heart: *Hoffmann: Through the Mansions of the Moon,* a sci-fi stage musical adaptation.)

The truck fire in *Night* was his first taste of it—an effect bigger than himself and his cohorts, big enough to make him, and future viewers, feel small, which I'd argue is the whole point of epic cinema. To feel small is to recognize forces bigger than ourselves. It is practically religion itself.

This is driven home by a second shot of Ben reacting to the explosion. The portraits of Ben that end up on posters, shirts, lunchboxes, etc., tend to be ones of gimlet-eyed resolve. I'm a sucker for those, but here Duane Jones shows his range, as he did when telling Barbra his origin story forty-four minutes back. Jones's expression is breathtakingly naked. His face is slack but not empty; you read his shock as well as the first screw turns of panic. The truck explosion is a mirror of what he described happening at Beekman's Diner—only this time the fault is his.

There's a second level here too. Five months before Romero's death, Jordan Peele's *Get Out* became one of the biggest horror debuts in decades. I was taken by the film's central marketing image: a close-up of star Daniel Kaluuya staring straight at the camera, two tears rolling down his cheeks. It felt revolutionary to me: a young Black man depicted not as violent, or cool, or tough, but as vulnerable, even grieving. This is the look Duane Jones gives here. As viewers, we aren't prepared for such honesty. Suspense has swerved into tragedy, and now we know no one is safe.

01:12:00

I OUGHT TO DRAG YOU OUT THERE

IN ROMERO'S SHOOTING SCRIPT, IT'S ZOMBIES WHO take down the fleeing couple. Russo's facsimile script simply adds the scrawled amendment *TOM & JUDY GET BLOWN UP*. Regardless, that's a wrap on Tom and Judy. Their intact bodies, anyway.

Harry vanishes from the window. Ben, meanwhile, realizes there's a football team's worth of zombies slouching his way. After seeing *Night* a dozen times, you clock that you've seen this group shot before. Conducting so many extras was a major pain in the ass, and there was no time to keep shooting new angles on them. Anytime Romero needs a wide shot of zombies, he returns to this setup, regardless of where the action takes place.

Technically that makes this a flub, but a cozy one: I like seeing all my favorite shamblers in a row like it's the *Thriller* video. Second from the left is Al Pankopf, not there due to a favor vis-à-vis Pankopf Ford Motor Sales, but because he was dating Judith O'Dea. On the far, far right, recognizable only by his sliding gait, is Zombie #1.

Ben gives the squib squad more work by shooting a zombie through the heart. This is Herbert Summer, a bar owner and menswear merchant whose 2019 obituary drops this double-take tidbit: "Herbert served in the Army Air Corps during 1947, which brought him into contact with the famed Roswell UFO incident." In his Psychic Vibrations column of the November/December 2003 issue of *Skeptical Inquirer,* Robert Sheaffer tells Summer's story. It is not, I regret to say, a story that aligns with the Venus probe. Summer worked on weather balloons at Roswell, and insists the alleged crashed UFO was, in fact, a weather balloon. There you have it: the Roswell incident debunked in the middle of a book about *Night of the Living Dead.*

The dead encircle Ben close enough for one of them to be sprayed with sparks from his torch—another case of even the smallest players hurling themselves into make-believe. The star of this zombie ensemble is Jason L. Richards, a heavyset dude with a Tor Johnson noggin, huge and square and with a fondant landslide of a brow. Richards, a brick manufacturer, died two years after filming, but is survived by his daughter, Paula, the Hardman Associates staffer who replaced Judy Ridley. Paula, who was pretty much ordered to appear in the film, appears as a typist in the newsroom scenes, but is best known as "Goth Ghoul," lovingly christened by fans for the straight black hair covering her face. (Goth Ghoul made the cover of Joe Kane's book and has scored two different toys, a vinyl doll from Japan's Club Daikaiju x M1, and an action figure from Zoloworld.)

In what are the best-staged action shots in the film, Ben lurches through the grasping hands of roughly fifteen zombies, swings wide arcs with the torch, and races onto the front porch. Inside, Harry is making for the cellar when he hears Ben from outside: "Let me in!" Ben slams his body against the door, hollering for Harry to unlock it already.

Harry's body surges slightly toward the front door. Then slightly more. It's delicate acting. You can call it cowardice (most do), but I appreciate the battle waging between Harry's heart and mind. He wants to help Ben but feels responsibility to his family first. He hesitates too long for redemption: Ben kicks open the door, and then, because Ben's a vengeful motherfucker, spares two seconds he can't afford to give Harry the glare of death.

Ben slams the door and manhandles a loose door horizontally

across it. Harry bolts over to help—example #954 of *Night* refusing to paint with anything but shades of gray. Together, the foes nail the abutment back into place. Never have we seen them work together so well. There is a moment of hope. I feel it every time.

Clearly, so does Harry. He meets Ben's eyes with wary optimism. It's easy to imagine Ben sighing, nodding forgiveness, and shaking the older man's hand. Instead, Ben gives Harry a left jab to the face. (Pause at 1:13:45 to see an entire film light in full view.) It's an awkward punch—Jones is too close to the door to rear back—but he makes up for it with a right hook that sends Harry to the floor.

Harry crawls into the den on all fours right beside the Zenith 7S363. The radio is past its prime, a relic, and so is Harry Cooper. Harry stands only to be felled by a third punch. This is plenty—Harry's down for the count—but Ben pulls him up off the chair where he landed to deliver a big fourth punch. Harry collapses beneath a mounted deer head. This prop, too, feels pointed: Harry's a few punches away from getting his own block knocked off.

Ben hoists him onto a chair and snarls, "I ought to drag you out there and feed you to those things!" Ben rushes away, maybe to stop himself from murder, and the next shot is one of *Night*'s best: tight on Harry, sparse hair mussed, half his face obscured. A small turn of his head reveals blood draining from his nose into his mouth. In the last seconds of the shot, Harry's expression of tight, hyperventilating panic abruptly loosens into a closed-mouth look of solemn dread. We just saw two young lovers roasted in a truck and yet this hits harder. Harry deserved to lose the world in which he ruled, but you still understand what the loss feels like.

01:14:18 WHAT THEY WERE EATING

It was the age of gimmicks. The 3D craze that crested with Hitchcock's *Dial M for Murder* (1954) had blistered into oddball agitprop like William Castle's "Emergo!," in which an inflatable skeleton soared above the audience during *House on Haunted Hill* (1959), and "Percepto!," in which certain seats were rigged to vibrate during *The Tingler* (1959). *Scent of Mystery* (1960) introduced "Smell-O-Vision," piping odors through air vents twenty years before John Waters made more infamous use of the concept in *Polyester* (1981), dispersing scratch-off cards that released on-schedule odors like "flatulence," "model building glue," and "new car smell."

Walter Reade's Continental Films prepared a grab-bag of stunts for *Night*. Contests like a "Scream-a-thon" and "Ghouls in Costume" (which wrongheadedly suggested adding a "third arm" to ghouls). A paper bag printed, *This VOMIT BAG and the PRICE of one ADMISSION will enable YOU to SEE . . . NIGHT OF THE LIVING DEAD.* The "Death Certificate" that reads: *I the undersigned take full responsibility of viewing . . . NIGHT OF THE LIVING DEAD. And by signing my own death certificate I hereby release this theater of any liability.* Sample newspaper ads that give would-be attendees this peace of mind: *IF "NIGHT OF THE LIVING DEAD" FRIGHTENS YOU TO DEATH—YOU ARE COVERED FOR $50,000,* a Lloyd's of London Insurance Company policy that, according to material provided to theaters, was legit.

If you were to stop watching *Night* right now, these shocktastic gags wouldn't make sense. The grossest thing we have seen is the gory skull, maybe the hand Tom smushed with a hammer. Those effects go out the window, with projectile-vomit force, in the sequence fans call "the Last Supper."

To hear Chuck Craig reference flesh eating is one thing. To see it (and, shudder, hear it) is something else. The scene begins with the camera looking over a truck still smoldering as zombies stagger close. While every cue of library music in *Night* is impeccably chosen, none are more effective than the deep, low, electronic pulse that begins here. A harbinger of synth soundtracks to come, it bears no resemblance to the Hi-"Q" library cues and goes unreferenced in the credits. The Varèse Sarabande album, however, puts an asterisk on the track with the attribution, "electronic sound effects by Karl Hardman." There wasn't much old Karl couldn't do. According to Jim Cirronella, one Hardman Associates employee believed the pulse was a "square wave" from a "tone generator." Something for you gearheads.

The second shot is handheld from inside the truck as zombies reach through broken windows. The zombies are *taking things* and bringing those things to their mouths. It's shadowy enough that, if it was your first time watching, you'd be excused for holding out hope that they are not doing what you think they are doing.

The third shot floats leftward over the truck bed, where we see several zombies, including Roger McGovern (*Great Caesar's ghost!*), coming away with small hunks they clutch like prizes. This is the first time zombies have shown interest in anything dead, and it's startling. They are *thrilled*. The fifth shot shows they have quit working as a wolfpack to separately enjoy Tom and Judy tartare. Six zombies (four of them seated, which is also new) chew their morsels.

The scene could have ended there and had a fabled impact. Romero's shooting script notes indicate restraint: *Scenes—quickly of ghouls grunting aspects of Tom & Judy.* But the next shot, the sixth, pushes into transgression, and no doubt pushed people from theaters. A zombie snarls and hisses over a rope of intestine. Incredibly, he is played by Chuck Craig, our stiff-backed, straight-laced newscaster gone feral, with the nice detail of black fingernails. (After retiring, Craig bought a rabbit farm. I just wanted to stick that in somewhere. A rabbit farm!)

No gore effect Romero ever concocted rivals this shock. This is no vampire pretending to bite a starlet's neck, no man in a monster suit gumming rubber bones. These are real intestines; somehow (survival instinct?) you just know it. The bowels rip and dribble viscous fluid. No low-budget filmmaker can make props this good and Romero knew it. At the end of his shooting script is a handwritten to-do list. Item one: *Marilyn will call—early afternoon—re entrails.* Item eleven: *Someone bring cooler & cake of ice—for entrails.*

An investor named Ross Harris supplied said entrails, mostly lamb guts. Harris ran a meat-packing company that serviced area butchers. (He can be seen answering phones behind Chuck Craig in the newsroom scene.) I didn't know this in 1996, when I shot a student film called *Endless Scenes of Carnage and Terror.* It included a terrific effect in which a "blood mutant" (my own "ghoul" disambiguation) pulls organ after organ from his own belly, then eats one. A Tipton, Iowa, butcher happily gave us two coolers of fresh guts and offered anything in the industrial-sized bins outside. This led to one of the most surreal scares of my life: lifting a lid to find *an entire cow,* minus interior organs, stuffed inside a trash can.

Vince Survinski didn't shrink from any task. He filled Coke bottles with water, and from those bottles, painstakingly filled the dry guts so they looked fresh. And do they ever. The next five shots are close-ups of zombies eating body parts. I mean *eating.* These volunteer extras—*Night* funders, ad men peers, the Evans City curious—bite into and chew up raw viscera. It's good to see Rudy Ricci again, delicately gnashing flesh off Paula's arm. But as usual McGovern (*Great Caesar's ghost!*) steals the show by happily snarfing down what looks like a liver. Here, at last, are the atrocities hinted at by Dr. Grimes.

You can imagine the effect this sixty-two-second sequence had on viewers. Had this been a buffoonish gorefest from the get-go, à la *Blood Feast,* that would be one thing—you'd be along for the tongue-in-cheek ride. But *Night* is realistic. Imagine if the third act of *Who's Afraid of Virginia Woolf?* began with Elizabeth Taylor and Richard Burton cannibalizing George Segal and Sandy Dennis. That's how it feels.

For a lot of reviewers, this was the ballgame. Ann Guarino of the *New York Daily News*: "The theme could not be in poorer taste." Lee Beaupre of *Variety*: "Until the Supreme Court establishes clear-cut guidelines for the pornography of violence, *Night of the Living Dead* will serve quite nicely as an outer-limit definition by example . . . The film casts serious aspersions on the integrity of its makers . . . and the moral health of filmgoers who cheerfully opt for this unrelieved orgy of sadism."

The most famous reaction came from our old pal Roger Ebert, who managed to catch a screening amid a crowd of kids. His *Chicago Sun-Times* article (famously reprinted in *Reader's Digest* but also elsewhere under the title "Ghouls Feast on Humans as Children Weep") begins, "There were maybe two dozen people in the audience who were over 16 years old. The rest were kids, the kind you expect at a Saturday afternoon kiddie matinee." You can predict how this is going to go. Ebert describes how the on-screen carnage is received by tiny-tot showgoers: "A little girl across the aisle from me, maybe nine years old, was sitting very still in her seat and crying . . . This was ghouls eating people—you could actually see what they were eating."

It was by the skin of their teeth that Walter Reade got the scene into theaters. Precisely one month after *Night*'s release—November 1, 1968—the ineffectual Hays Code that had determined cinematic acceptability since 1930 was supplanted by the MPAA ratings system, which offered up four categories: G, M (soon to become PG), R, and X. The Last Supper would have indubitably earned an X, hamstringing its screening potential.

Ebert came around to *Night* and said his original piece was only a condemnation of admittance policies. He's not wrong about that, but he was wrong about horror. Ebert lost me in the piece's second paragraph, where he admits to going to *Night* because it had been a long time since he'd seen a horror film. He only "vaguely remembers some stuff from the 1950s, like *Creature from the Black Lagoon* or *Attack of the Crab Monsters*. They were usually lousy, but it was fun to see them." Say what you will about *Crab Monsters*, Mr. Ebert—but *Black Lagoon*? Lousy?!

It's possible Romero created the Last Supper solely for shock value. It was certainly an appeal factor for Walter Reade, which pushed the gore angle from the jump. For Romero, it presaged a filmography replete with gory "gags," as he called them. It even led to what he admitted was the "most embarrassing moment" of his career, taking a gig directing violent insert shots for the U.S. release of Umberto Lenzi's *Spasmo* (1974)—without Lenzi's okay. The reason for this moral lapse could be found in Romero's checkbook. He was half a million in debt.

The Last Supper is no "gag." I'm here to tell you that without this scene, *Night* would not succeed. Until this moment, the film is just a film. A very good film, but one people could watch, categorize, and file with other films of the time.

During the Last Supper, the film transcends not only genre but its very film-ness in what I can't help but compare to erotic asphyxiation. The film chews through the guardrails of sensible cinema, abandoning the land of good taste for the seas of amygdala-powered id. Script and plot are gutted. Main characters are gone, lost in the night. Dialogue is replaced by slurping sounds. The maddening electronic pulse begins to feel like electroshock therapy.

If you agree at all that *Night* vibrates with the mood of the Vietnam era, here is the comeuppance dreamed of by a generation used to seeing dead bodies on nightly TV and receiving regular word of the wartime deaths of people they knew, picked off as if by a movie slasher, and in the name of the American flag. An estimated 250 different people played zombies in *Night*, a staggering number for an indie film, one after the other treated like Army privates, hastily outfitted and shoved into a field until the filmmakers themselves lost count.

Even today, Image Ten is trying to ID all those bodies, with John Vullo emerging as the crackerjack gumshoe. Vullo's ability to track down previously unlogged ghouls is downright mystical. Just ask "Housedress Ghoul," an unknown twenty-three-year-old that Vullo tagged in May 2024 as Sharon Brubach Rapone (formerly Sharon Carroll). Only weeks later, the eighty-year-old

Rapone found herself signing autographs at Living Dead Weekend. Life is strange.

Vullo's biggest find, uncovered on August 29, 2024, is five minutes of candid 8mm footage—*color* 8mm footage, no less—shot on a lark by Stephanie Barrett, daughter of Jack Barrett, a local artist whose zombie cameo didn't make the final cut. Shot in daylight over what seems like about an hour, Stephanie's footage focuses on tables set up outside the farmhouse, crammed next to at least eleven vehicles parked on the lawn. What an unexpected pleasure it is to watch Hardman and Eastman ply Derma Wax and makeup. The biggest surprise: Some zombie makeup was mustard yellow! The biggest gut-punch: The footage reveals someone *else* shooting 8mm footage as well—a whole new treasure for Vullo to hunt down.

These, the needlessly killed of the Vietnam era, are owed life, and pleasure. Pleasures include eating. Our zombies take bites from a society that felt justified in serving them up on plates. For all its viscera, *Night* is subtle in this regard. More overt successors followed. Six years after *Night*, Bob Clark (possessor of the wonkiest CV in Hollywood, having also directed *Porky's* and *A Christmas Story*), released the fabulous *Deathdream*, which follows the return of a soldier who died in the Vietnam War. Another standout is "Homecoming," a 2005 episode of the TV show *Masters of Horror*, directed by Joe Dante, in which dead American soldiers rise as zombies to vote out the current administration. (A headstone in a cemetery scene reads GEORGE A. ROMERO.)

What I value most in art is an artist's willingness to drive their premise to the hilt. Image Ten knew what they were doing when they titled their film *Night of the Flesh Eaters*. To not show flesh-eating would be a cop-out of the first order, the kind common to shockers with no intention of paying off their titles. (I'm looking at you, *Curse of the Cat People* and *Friday the 13th, Part VIII: Jason Takes Manhattan*.) Why Romero shows gut-munching in *Night* is why some auteurs show unsimulated sex (*Cruising*, *The Brown Bunny*, *9 Songs*, *Anatomy of Hell*, *Shortbus*, *Nymphomaniac*).

To get past what you think you know about the most basic human activities, you have to see it larger than life, let it hit you like a bucket of ice water, then reevaluate.

It's a matter of being honest with yourself. Do you want to die in delusion? If you're a meat eater, for instance, you should know how meat is processed. I eat meat, and consider *Blood of the Beasts* (1949), a documentary about Paris slaughterhouses by Georges Franju (best known for *Eyes Without a Face*), one of the most important films I've seen. You must open yourself to self-recrimination if you are to live a considered life.

After TV coverage turned the American tide against the Vietnam War, the U.S. government learned to hide their dead. When a million-plus Americans died of Covid-19, where were the videos of morgues overflowing with bodies? Where were the photos of refrigerated trucks jam-packed with corpses? We know it happened. Chuck Craig says in *Night*, "A widespread investigation of reports from funeral homes, morgues, and hospitals has concluded that the unburied dead are coming back to life." That's us, you know. We're the unburied dead.

Night of the Living Dead's Last Supper asks us to look at our dead in all its avoidable barbarity and ugly decay, in the hopes we'll ask *ourselves* the necessary questions.

Is it wrong to be shown images of death?

Or is it wrong *not* to be shown them?

01:15:20 GET OVER IT

Night of the Living Dead: 30th Anniversary Edition responds to these questions. This controversial variant, released on DVD by Anchor Bay Entertainment in 1999 (the thirty-first anniversary, technically), weaves newly created footage into the film, much of it gory. As it turns out, it's not just *how* gore is applied, but *when* it's applied that matters. *Night 30* (as I will hereafter dub it) doesn't insert its splashiest carnage into the Last Supper, but rather thirty-two minutes earlier. Right after Ben finishes his Beekman's Diner monologue, *Night 30* takes us to a road near Beekman's, where at least twenty-six zombies (a new high for *Night*), including a Beekman's waitress, shuffle past a crashed car. A few zombies stop to drag a corpse from behind the wheel, causing brains (the commentary track tells us it's ham barbecue, probably the sickly-sweet Pittsburgh staple Isaly's Chipped Ham) to spill from a hole in its skull. It's more disgusting than anything in the original: mission accomplished.

It explains one of *Night*'s more puzzling questions: Where are all these dead people coming from? Their general freshness indicates they didn't claw themselves from rotten cemetery caskets. They came from Beekman's. I like this explanation. It makes good, economical sense.

Unfortunately, the new Beekman's gore neuters the Last Supper. Instead of Romero's gore instigating a payoff, catharsis, and revelation of a truth beyond words—pure cinema, in other words—it's introduced as a standard ingredient, just like in thousands of other splatter fests.

We might as well get into *Night 30*. No single product draws more condemnation from fans. It was instantly reviled upon release. That's not even accurate; it was reviled when it was *announced*, to such a degree that nothing in it could reverse the global gag reflex. The negative reaction came so early that it's referenced in the thirty-two-page booklet packaged with the DVD! In one of the booklet's interviews, inserted costar Debbie Rochon says, "I never realized how anal fans would be about it 'til I saw some reaction to the project on the internet."

I was one of those fans. At age twenty-three—the pinnacle of my unimaginative, knee-jerk snobbery—I dashed off an online article cheekily bashing the project. At least I watched it first. But I hadn't, if you catch my drift, *seen* it. I believe very few people did.

The project was inspired by George Lucas, who, in 1997, released three *Star Wars: Special Edition* films awash with digital extrapolations, new effects, and reinserted and CGI-enhanced deleted scenes. For people to whom it was important that Han Shot First, the results were a mixed bag. Regardless, it was a big honking deal, and soon Jack Russo and Marilyn Eastman thought of doing something similar for *Night*.

In their original proposal for the project, they write that an amended version "would reopen all the markets that have been supersaturated by the 1968 version, and they would be ready to be saturated again. It would also reopen opportunities for ancillary tie-ins such as comic books, model kits, trading cards, poster books, etc., etc." Big ideas, none of which would occur. (By the way, according to Johnny Martyr's Mass Hysteria site, at least twenty-eight different sets of *Night* trading cards have been produced since 1987.)

Because no deleted scenes of *Night* existed, the gang (including Karl Hardman, Russ Streiner, and Bill Hinzman) shot eighteen minutes of new scenes. Russo says in the booklet, "I wrote the new scenes based on ideas that, for the most part, were discussed back in 1967 during our first story sessions, but were not carried out due to lack of time and money."

Russo's autobiography adds that Image Ten had gotten wind that an outside entity was considering giving *Night* the George Lucas treatment. Therefore, out of "fiduciary obligation" to shareholders, Image Ten took the $200,000 deal Anchor Bay offered—far less than the $5,000,000 asked for in their proposal. Given the perpetual opportunist tampering of *Night* by entities outside Image Ten, this financial impetus feels feasible.

It's the "for the most part" two paragraphs above that gives Russo his escape hatch. The proposal lists among its planned new sequences Ben's truck escape from Beekman's Diner and the awakening of the limbless cadaver that Dr. Grimes describes to Chuck Craig. Anchor Bay's budget made those scenes impossible. In addition to the post-Beekman's zombie scene (set up by a new bit of radio reporting recorded by Craig), *Night 30* adds two plot threads. The first supplies a backstory for Hinzman's

Zombie #1, who has been executed for the rape and murder of a child (shades of Freddy Krueger). The second tracks the new character of Reverend Hicks, a fire-and-brimstoner who gets bit, doesn't turn into a zombie, and credits it to being God's chosen one.

There are good reasons to be uncomfortable with all this. The biggest red flag for fans was that it was Russo's butt in the director's chair, not Romero's. Russo is adamant that Romero was on board to direct until scheduling got in the way, and the proposal insists Romero "will be executive producer this time around." This conflicts with Romero's take. In an article on the *Entertainment Weekly* website dated April 23, 1999, Romero says, "I didn't want to touch [*Night*]." Later, to *VideoScope*, he said, "That was one of the things I told [Russo] I thought was dumb! . . . I just thought it was ridiculous." In private, he flat-out claimed he hadn't even been asked to be involved.

I'm not picking sides. There's evidence the *Night 30* collective honestly believed Romero was going to nominally participate. A letter from Russo dated May 28, 1997, is addressed to Streiner, Hardman, Eastman, *and* Romero. In it, Russo writes, "Of course, if George wants to take a more active role, a lot would change." A month earlier, Karl Hardman wrote to a group (including Romero), "[George] is 'on-board.' While on the west coast for the next two weeks, he will contact some of his own connections in regard to the project. He agreed that his participation is crucial to the success of the project. (That's correct, is it not, George?)" The letter is signed, "Hopefully yours, Harry Cooper."

In many ways, *Night 30* feels like the climactic scuffle between Romero and Russo. Their relationship is best synopsized, however, by an email chain that is part of the John A. Russo Papers at the University of Pittsburgh Library. In late 2011, Russo was trying to produce his satirical script *TAU KAPPA ZOMBIE*, in which Willard is treated as "the Roswell of zombie lore"—a clever notion. Russo wanted Romero involved as executive producer, writing, "If you do not participate in the project

I will probably be lambasted in a similar fashion to the 'hits' I took for *NOLD 30th Anniversary Edition*."

Romero's November 2 response to the script is harsh: "I've never been into this soft-porn, Scream Queen stuff . . . it just feels like what it is . . . an attempt to ride on coattails (many of them tattered by bad films) when we should own the coat! The script strikes me as less funny than sad in that you've had to resort to such a thing." Russo emailed back: "This is not soft-core porn of any sort, it is satire and honest fun, so I don't know where you are coming from on that . . . I am just having fun with what I consider to be a humorous approach to my material, so I don't see anything 'sad' about that, and am sort of offended by that comment . . . I am not a coattail rider. I am a serious film-maker and writer, and I think you have missed the point and have unnecessarily denigrated my efforts."

Reading this interchange is like hearing your parents fight. It's heartbreaking, apocalyptic. You want to butt in, as I remember doing as a child, offer yourself up as sacrifice, take the blame, anything so these two people who love each other can return to affectionate states. But Romero and Russo couldn't, not really, not ever again.

After watching *Night 30* for the first time in twenty-five years, I still side with the masses. *Night 30* is misguided. But it's not, as Russo put it, to be unnecessarily denigrated. While the library-music score of the original is more expressive, the only thing really wrong with Scott Vladimir Licina's new synth score is that the film reverts to Hi-"Q" cues anytime dialogue makes it impossible to disentangle them.

Subsequent efforts at rescoring *Night* have had mixed results. For a real *Wizard of Oz–Dark Side of the Moon* experience, cue up *Night* with the exceptional *Night of the Living Dead* alternate score released in 2016 by OGRE and Dallas Campbell (or Morricone Youth's deeply cool 2016 translation of the Capitol Library Services score). The electric-guitar-forward score for the curious twenty-one-minute abridgment of *Night* released in 1995 via the TV show *Attack of the Killer B's* (retitled, oddly, as *Zombie Attack!*) isn't bad either, but, you know, has seventy-five fewer minutes to cover. For something more ethereal, try *Tonight of the Living Dead*, a haunting 2008 album by 400 Lonely Things described as "a collage of restructured audio taken from a public domain edition of the 1968 film *Night of the Living Dead*."

Night 30's new footage, shot by Hinzman with the same kinds of lenses, lights, and film stock used on the original, matches well, and some of the transitions between new and old footage are bracingly seamless. The zombies created by *Saturday Night Live*'s makeup department (strange but true) effectively mesh with the original ghouls. And the new finale with Reverend Hicks crying the slogan "Spike the dead!" (while cradling a tiny white doggie named Moo Shu—Russ Streiner's pet—a detail absurd enough to work) is at least intriguing. ("Spiking"—driving a nail through a corpse's head to prevent revival—is a concept Russo ported over from his original *Return of the Living Dead* novel.)

It's also nice to see Rochon pop up as the reporter interviewing Reverend Hicks. Rochon's star quality is always a joy to observe, and her humor and intellect serve her well off-screen. Once upon a time a regular *Scream Queens Illustrated* contributor (you could order a Debbie Rochon "nipple print"—like a fingerprint—from the back pages of *SQI*), she is magnetic even in dreck like Russo's *Santa Claws*, a film notable for rare Karl Hardman and Marilyn Eastman appearances. In it, Hardman plays a Russo-like character to no avail, but Eastman is good as Rochon's disapproving mother-in-law.

There: I have now written more kind words about *Night 30* than anyone in history, and I stand by them. But let's not go crazy. Miscues abound. Anyone who's seen *Night 30* knows what they are, so I'll rush through them. While it's fun that Hinzman returns as Zombie #1 (his zombie gait remains perfect), no sixty-two-year-old man can stand in for his thirty-year-old self, and the physical contrast would baffle new viewers. (The older Hinzman is just as unrecognizable in a zombie-themed commercial he shot for Goodfella's Brick Oven Pizza.) Reverend Hicks's Anton LaVey-like shaved head and stylized goatee are wildly inappropriate for a 1960s Midwestern preacher. The juiced-up sound effects (punches, et cetera) go too far. The urge to wedge new music everywhere possible botches the silences Romero so assiduously employed. Most perplexing, instead of simply adding new scenes like Lucas, Russo and company felt the need to adhere to the 1968 running time, which meant cutting eighteen minutes of original footage. This cashiers huge amounts of character development. Helen, for instance, is reduced to a Judy-sized role. Russo often points out that the disc also features an uncut version of the original film restored to the best quality 1998 could offer. It's true—except for the fact that it has Licina's new score!

Suffice it to say, *Night 30* did not generate the $30,000,000 the proposal predicted. Everyone involved took a beating. Russo's reputation never recovered. In a one-off 2012 magazine called *Fangoria Legends Presents George A. Romero*, Rochon writes eloquently on her experience and brings a new wrinkle into the conversation: Her understanding was the eighteen minutes of new footage legally changed the film enough to establish a new copyright for Image Ten.

I traced this notion back to an April 11, 1997, note Karl Hardman faxed to Romero, Streiner, Russo, and Vini Bancalari, in which Hardman sums up a meeting he had with Bill Lustig, the grindhouse auteur behind films like *Maniac* (1980) and *Maniac Cop* (1988). By 1997, Lustig had become an important DVD producer (and, by the way, was the nephew of Raging Bull himself, Jake LaMotta). Wrote Hardman, "It is [Lustig's] feeling also that this new NOLD would render useless many old versions of the films based not only on the additions but also the fact that this new version would be pristine in every sense of the word."

In 1999, Romero himself referred to *Night 30* being made because of "the copyright issue being all messed up," before coming to a different conclusion in the *VideoScope* interview, insisting,

"That one wasn't about the protection of copyright or reestablishing copyright or anything. The remake was."

Rochon's chronicle of the film's reception is damning. She quotes one review: "This version is a raping of a great film. No scratch that, they raped it till it bled, knocked its teeth out then orally rapped [*sic*] it, and then used it as a toilet." The tone of this review is so repellent, I assumed it had been written by Harry Knowles of *Ain't It Cool News*. I was wrong, but stumbled upon Knowles's review, which is just as bad: "I feel as though I have just watched a personal family member gang-raped by a pack of super sodomites."

It makes me want to burn my horror card. If I have to line up behind blubbering man-children who believe they spiritually own *Night*, or line up behind Jack Russo and Debbie Rochon, I'll choose Russo and Rochon every time. I may not like everything Russo has done, but goddammit, he has the right to do it. As Rochon writes, "For all those who have directed insults, death threats, and glib anonymous hate on the internet toward [Russo], all I can say is, get over it. Hate the movie, hate the music, but there's no need to take it as far as some have."

This is what is important about *Night 30*. Not the film. But our entitled, over-the-top reaction to it.

In the *Night 30* booklet, Rochon asks Russo, "Now can you do me just one more favor? Can you put me in *Casablanca*?" A joke in 1998, but a legitimate concern in 2026. AI is rocketing us into a world of personalized entertainment capable of fulfilling individualized dreams, and the likely cost will be the communal fellowship that has always brought us together—what made me write this book, and what made you read it.

In fact, *Night* has already been a part of two such experiments, though fictionalized. "Bite Me," the October 30, 2009, episode of the NBC/CBS drama *Medium*, coproduced by Pittsburgh native Craig Sweeny, who reported he'd watched *Night* fifteen times (dilettante!), involves series protagonist Allison DuBois

(Patricia Arquette) dreaming her way into the Barbra role, complete with hot-rollered flip wig and black-and-white photography. Allison is cleverly edited into *Night*'s cemetery, farmhouse, and cellar scenes—all three sets nicely re-created—before the deviation of making her the asshole who won't let anyone into the cellar.

Twelve years later came "Night of the Living Late Show," the Season 3 finale of *Creepshow*, the anthology TV series inspired by Romero's film (disclosure: I wrote two segments of the series). A virtual reality inventor named Simon (Justin Long) creates the Immersopod, a tanning-bed-looking capsule that ports users into their favorite films. Eventually, Simon's jealous wife ports him into *Night*, right at the Last Supper. Simon asks of Ben and the gang, "Who are you people? Why are we in black-and-white?" Aided by tech beyond anything Russo had in 1998, director Greg Nicotero's integration is flawless.

While this episode is a different beast than *Night 30*, it's worthy to note no one got up in arms about it. We're all getting used to this sort of thing. In 2010, Mike Stanley created *Dead of Night*, a feature film edited together from *Night* and *Carnival of Souls*. No one's bothering Stanley, are they?

These remixes were hardly the first times *Night* had been used as a bridge between the comfortably fakey film horrors of the 1950s and the palpable horrors of the modern age. In the climax of Peter Straub's *Ghost Story* (1979), which I read in high school, young and innocent Peter is hurled *through* a movie screen playing *Night of the Living Dead*. Peter climbs back through the gash altered; *Night* has infected him with a modernism that makes him more of a "man"—never a good thing in Romero films. Peter's subsequent Ben-like act is to chop up the villains: "He took the axe from Don and brought it weakly, glancingly down, his hysteria and loathing spoiling the blow; then he felt suddenly stronger, as strong as a logger, felt as if he were glowing, filled with light, and raised it effortlessly, all the pain leaving him, and brought the axe down again; and again; and again; and then moved to Fenny."

Whether you're watching *Night* or *Night 30*, the Last Supper isn't a private affair. The film's next shot is of Ben staggering from the window through which he's watched the bacchanal. The buzzy pulse cuts off, leaving the lonely echo of omnipresent crickets, always the crickets—perhaps the most important stretch of audio replicated on Hardman and Eastman's sound effect cassette tape. (A shot checklist in Romero's script has an unchecked item called "insect studies," which suggests he wanted a shot of crickets to excuse the noise but never got it.)

Ben is all of us: He palms his stomach as if to heave before lowering himself into a chair. (Another Latent Image script binder lies by his feet.) The two young people—the symbolic hope of the future—are dead, reduced to nothing but gristle.

Romero lets the numb stillness extend for thirty-eight seconds, a choice baked into the script: "For a long time, we dwell on the scene, on the absolute dejectedness of the prisoners within the barricaded house." Russo and Romero were right to plan this break. We need it. We have been through a lot. The world is full of people who want to eat us alive.

01:15:35

WHAT KIND OF DISEASE

I KNEW WHO WANTED TO EAT ME ALIVE IN MIDDLE school: everyone.

Fairfield Community Middle School sits across Fillmore Avenue from Pence Elementary, where I spent seven more-or-less decent years. I'd served as a crossing guard on Fillmore in sixth grade, clad in a reflective sash to help littler kids who went home for lunch to cross the street. Mostly, though, I just stood on that corner staring at large kids enter and exit the middle school, which resembled (and still does) a military bunker.

Because the middle school was amid the process of transitioning from a junior high, my class spent only two years in the bunker instead of the standard three. A lucky break. I don't know if I could have survived three. My memories of the place are uniformly awful. FMS was a one-and-a-half-story square of hallways surrounding a courtyard you couldn't access—a loop of madness. And I do think kids went mad there. I recall two boys in particular bullied within inches of their lives. Today, they would have been on suicide watch. They both moved before high school.

Unlike them, I'd mastered the art of lying low. Though I'd grow an entire foot my freshman year of high school (and start Danman Productions, and find more friends, and be generally happy), at the time I was the shortest, skinniest boy in school.

In other words, a target. I took solace in classes, as everywhere else felt lawless. On October 22, 2024, my old friend Jay, now a counselor at FMS, gave me a tour of the building, my first time inside in thirty-five years. A nostalgia trip, in theory, but I shuddered throughout. There was my eighth-grade locker, somehow undented from the body slams. There was the locker room, the little metal cabinets like lab-rat cages, where I was body-checked with impunity. The worst place of all was the industrial arts room. In 2024, it looked shockingly small. In 1987, it was a jungle of sawdust and metal that was, through an unlucky draw, thickly populated with aggressors. I don't think I'll ever forgive the shop teacher for caring so little about what was going on amid the machines.

Each night, I worried about how to navigate the next day's gauntlet. Those first months, I cried all the time, hot whirlwinds of anxious fear. By the end of the first year, I'd hardened like a soldier in war: I let nothing make me cry, an unfortunate conditioning that exists to this day.

Not all of it was bullying.

In fall 1988, I was overwhelmed with dread about the first aid unit in health class. On the docket was a lesson on tourniquets. *Tourniquet*: The word was the emblem of my blood phobia, which was more a phobia of passing out in public and never living it down. Even worse was the sex ed unit, which notoriously included a film of a live birth. (I swear the film had the unlikely title of *Heidi in Switzerland* but I can't verify that.) I kept my ear to the ground so I might fake sick on the right day. I failed, was forced to see the film, and managed to get on top of the fear, which was often the case.

One worry was always replaced by another. The driver's ed slideshow of gory car crash photos. The day in science class we had to prick our fingers to find our blood type. The infamous fetal pig dissection.

Nauseated by blood in the daytime, I mainlined bloody movies at night. It doesn't take a psychology degree to figure it out.

Waving the flag of horror gave me a smidgen of confidence. I could honestly say I'd seen the nastiest shit Adventureland Video had to offer, a feat of bravery even the guys giving me headlocks couldn't claim. (Even Adventureland's eventual competitor, a local grocery store, stocked grisly titles like *Faces of Death*—a quasi-snuff film propped right alongside the bananas and marshmallows.)

My VCR was a trainer, toughening me up. For every film that sent me dry-heaving over the toilet (*Halloween III: Season of the Witch, The Stuff, Deadly Friend*—there was no rhyme or reason), there was another that made me feel like part of an exclusive club that was happy to have me (*House, The Lost Boys, Poltergeist, Christine*). I watched them until I understood how they worked, then set about replicating them—in goofy Danman Productions, yes, but more seriously in my fiction.

In 2018, the horror apparel company Fright Rags (believe it or not, I haven't purchased *every* iteration of *Night* shirts they sell) produced a clever six-minute short called *Dead Neighbors,* which imagines a roughly ten-year-old George Romero whose daily anxieties (like running across a cemetery worker played by Russ Streiner) inspire his future creations. As a George Romero story, pure invention. By accident, however, it's dang close to the Daniel Kraus story.

The lighthouse of *Night of the Living Dead* always waited for me at home. At school, I made do with reading Stephen King and Clive Barker between classes. Barker, by the way—ultimately more of an influence on me than King—cowrote with Steve Niles the greatest of all *Night*-related comics, the two-issue *Night of the Living Dead: London* (with art by Carlos Kastro). *London* returns to "Anubis," Romero's original allegorical short story, by focusing on Britain's Royal Family, ensconced "Masque of the Red Death"-style inside Buckingham Palace and obsessed with perpetuating their bloodline at all costs.

In March 1988, I bought an odd item at Kramer's Books, a black hardcover sleeve you slipped over paperbacks. I didn't realize what effect it had on books like Barker's *Weaveworld* and King's *It* until a classmate asked if I was carrying around a Bible. I said no. But that was a lie, wasn't it?

Helen Cooper's trauma is different from mine, but the numb way she enters the dining room feels familiar. She's past crying over the bullying Harry or the loss of Tom and Judy; only weariness remains. Her first words give us a time check: "Isn't it three o'clock yet? There's supposed to be another broadcast at three o'clock," to which Harry, holding an ice pack to his face, mutters, "Ten minutes." Three hours and eight minutes have passed since we saw the clocks behind Chuck Craig. (Helen wouldn't need to ask if she owned a watch with her own face on it—a spectacularly rare item Marilyn Eastman and Karl Hardman produced and sold in the 1990s.)

Barbra natters nonsense about how it's time to leave, which Ben cuts off with a loud *crick-crack* of the Winchester. I keep thinking the gorgeous shot that follows will show up on a Fright Rags shirt: Ben centered on a chair, posture busted but not broken thanks to an outstretched right leg. The rifle barrel counterweights the other side of his body. The pose exudes the ragged determination of the Marine Corps Memorial of the Iwo Jima flag-raising. The room vortexes to a point behind Ben, half the backdrop a white wall, half a black door, a visualization of his competing impulses of altruistic protection and self-serving vengeance.

Ben's got life in him yet. He scoots the Air Step ammo box between his legs like a basketball dribbler. He asks Helen if Willard is really the nearest town. (Oddly, in *Night 90*, Savini replaces the fictional Willard with the real-life Zelienople, a half hour north of Pittsburgh.) Helen supplies all the Cooper family backstory we're going to get by saying she has no idea—they were just trying to get to a motel. Am I wrong that her sleepy demeanor is sexy toward Ben? It's hard to resist the idea of them flirting with cuckold Harry sitting right there.

Indeed, Ben quickly takes over the daddy role. In a scene

composed on the back of page 81 of Romero's shooting script, Harry gripes that he can't carry his girl all the way to the Cooper car (which, you recall, is overturned). Ben says he'll carry Karen. This spurs Harry to reveal what happened to Karen: a zombie bit her. Ben fails to lighten the mood by shouting, "Who knows what kind of disease those things carry?"

Barely keeping up per usual, Barb sweetly asserts that Johnny has the keys. This time, it cuts through. Ben kneels before Barbra, as he's done before, and questions her about the goddamn LeMans. Ben and Barb are a comedy duo by now, their every interaction a delight. "You won't be able to start it," Barbra singsongs—and, indeed, a video exists of Judith O'Dea at the 2013 Living Dead Festival, in the Evans City Cemetery, being handed the keys to a suspension-lifted LeMans—way cooler than Johnny's—and having, you guessed it, trouble getting it started. Ben, the Jack Lemmon to Barb's Walter Matthau, replies, "Yeah, yeah, I know. But where is it?"

The film underplays this moment—a moment that might save them all. Turning over the Cooper car was a nonstarter. But Johnny's car? It's just sitting on the cemetery path. The way Ben pushes here suggests he knows how to hot-wire. If that's the case, at least Ben could get to the car, start it, and find help. Problem solved! Movie over!

Unfortunately, a noise outside grabs everyone's attention. There's no telling what the noise was intended to be, but in the final film, it's just a zombie moan, which shouldn't bother our group at this point. Romero cuts outside to a composition we have seen before, the shot with Nude Ghoul, now joined by a zombie wrestling a snake. There's no good reason for this shot to appear, which supports my hunch that something got cut. My best guess, based on the script, is that this is where the first zombies began to break into the house. (Spoiler.)

Ben and Harry race to the window. This piece of film, even in the Criterion version, has a vicious scrape down the center, a piece of damage I have come to love. (This is also where the *Night of Anubis* mass zombie shot originally went.) Ben switches on the TV, the LeMans plan tragically forgotten.

Chuck Craig's back on the air, talking about radiation that could grow the zombie hordes: "So long as this situation remains, government spokesmen warn that dead bodies will continue to be transformed into the flesh-eating ghouls."

Fans like to recite the fact that *Night* never calls the undead "zombies," but rather "ghouls." (Stephen King, an O.G. *Night* fan, got in on the fun in *The Shining*, with Jack Torrance quipping, "A dead woman who's alive again, zombie, undead, ghoul, you pick your term.") These fans aren't wrong, but it's easy to go overboard. The word "ghoul" isn't heard until now, seventeen minutes from the end of the film. Evidence shows Romero and Russo lost no sleep over terminology. By the time I first saw *Night* circa 1980, "ghoul" had become a catch-all to refer to any Halloweenish figure. Someone might open their door to trick-or-treaters, gaze at a coterie of vampires, witches, and aliens, and say, "What a spooky-looking group of ghouls!"

In Romero's formative years, the term had a different connotation. Like a lot of 1950s kids, he loved EC comics like *Tales from the Crypt*, *The Vault of Horror*, and *The Haunt of Fear*. (Romero discussed his EC fandom in Bravo's 2014 miniseries *100 Scariest Movie Moments*, which you can skip, but do watch the online outtake in which Romero is interrupted by a runaway ferret.) In college, I borrowed hardbound reprints of these comics from the Iowa City Public Library and, in the piecemeal pattern of anyone living paycheck-to-paycheck, acquired my own copies over the next several years. So I can say with authority that "ghouls" (from the Arabic *ghūl*) pop up all over these comics and have a specific definition: a person who digs up a corpse and eats it. Unpleasant!

Romero's EC enthusiasms paid off with his Stephen King collab *Creepshow*. I should fess up that *Creepshow* is my second-favorite movie of all time. I first encountered it via the 1982 graphic novel adaptation, which I found at my public library. I brought it home and hid it from my parents. My grandparents on my mom's side were visiting from Chicago, and Grandpa Harold spotted the gory thing. To my alarm, then delight, he began performing it aloud. I still remember his tickled reading of a scandalous line ("Cassandra, darling . . . how can such a beautiful woman be such an UTTER TURD?") and the subsequent rush of bonhomie and acceptance.

Grandpa Harold was my favorite grandparent, the lot of whom would be dead by the time I was twenty-seven. He appreciated my interest in horror even more than my mother. He'd had a decent job at a Johnson & Johnson diaper factory before open-heart surgery at age forty-six rendered him unable to work, putting the moneymaking onus on his wife, Dorothy, a warehouse worker. After losing a leg to diabetic complications, Harold died of lung cancer on March 9, 1988, when he was fifty-five and I was thirteen. The next time we visited Grandma Dorothy in the trailer she'd moved into, she gifted me my own copy of the graphic novel. Even today, the *Creepshow* book *feels* like Grandpa Harold—his unconditional support for my deviant pursuits translated into Bernie Wrightson drawings of severed heads, killer weeds, and body-invading cockroaches.

My first glimpse of the movie came on July 11, 1987, at age twelve, when it played on Cinemax on my neighbor's TV. It was the scene where the grad student gets eaten by Fluffy. Never in my life had I seen so much blood. I cited this—and generally felt like I'd come full circle with the film—on October 16, 2024, when I cohosted a screening of *Creepshow* with Bev Vincent at Houston's River Oaks Theatre.

Creepshow doesn't include *ghouls* (the corpse-eating kind), but it's brimming with *ghouls* (the oogie-boogie kind). I deal a lot with this terminology in *The Living Dead,* so I won't belabor the subject here. Instead, a mea culpa. In the novel's author's note, I repeat the factoid about *Night*'s use of "ghoul" and report how Romero didn't use "zombie" until 1978 in *Dawn of the Dead.* I wasn't wrong, but also didn't realize how quickly the Z-word got applied to *Night*'s undead. Very quickly, it turns out. A July

2, 1968, article about *Night* in the *News-Tribune* of Beaver Falls, Pennsylvania, is headlined, "Zombies, Ghoul Friends Have a Ball at Gass House."

There you have it. Three months *before* the film came out, people were already calling the ghouls zombies. It all tracks. At least two other horror films involving zombies of some type came out in 1968: *The Astro-Zombies* and *The Mad Doctor of Blood Island,* though only Ted V. Mikels's *Astro-Zombies* bears any resemblance to Image Ten's take with its Frankenstein-like Quasi-man. ("Quasi-man?" a character asks. "You mean a sort of zombie?") It was the world, not Romero, that first conflated *Night*'s hungry shamblers with the poisoned, enslaved zombis of Haitian Vodou lore.

For Ben and the others, it's old-school flesh-eaters they picture when Craig starts talking ghouls. The reaction close-ups of each character mirror the first time we did this round-robin, the biggest difference being the state of Harry's cheek. Rather than the dark smudge Barbra sports, Harry's glossy, pitted bruise looks more like his skin has been burnt. Since Hardman's the actor here, it stands to reason Eastman did this makeup.

It's too much. Yet I love it. Moments ago, Ben asked, *Who knows what kind of disease those things carry?* Harry's makeup asks a different question: What kind of disease do we *all* carry? It looks as if the rot inside Harry has begun to fester through his flesh.

01:18:26 'CAUSE I'M A MAN

"Our news cameras have just returned from covering such a search-and-destroy operation against the ghouls, this one conducted by Sheriff Conan McClelland in Butler County, Pennsylvania," Chuck Craig says. "So now let's go to that film report."

Craig's hermetic news desk gives way to 16mm footage of a posse of nineteen white men (many of them repeat players, including, well, Chuck Craig, who shows up in a fifth role, tying

Jack Russo and Jack Givens for the record), many of them wearing flannel and toting guns. Nineteen—that's more extras than Image Ten ever scared up for zombies. Pittsburgh's WIIC TV11 News filmed a news story on *Night* that day and, besides a precious fifteen seconds of young George A. Romero directing, their two minutes and forty-eight seconds of film show way more than twenty people, including a bevy of police officers donating their time to the local oddity.

To put this into context: If I could reliably get this many people for book events, well, I'd do a lot more book events. So why the impressive turnout? Part of it was because the sequence was shot on a weekend day. But there's another part. Most of these extras came from the steel town of Clairton, both the setting and one of the filming locales for Michael Cimino's *The Deer Hunter* (a film set in 1968). I wonder how many people simply got excited about walking around Evans City with firearms. There had been, after all, glimpses of a Black man being driven back to Duquesne most nights, a sight that must have agitated certain locals. In the Ferrante tapes, Jones recalls a teen approaching his car with a tire iron. "The paradox and the irony of that," Jones mused. "I had been walking around brandishing a tire iron at ghouls all day."

A never-published behind-the-scenes photo of the scene shows a detail hidden from view in the film: a wooden sign stabbed into the grass and slashed with insistent white paint: PRIVATE PROPERTY CAMPERS ONLY STAY OUT. "Campers"—a handily harmless word to brandish against anyone who didn't look or act like you.

Speaking of Black men in Evans City: On a 2018 episode of *Mike Judge Presents: Tales from the Tour Bus*, Funkadelic tells a story with such casual authority that I can't help but believe it. While driving to a Pittsburgh gig ("high as hell" on LSD, George Clinton admits), bassist Billy Nelson decided to take a shortcut. One wrong turn later, they were surrounded by *Night*'s zombies. "We didn't know what the fuck was happening," Clinton says. "They scared me so bad I was peeing in my pants and screaming." *Night* has intersected with other popular music too. In the video for Run the Jewels's "Never Look Back," director John Hillcoat impressively cuts Killer Mike and El-P into *Night* footage, roping in an impressive Johnny doppelgänger as well as zombie cameos by Norman Reedus and Greg Nicotero. And then, of course, there's "Night of the Living Dead" (1981) from punk legends the Misfits, a band so enamored with Romero they gave him two songs for *Bruiser* in exchange for Romero directing the video for their song "Scream."

Nothing in *Night*'s screenplay suggests its writers intended Sheriff McClelland's posse as social critique. But that's to be expected; most critiques came through the director's sensitivities and instincts. The second this ad hoc militia hits the screen, you feel the whole zombie universe, begun only seventy-eight minutes ago, flop over. The astonishing thing is that it didn't take some new voice twenty years down the road to turn the zombie film on its head. It happens in the very same film that spawned the genre.

These men behave nothing like those in the farmhouse. Protected by their numbers, firearms, flannels, and color of their skin, they swagger about, eager to search, antsy to destroy. I've stood on this patch of grass at the same time of year the film was shot and can still smell the steel of the Connoquenessing Creek bridge, feel the sun wrap around my arms like cellophane, taste the road gravel, and most of all, hear the bugs scream in echelons. It's both quiet and loud on Ash Stop Road in the summer, a nerviness that makes you want to *do* something. Now add guns. (That said, at least one posse extra had a sensitive soul: Harry Zinzella, a contemplative sort whose 1982 self-published book of poetry was titled *Distant Skies: Exercises in Meditative Comprehension*.)

George "Kuss" Kosana plays Sheriff McClelland. (A nicer name than "Sheriff Suck," a character from an early movie concept that fed into *Night*.) I would have bet my life that Kosana was another of *Night*'s uncannily good non-actors. Instead, Kosana's name is the fourth to show up in the film's opening credits. He was *Night*'s production manager, which, on a production like this, meant doing everything, right down to donating his taxidermy (of animals he slew himself) to the set. Image Ten could have flown in Sir Laurence Olivier and he couldn't have bested Kosana's mumbly, half-improvised Sheriff McClelland.

For two years after college, I worked as a videographer for an NBC affiliate in North Carolina, where I routinely cheated death driving through hurricanes, doing live shots at murder scenes, and recording B-roll inside a fire-damaged building that collapsed while I was inside it. Countless times I videotaped law enforcement personnel on manhunts or missing-person searches while my reporter colleague asked questions. This is how sheriffs often interacted with the media, not with hostility but only giving them half their attention. While talking to a newsman (who calls him "Chief McClelland," though "chief" is a different job than "sheriff"), McClelland casually shouts directions off-camera, ominous stuff like "Hey, Cas, put that thing all the way in the fire!" (*Cas* is a nod to an extra who couldn't make it that day, Kosana's pal Casper Casiraro.)

McClelland's the most competent and capable character since Ben. He wears a jacket and tie but with the collar loosened in the style of a working-class hero. Across his chest, a bandolier of bullets. In his hat band, three wrapped cigars, ready for celebratory smoking. Yet instead of feeling Ben-like relief when McClelland barks orders in his country twang, I feel despair. McClelland might fix the ghoul problem. But fix it into what?

The McClelland interview is shot in daytime. Given how long it would take this piece of film to be developed, edited, and broadcast, his posse action had to take place *before* Barbra's cemetery attack. Based on everything we know, here's the timeline:

Two days ago (Friday) a family of seven is slain by zombies in Gulfport, Louisiana.

This morning (Sunday), a morgue body starts twisting its trunk.

Tom and Judy hear the news en route to the swimming hole and head to Seven Pines.

The Cooper family truckster is overturned, and they, too, go to the house.

The McClelland posse is unleashed.

Zombie #1 attacks Barbra.

This means McClelland's interview takes place mere hours after the zombie situation was understood. And already he's calling our dead neighbors *things*?

McClelland and his militia are too ready, too raring to go. I have no doubt this is how some people would react—and not only in 1968. On August 25, 2020, seventeen-year-old Kyle Rittenhouse took it upon himself to grab his AR-15–style rifle and join a self-deputized citizen militia to "protect" Kenosha, Wisconsin (even though he lived in Antioch, Illinois), against civil unrest following the police shooting of a twenty-nine-year-old Black man named Jacob Blake. Rittenhouse shot three men, killing two. He was acquitted, but anyone with an ounce of common sense can intuit how excited Rittenhouse was to be patrolling the streets, which he had no right to be doing. Right-wing media turned Rittenhouse into another working-class hero. Just add a hat band of cigars.

That's what I see in this scene: Sheriff Kyle Rittenhouse marshaling a force of Rittenhouses. Footage of the actual Rittenhouse shows him proudly striding down the center of a street, and, hours earlier, happily giving interviews. He wanted to be *seen*. So did eighteen-year-old Dick Heckard, who got wind of *Night*'s posse scene from his dad (who supplied the production with one of Ben's trucks). Heckard showed up in a black cowboy hat with half of the rim pinned up, inspired by the slouch hat Christopher George wore in the TV show *The Rat Patrol*. If this movie became big, he wanted to be sure people noticed him. It worked. Once you notice this black-hatted bandit, you can't stop. I've spotted him in no fewer than twelve shots.

Things don't change as much as you'd hope. In 1972, Romero returned to Evans City to film *The Crazies*. When a scene called for actor Lloyd Hollar to undress, the whole goddamn city council objected so fiercely Romero had to lawyer up. In the Felsher tapes, Romero adopts a redneck twang to imitate them: "We don't want no Black man strippin' down naked in front of our women!" Jump to 2010, when Tony Todd, star of *Night 90*, told the Reel Horror podcast of his experience in Savini's remake: "I'm surrounded by a bunch of zombies who were rednecks in another life . . . I knew it was going to be fucked up because they were all waiting to try to tackle me for real. Some of the tension you see is real, genuine stuff."

With the easy jocularity of a pre-murder Rittenhouse, McClelland boasts that he and his men have already harvested nineteen ghouls: "We came over and beat 'em off, blasted 'em down." He seems incapable of comprehending anyone who *wouldn't* enjoy this. "Beat 'em or burn 'em," he says. "They go up pretty easy."

In two swift minutes, Romero proposes the whiplash notion that the zombies are not the bad guys. It wasn't unheard of; viewers sympathized with Karloff's Frankenstein monster and Chaney Jr.'s Wolf Man. But those were pictures from another era. The 1960s, with its rafts of Poe adaptations, Hammer films, science-gone-wrong creature features, and prestige works like *Rosemary's Baby*, kept its monsters monstrous. The technological trappings of McClelland's militia emphasize the naturalness of the undead. Zombies only do what is in their nature to do, no different from a deer, or a boar, or any of the other animals taxidermied on the farmhouse walls.

Romero seized upon these ideas more forcefully twenty minutes into *Dawn of the Dead*, abruptly abandoning our protagonists to spend a few minutes with a boisterous batch of gun-wielding country folk swilling coffee, taking group photos, and cracking open cans of Iron City—only pausing the party to sniper encroaching zombies. The scene is set to a country-western song titled "'Cause I'm a Man." (This song hews close to the "I'm a Natural Man" jingle that shows up in commercials Romero directed for Duke Beer in 1967.)

Twelve years after he uttered it, Sheriff McClelland's "beat 'em or burn 'em" line inspired *Dawn of the Night of the Dead . . . the*

Musical (1980), a five-minute short by University of Bridgeport student Dan Karlok that would have been lost to time if Karlok hadn't somehow sold it to the TV show *Night Flight*, where it periodically popped up to fill time slots. It imagines McClelland's posse in choreographed harmony with zombies as they sing a driving chorus, "Beat 'em / or burn 'em! / beat 'em / or burn 'em!" (The main zombie is played by Howard Sherman—today a Manhattan arts administrator—not to be confused with Howard Sherman, who played Bub in Romero's *Day of the Dead*, but whose given name is actually Sherman Howard, if that makes any sense.)

The short, if you can find it, nicely defuses the discomfort of the actual scene.

Out of obligation, I'll mention Kosana's most iconic improvised line. To the question of "Are they slow-moving, chief?," McClelland replies, "Yeah, they're dead. They're *all* messed up." I get why it's funny, but it's never made me smile, and now I understand why. Compared to the raw hurt bleeding from the farmhouse contingent, McClelland's aloofness is loathsome. Brilliant filmmaking, though. The well-scrubbed, well-dressed, well-fed folks talking safely from inside the TV have no idea how the other half lives, nor do they seem to care.

01:20:12

YOU WERE A SUPERSTAR

THE LAST THING THE REPORTER WANTS TO KNOW from McClelland is if the zombie roundup will wrap within twenty-four hours. The sheriff declines to say, though I read this less as humility than a reticence to imagine the fun ending so quickly. He concludes by saying the posse is "working their way" (read: shooting their way) toward Willard. In Roy Frumkes's seminal Romero doc *Document of the Dead* (1985), Judith O'Dea reveals that her own father was in that posse, a claim backed up by a typewritten page in Romero's archives titled *ADDRESSES OF POSSE AND GHOUL MEMBERS*, which includes a "Mr. Stanley J. O'Dea." If you're like me, you wonder the worst. Did Daddy have to put down his little girl?

In a fresh shot with Sheriff McClelland back to work behind him, the reporter signs off, "This is Bill Cardille, WIIC-TV 11 News." That's *Bill Car-DILL*, the phonetically irresistible name of an irresistible fellow—a real one too.

His nickname, as reproduced in *Night's* closing credits, is even more fun to say: Bill "Chilly Billy" Cardille. There are a lot of ways one could describe what Cardille meant to Pittsburgh in 1967, but the simplest way to put it was that he was a local celebrity. Cardille and his velvety buzz of a voice began broadcasting in college and never quit. His list of on-air activities is head-spinning. He hosted spelling bees. He did live commercials during Cleveland Indians games. He read the news on WIIC, where he was the first voice aired when the channel hit the air in 1957. He deejayed dance music programs. He hosted a kiddie show called *Tip Top Time*. He did weekly radiocasts on psychic phenomena. He headed up twenty-four-hour muscular dystrophy telethons. He did play-by-plays for football, baseball, and basketball. His ringside commentary for the regional *Studio Wrestling* circuit was so renowned Vince McMahon Sr. drafted him into what was then the WWF. Many photos exist of the well-coiffed Cardille between shirtless, greased-up musclemen. Wrestling was big business in the 'Burgh: Romero once wrote, directed, and costarred in a fun twenty-two-minute TV pilot called *Iron City Asskickers*.

No genre celebrates its own like horror, and Chilly Billy is best remembered as the host of *Chiller Theater*, which aired at 11:00 p.m. on WIIC/WPXI from 1965 to 1983 (after which he went on to be a morning weatherman and host a nightly bingo program—this guy!). Chilly Billy's persona was Johnny Carson meets Richard Dawson, dapper and handsome, fast with a double entendre, willing to wear any number of (literal) hats to service whatever chucklebutt the skits required.

I wish I could have seen it in real time. All I had in late-eighties/early-nineties Iowa was the USA Network, which carried two programs that featured horror films: *Night Flight* and *Saturday Nightmares*, the latter of which ran for a decade, 1984 to 1994. Not bad, but a far cry from *Chiller Theater*'s nineteen-year spree. Cardille's show was so popular that Channel 11 was the last NBC affiliate in America to air *Saturday Night Live* while it was, you know, live. Such was the dedication of the Pittsburgh faithful.

The faith went both ways. When Cardille heard the first feature film to be mounted in his fair city was called *Night of the Flesh Eaters*, he wanted to support it. It helped he'd worked before with some of the creators. Marilyn Eastman had appeared on *Chiller Theater* (sporting a widow's peak, branched eyebrows, long black fingernails, and black gown) to advertise Commonwealth Heating and Plumbing as "Commoneltha"—Dracula's girlfriend, or so went Karl Hardman's script.

Cardille began hyping Image Ten's production in 1967, which greased the wheels of investors and piqued the interest of lookyloos who ended up as extras. But it was Cardille himself who excited the filmmakers. They were fans. They never dreamt their horror film would be added to the Library of Congress National Film Registry (which it was in 1999, alongside *The Ten Commandments,* which must have blown Romero's mind). What they dreamed of was their film on *Chiller Theater.*

Night's first known TV broadcast was on January 1, 1972, as part of a Creature Features double feature with *House of Horrors* on San Francisco's KTVU, hosted by Bob Wilkins. A few years later, *Night* had its late-night network premiere as part of ABC's "Haunted Hollywood" series, hosted by John Carradine. Many *Night* insiders insist it's this legal syndication, offered in 1971 as part of a Teleworld package, that brought true fame to the film, not the copyright blunder. Regardless, it took twenty-six years—October 25, 1998, to be exact, long after *Night* had become the most frequently horror-hosted film of all time—for Image Ten's most ardent wish to come true.

That was the night Chilly Billy returned for a "One More Time" special fifteen years after the show's end—and thirty years after *Night* premiered. Cardille, gray-haired, bearded, and debonair as ever, is joined at each break by fifty-eight-year-old Romero in a seaweed-colored corduroy blazer and the gigantic black glasses that were becoming his trademark. It is unknown how many times the two met after the taping, if at all. Cardille died on July 21, 2016, from liver cancer, and Romero died almost exactly a year later from lung cancer.

"You were a superstar to all of us," Romero gushes to Cardille with that raspy rise in volume he used to hide softer feelings. "I used to watch *Chiller* faithfully."

At that moment, Romero was mired in the most frustrating seven years of his career. Though he'd been churning out scripts, he hadn't directed since 1991. In the friendly confines of Chilly Billy's castle, however, Romero is happy. He's glowing. He's accomplished everything he ever wanted.

01:20:42 HAVEN'T YOU HAD ENOUGH?

So much time, energy, and anger has been spent sparring over the 7S363 radio and the 17T5E television—the two strings tying our survivors to the outside world. Both strings are cut in an instant as the power goes out. Ben, Helen, and Harry glance about in shock (Barbra, presumably, is unmoved), as if the house itself has vanished.

Until now, the filmmakers have enjoyed a license to flood their actors with lights. Ben made a point of turning on every light he could. From this point onward, the presumed source of light is the moon raking through gaps in the boarded windows. Light and shadow become subjective art, and from a production perspective, more challenging.

"Lighting is a feeling," lighting supervisor Joseph Unitas declares in *Autopsy of the Dead*, and the instant feeling here is claustrophobia. Gone are the rooms in which characters paced and gestured. Darkness overrides like soil poured into caskets. Shards of light reveal each survivor's panicked, searching eyes.

Ben goes into the cellar to seek out the fuse box. It's the first time he has ventured into the lair of his nemesis, but we don't follow. We stay with Harry as he vultures over Helen on the sofa. His mind isn't on the electricity, the darkness, the isolation, or even the zombies.

"I have to get that gun," he hisses.

The negative shape between the married couple is puzzle-pieced by the slumped Barbra. Her limp form feels like the ghost of feminine obedience that Helen Cooper has at last discarded.

"Haven't you had enough?" Helen snarls—and at this, Barb perks up. Great instinct by O'Dea: Maybe there's something Barbra can learn from Helen. (The novelization adds a line that weakens Helen's motivation to self-protection: "He'd kill us both.")

The house lights must have served as a fire-like deterrent: The zombies, habitual loiterers, begin to mobilize. Outside, a hand picks up a rock. We know it's a zombie hand from the ragged gash between two fingers. The hand belongs to farmhouse neighbor and carpenter Philip Smith, who, unlike wife Ella Mae, was reluctant to participate in the film being shot next door, even for twenty-five bucks a night. Ella Mae, delighted by their involvement until her recent death, kept Philip's hand-wound makeup preserved in a plastic bag, which, frankly, looks like someone sneezed into it. Ella Mae's casual snapshots are some of the only color photos that exist from the production, and on a 1988 episode of Cinemax's "Max Zooms In," she recited a poem she'd written about being drafted onto the set, which concludes:

We'll always remember and never regret
No matter how old and feeble we get
The time we spent acting like silly old fools
And got in the movies resembling two ghouls.

A second zombie (Jack Givens, one of the reporters in the D.C. scene) picks up the table leg of Ben's former torch and clubs it against the front door. The reaction shots of the gang (Ben has rejoined them) grow tighter, sweatier. The porch fills with ghouls. One of them is John Kirch, at age fifteen the production's youngest zombie. He was also the most passionate. After seeing the local hype (probably from Chilly Billy), Kirch called Hardman Associates for weeks angling for a part—and his elation never let up. Before his death in 2021, Kirch attended every convention he could, was universally adored, and created the video short "I Was a Teenage Zombie," in which he explains how he parlayed three seconds of recognizable screen time into schoolyard fame, complete with 8mm footage of him and his friends re-creating his big scene. From the stage of *Night*'s fiftieth anniversary screening, Kirch said, "My fondest memories of my high school years involve murder and cannibalism."

Inside, our foursome is frozen with fear—until Philip Smith's bloody hand lobs his rock through a window. Ben rushes forward to brace the rattling boards with his rifle. Helen follows suit, using her body weight to keep the front door shut. The amount of arms sprouting through the gaps at Ben and Helen make it feel like the house is being coated by a thousand-handed blob.

Psychologically, it's the most profound image in the film, one Image Ten appreciated on instinct. The earliest promo items the gang made were bookmark-sized vinyl banners reading COMING! THE NIGHT OF THE FLESH EATERS along with a cartoon image of a boarded-up window. You could draw the image today in a game of Pictionary, and your teammates would know which movie you were portraying.

Hands coming from walls are a mainstay of dreams. My earliest remembered dream (I was probably three, so it might be my earliest memory, period) attests to this. It's night. I'm walking in footed pajamas back from the bathroom and see two long, pale arms reaching from the ceiling toward the crib of my baby sister. Each hand, absurdly but terrifyingly, is holding a bottle of lotion that pours onto the baby's belly in a sloppy pile. This dream scared me so badly that, the following night, I had a dream in which the previous night's dream played on televisions stacked all over my room. Hiding under the bed didn't help: The TVs were there too.

Psychoanalytic takes on disembodied arms run the gamut from Freud's sexual slant (valid here, as both Helen and Barbra are about to be groped by anonymous men) to notions that equate arms with social relationships. Not to play armchair shrink, but I'd say *Night*'s clawing hands are shredding the social web that binds us.

Then there's this. On the LaserDisc commentary, Keith Wayne mentions a college student he sat next to on the flight in. She'd recently watched *Night* in a film class, and her professor had compared the hands reaching for Ben to images from D. W. Griffith's *Birth of a Nation*. The commentary gang laughs this off, and I didn't give it much credence either, until I, kicking and screaming, rewatched the famously racist 1915 epic. The echoes are overwhelming: Consider me #TeamFilmProfessor. In *Birth*, mobs of cartoonishly violent Black men assault two different homes barricaded by (as the title card calls them) "helpless whites." Repeatedly, arms shoot through boarded windows. Most of the Black men are played by white actors in blackface that turns them into uncanny boogeymen—the kind of soot-black makeup David Lynch layered on the woodsmen in *Twin Peaks: The Return* (2017).

Lots of artists in touch with their subconscious play with similar imagery. Think of the countless bodiless arms of Bosch or Dalí. The cover of Ultravox's "The Thin Wall" single. The music video for Taylor Swift's "The Man." The Helping Hands from Jim Henson's *Labyrinth*. Unsettling scenes in Roman Polanski's *Repulsion* and Jean Cocteau's *La belle et la bête*. Even Dan Brown's *Da Vinci Code* posits that there's a disembodied, dagger-wielding hand in Da Vinci's *Last Supper* (not to be confused with *Night*'s Last Supper). Finally, there's the prologue to Romero's *Day of the Dead*, in which at least twenty-six hands simultaneously explode from a brick wall toward Lori Cardille—before it's revealed to be a dream.

Consciously, the focus of this scene is Harry. While the Bluestone-Cadkin cue "Heavy Dramatic (CB-54)" blares, our Father of the Year stands up, lips fretting like they did when he hemmed over helping Ben barricade the door. Ben shouts, "Get over here, man!" but the last time Harry helped, Ben beat the crap out of him.

Ben has to toss the rifle to the ground to better hold back the onslaught. The Winchester 1894 lies on the Persian rug in a way identical to that of the tire iron Ben dropped at 00:17:56. That's two lethal items we have watched fall to the rug. Remember this—a third fall is coming, the fall of the most lethal weapon of all.

Harry darts like the Lizard he's always been, snatches up the rifle, and lurches to where he can level the weapon at Ben. "You wanna stay up here now?" he challenges. He tells Helen to get in the cellar. When she stays pressed to the front door, Harry tells her again. In this critical instant, Helen refuses to turn her back on the larger world, even if it means death to her family unit. It's a heroic turn, but one that *Night,* in its nihilism, refuses to reward.

Quite the opposite. With Harry's attention on Helen, Ben javelins the board he's been using to quell the horde right at Harry. It knocks the rifle to the side and allows Ben to lunge forward and fight the older man for the gun. During one take, the board struck Romero, which rattled the peacenik Jones so badly he embraced Romero and needed an hour to recuperate.

We watch them struggle. (The Criterion dailies include a funny take in which Kyra Schon is seen happily watching from the sofa.) We are thrilled and hopeful the right man will prevail. But in this petty battle over the boom-stick, the whole game is lost. No one's protecting the broken window.

Nothing that happened in this house meant anything at all.

Ben gets the rifle. Of course he does. He's younger, stronger, and from a generation that has always felt like people were tearing through walls to get them. Harry rises from his puny crumple and regards Ben with naked fear. No matter how many times I watch this sequence, I never get the feeling Harry intended to shoot Ben, as long as he got his way. But Ben knows he'll never get *his* way, not in this country, not so long as people like Harry give the orders.

In the first line of the film, Barbra spoke of wanting a "time change."

She had no idea what she was asking for.

That change has come.

In the script, Ben's shooting of Harry is accidental. *Accidental.* I understand it from the perspective of screenwriters still months away from filming. Their message might have been that accidents happen in war (an estimated three thousand Americans died from friendly fire in Vietnam). But the reality of a film set crowded with people of flesh and blood and skin—never forget skin—rarely matches that of the black-and-white page.

There is no evidence Duane Jones insisted that Ben kill Harry in cold blood. But it feels like something he might request. Consider again what Jones told Romero about the prospect of Barbra saving Ben: *The Black community would rather see me dead than saved.*

He knew what the Black community needed to see.

Ben takes a six-second pause. Amid a zombie blitz, it's an epic length of time. Then, with the detachment of an exterminator stomping a roach, Ben makes good on the promise of his earlier beatdown and shoots Harry below the heart. In Romero's shooting script, this monumental moment is conveyed with two scrawled words: *Blasts Harry.* The only emotion we see from Ben comes from an unused take in the dailies, in which Duane Jones instantly plants a hand over his right ear, in pain from the thunderous blank.

01:23:05 PLEASE GUIDE US ALL

It's not terribly realistic that Harry surges *toward* Ben after being shot in the torso, but it allows for some fun theatrics as he collides with the piano. Harry wraps his arms around a coat tree as if, in this moment of mortality, he needs the embrace of someone—Helen probably, if it weren't far too late. As his arms slip from the piano top, his right hand swipes a doily to the floor, a detail fraught for reasons I've discussed ad nauseam. The refined niceties epitomized by the doilies are revealed to be the cheap trash they always were.

Ben stands inside a wisp of smoke (cigarette smoke Russ Streiner blew for effect). Watching Harry suffer, Ben looks lifeless. Not alive, not dead, not undead, but somewhere close. *Night,* we realize, isn't about zombies at all. It's about ghosts. Of the past, of enslavement, of rage, of violence whitewashed in time for new violence to create new ghosts to haunt new killers. Ben beats Harry, but for what ultimate good? His cold-blooded murder damns Ben just the same.

From a character perspective, Helen's reaction to Harry's death is even more fascinating. Her lack of a reaction, I should say. In the script, Helen runs for the cellar without being told. Eastman's portrayal was too strong to make that a viable option. Helen doesn't even blink at Harry's death before going back to watching the door planks over her head splinter. Soon four hands reach for her, paw her neck, face, and hair.

Barbra, still on the sofa—a doily island in a stormy sea—covers her face with her hands. Her wedding ring is huge in this shot, a gewgaw too absurd to have meant anything real. In the LaserDisc commentary, O'Dea says, "I still have that signet ring," which, I admit, does cast doubt on my theory that Barb is married. But it *is* on her left ring finger, and Harry's wedding ring is also flat-faced. Maybe that was the style of the time?

Harry reels drunkenly through the cellar door and, in a fine physical performance, spider-walks down the stairs. The Harry that clings to the wall at the bottom of the steps (please note the cement trowel hanging there) has radically changed in the seconds since being shot. His face stubble is newly pronounced, darker to match the gray ringing his eyes. This makeup was certainly applied by Eastman, and who can blame her for going overboard? Here was the death of the most important man in her life. A brutal death, but more merciful than Hardman's death forty years later from cancer.

Romero alternates between a locked-down, Dutch-angle view of Harry staggering to make it to Karen, and a woozy, handheld view from Harry's dying eyes. The scariest thing is the lack of music (even *Night 30* knows better than to blow this silence with synth); the only noises are the muffled groans and thumps of zombies above, standing in for Harry's flagging heartbeat. For all the complaining about Tom and Judy's mushy scene, the most cliché moment in *Night* is Harry's final one, reaching for his daughter, inches away, hand shaking . . . until he collapses dead.

Exit Harry Cooper. An S.O.B., but an S.O.B. you miss the second he's gone. It makes you miss Karl Hardman too. I can't put it better than "Anna Liza," a commenter on Hardman's online obituary: "Fans all over the world miss you. Please guide us all to that 'safest place.'"

Back upstairs, Helen faces her own mortality. A man's hairy forearm has hooked her neck from the gap in the door. She's not fighting hard. Her legs don't push, or kick, or run. She looks defeated. In the end, there is no escaping men's arms, no choice but to yield to their wishes.

Romero's angles have gone cockeyed. Another board drops from the front door to reveal none other than the horde's erstwhile leader, Zombie #1. Bill Hinzman's crewcut doesn't match the longer locks he had back in the cemetery scene, but at this pitch of excitation, I'm willing to believe in zombie barbers.

One hour and fourteen minutes have passed since Barbra laid eyes on Zombie #1. Seeing him again does what Ben, Harry, Helen, Tom, and Judy could not: it gets her off the Sofa of No Opinions. Barbra's lips curl inward with hatred. She seizes the same board Ben used to disarm Harry, and with the gusto one might expect of sporting a weapon from *Night of the Living Dead: A Zombicide Game*—maybe the Japanese katana—Barb rushes the door, planting the plank over the hole through which Zombie #1 reaches.

Barbra does no such thing in the script. But Romero wasn't going to let her go out like that. Everyone who complains Barb is a bump on a log in *Night* simply forgets this scene. She fights. And for whom? For Helen Cooper, the only other woman alive, who sat with Barbra and soothed her, *Don't be afraid of me.* Everyone else? Sure. But you and me, we need to look out for each other.

Barbra is swarmed with arms, men's claws entangling in that dopey hot-rollered wig. Her screams come in short, angry bursts: This is as much fury as fear. With Ben locked in his own window struggle, it's hard to imagine Barb getting free. It doesn't matter. She's already won. She's done more than anyone observing would have believed possible. Helen is freed. And though we may want her to return the favor by helping Barbra, Helen has a daughter to protect, and she bucks off the wall toward the cellar. As first-time viewers were starting to suspect by this point in the film, she is too late.

01:24:28 HONEY, YOU'RE GOING TO FLIP

There's no following of Helen down the cellar stairs. No close-up of her confused expression as she tries to interpret gruesome noises. In the bluntest edit of his career, Romero smash cuts from the first-floor shot of Helen taking off to *Night*'s most shocking image, arguably one of the most shocking images in cinema up to 1968: Harry dead on the cellar floor, right arm a bloody stump (made from fiberglass insulation), the kneeling Karen eating part of the arm (leftover meatball sandwich) like the child she is, both hands cupping the hunk of meat.

Mike Nelson's best RiffTrax joke comes here, imagining a Karen/Helen conversation: "'Can I go play hopscotch with my friends?' 'No, now you get down in that dingy basement and pretend to eat your father's flesh, or there'll be no supper for you.'"

In an essay inside the Criterion edition of *Night*, Stuart Klawans points out how the composition echoes the interfamilial cannibalism of Goya's *Saturn Devouring His Son*. As Klawans notes, Romero likely knew this painting from art classes. The question, then, becomes: Where did *Goya* get it from? It's one of those images, I think, that exists in our cerebral cortexes. By simply existing, we know it, we fear it. Brutality exists in us all.

Like all the most upsetting horror images, the cellar tableau is bewildering before anything else. The bedridden girl is up and moving? Harry's arm, which we saw reaching for Karen twenty-seven seconds ago, is gone? The unsourced white spotlight on the characters only ups the disorientation. The millions who have watched *Night* all ask the same question: *Am I really seeing this?*

There is no upset or admonition in Helen's voice, only honest wondering: "Karen?" Karen drops the dadwich and stands. We finally get a good view of the bloody bandage on her arm (a continuity killer, it will move up and down till the end). Helen's tone shifts to the sort a mother uses to cajole her child to put down her phone: "Karen." No reply. The girl, with gray-shaded eye sockets and a blood-dribbled chin, walks toward her mother—and toward us.

Newscasters aside, it's the only shot in *Night* where an actor looks straight at the camera. The tactic is every bit as disconcerting to me here as it was in 1995, when I saw Rouben Mamoulian's *Dr. Jekyll and Mr. Hyde* (1931), which destroyed enough fourth walls to rouse me from teenage stupor. (This technique reaches its devastating zenith in Elem Klimov's *Come and See* [1985], which forces you to stare into the abyss until it stares back.)

It's masterful to employ this tactic after showing disembodied hands tear down the house and, by sensory extension, the home/theater/airplane in which you are watching the film. Karen's direct eye contact finishes the job. The zombies aren't only in your space. They *see* you, cringing there in your seat. The one they're coming to get is *you*.

Karen extends her arms like Karloff's monster, exactly how Romero instructed his zombies *not* to walk. But this is Kyra Schon, Karl Hardman's daughter, and by her own account, her dad directed her, and perhaps he had laxer standards when it came to undead ambulation. Or maybe he intuited the DNA-level emotions the sight of a child holding out her arms for her mother would stir up in viewers.

The name "Karen" shows up zero times in the script, but this isn't a Judy situation. The character as written was "Timmy" (and, in one random sentence, "Kevin"), but as Image Ten was low on sons, the decision was made to cast young Kyra (Eastman claimed it was her idea), and the girl had the fortune of being woken up by her mother one morning with the very 1967 statement, "Honey, you're going to flip."

Flip she did. She was a *Chiller Theater* devotee the same as everyone else in da Burgh and knew how cinema sausage got made thanks to her father's work. Periodically, Hardman would involve her in one of his pursuits. In 1963, Hardman recorded local tenor Mike Driscoll for a novelty 45 called "Figgy Pudding" (set to the tune of "We Wish You a Merry Christmas"). The record label he put it out on was called KYRA.

Karen was the ideal role for a young non-actor. Lie on this table, utter two words of dialogue, attack your on-screen mother with as little emotion as possible, then take your friends to the premiere. Schon fulfilled each requirement. To hear her tell it (and she's open, honest, and funny in her tellings), she had a ball filming her scenes, aside from losing her mind with boredom during what felt like interminable argument scenes between her on-screen parents. One behind-the-scenes cellar pic of Harry and Helen is simply missing Karen, as if the little girl, zombie bite or not, had reached her limit and exited stage left.

Of all the major players involved in *Night*, only Schon has kept a steady, accessible website since 1997. (Romero's own website didn't debut until 2000 and, despite fantasies of bringing his work straight to the masses, he spiked the site after the inevitable troll invasion.) Schon's site includes "Zombie Zen" poetry (including a fine one by *The Texas Chain Saw Massacre*'s Gunnar Hansen), photos of Karen tattoos, signed memorabilia, links to her handmade jewelry ("ghoulry"), and good stories (including one about accidentally cutting herself at a convention and, by request, bleeding onto a fan's photograph).

Tellingly, the first story told in the site's intro is one of hiding her *Night* involvement. The notoriety made her stick out at an age when that was the worst thing possible. "Two awful girls (twins—both evil) I went to high school with picked on me mercilessly until someone told them that I'd been in the movie," Schon writes. "Suddenly they wanted to be my best friends." Her mother, meanwhile, had to defend her decision to allow Schon to be in the film.

Schon concealing her role in *Night* mirrors the efforts of

Duane Jones. The curious nine-year-old Schon and the sensitive thirty-year-old Jones had a mutual affinity. She admits to having a crush on the man who seemed so much more sophisticated than the rest of the playful yahoos. "I never did see him again," she writes, "and I feel cheated." There is no doubting her sincerity: Her website is officially dedicated to Jones.

Schon never felt compelled to act again. She spent twenty-five years teaching pottery and sculpture in Pittsburgh Public Schools, a fact I first picked up from an Uber driver in Pittsburgh, who said he'd been a student of Schon. (Every driver I have in Pittsburgh has a Romero connection, from an alleged friend of Judith O'Dea to a woman who helped finance Jack Russo's home.) Schon once observed how much more interested her girl students were in *Night*. I imagine this is due in part to the girls' identification with Schon, but credit goes to Romero too. If female viewers don't regard your horror movie with reflexive disgust, that's a good sign.

It's a quirk of history that Karen, the Farmhouse Nation resident with the least screen time, ended up as the face of the film. *Night* began its long, painful home video journey with a 1978 VHS and Betamax release on MEDA Home Entertainment (soon renamed Media Home Entertainment), eventually featuring three different covers. My first *Night* VHS, featuring a barely trying image of some trees, came from Memory Lane Video, which began issuing public domain films in 1984. My second was a chintzy United American Video Corporation version that misspells "Duane" on the cover as "Duanne." The 1993 Blockbuster Classics edition was the first wide-release cover to use the now-classic headshot of Schon (taken by Hardman during lunch outside the farmhouse). Anchor Bay's VHS and DVD editions, starting in 1995, solidified it as the film's de facto cover image.

In the ubiquitous photo, Schon is looking—you guessed it—straight at the camera. It makes sense why savvy companies embraced the image. Duane Jones and Judith O'Dea, the only other viable choices, are too specific to be universally satisfying.

A child's face, however, is an embryonic canvas on which anyone can transpose their feelings. As this is also the general MO of zombies, Karen becomes the zombiest of zombies. The Image Ten site even offers a free stencil of Karen's face for pumpkin carving. (Meanwhile, the 2010 stoner parody *Weed of the Living Dead* uses the image but inserts a joint between Karen's lips.)

Schon *is* the film in a way, and that honor (and burden) will only increase. As the youngest cast member, Schon will likely be the last person standing who was actually there. The literal day I'm writing this sentence, Kyra Schon, Judith O'Dea, Judy Ridley, and Russ Streiner—the four major cast members still living—are appearing at Living Dead Weekend in Evans City. I wish I was there, if only to add to the latest tidal wave of appreciation. Better to receive too much of it than none at all.

01:24:43 JUST KEEP GOING

"Poor baby," Helen says. More like a whine. It's as if time, accelerated to the speed of the upstairs shuffling, has aged Helen to the point of begging her offspring for mercy. Don't break my fragile body. Don't send me to that old folks home. There is a chance here for Helen to resist. She's bigger and stronger than Karen, and the cellar is filled with potential weapons. For a split second, *Night* is a film about euthanasia. Can a mother put a sick daughter out of her misery?

But then Helen slips and falls, because she's old, she's so old, and it's old people who need to be euthanized, not the young, nor the double-young—freshly birthed as the undead. Helen collapses onto a step leading to a storage door, her neck awkwardly bent. This is how it ends, isn't it? So many old people's final spirals begin with falls.

That trowel on the wall. It's sharper than we realized.

Karen lifts the trowel from its pegs, holds it daggerlike in both hands (turning her whole body trowel-shaped), and walks toward the camera. Freeze the frame. Now go find the shot, one hour and forty-one minutes into Alfred Hitchcock's *Psycho* (1960), in which Norman Bates enters an almost identical cellar wielding a knife. The similarity is astonishing, from the cluttered shelving and visible ceiling pipes to the centered characters who are not what they appear to be. In *Psycho,* Anthony Perkins is wrestled down by John Gavin before any gory culmination.

In *Night,* no square-jawed hero is coming to save you.

Helen cries out. Loud, wordless bursts. When the camera (Karen's point of view) arrives above Helen, the sound dramatically changes. Thanks to seven hours of work "to record and electronically manipulate" the audio (per the Hardman-Eastman sound effects cassette), Helen's screams are like no scream in cinema history, distorted into the pitch of a leaking balloon, the porcine screech of slaughtered livestock. The scream warps, and echoes, and is the most hideous thing I have ever heard.

I often say movies don't scare me anymore, but I forget the rib-rattling shrieks tucked into the final minutes of my favorite film. It reminds me of how, when I was very little, nothing was more exciting than flipping through the toy section of the Sears Christmas catalog. But my mom had to bend the corner of the page that hid the ventriloquist dummies—otherwise, they'd leap out and catch me off-guard, just like Helen's screams.

Punctuating the shrieks like a fleshy metronome are the impacts of the trowel into Helen's body (one more honeydew melon). Schon recalls asking how many times to stab the pillow standing in for Marilyn Eastman. Her dad replied, "Just keep going." Hardman sensed the power of drawing the scene out, and in the single behind-the-scenes photo of this moment, Schon's arms are blurred in motion. On-screen, Karen stabs her mother fourteen times at a leisurely pace. Helen's expression (strobed by diamond-shaped trowel shadows) never conveys pain. She seems appalled, lips curled inward to look toothless—*old,* I said, she's *old.* Helen looks and sounds as if she's gotten word her daughter has died, which she has.

Throughout these twenty-six seconds of audiovisual hell, a mix of black Pratt & Lambert Vapex Flat Wall Paint and Bosco chocolate-syrup blood (technically Bosco "Milk Amplifier") flings onto Helen's face, her dress, the trowel, a big glob running down the wall. (It's fascinating, albeit pointless, to note that 1968's *The Astro-Zombies* kicks off with a trowel stabbing that is the spitting image of this, though far less effective.)

If you need more evidence of Romero's directorial instinct, Helen's death is entirely off-camera in the script. Despite the going wisdom, less isn't always more. (Helen's death scene in *Night 90* is far less gory and totally forgettable.) Eastman was never able to clean Helen's dress, but thankfully, this was one of the final scenes, if not *the* final scene, shot inside the farmhouse. Luckily, when she'd gone shopping for costumes with O'Dea at Horne's and Kaufmann's, they bought two copies of each outfit. These days, Eastman's son, John, displays the pristine dress at conventions. It's neat. But sad, too. What a slight slip of a garment to have held such a woman.

Action resumes upstairs, such a typhoon of classic cinematic techniques—Ben struggling with invading arms while "Heavy Dramatic (CB-15B)" crashes and booms—we're left to wonder if what we saw in the cellar connects to this other movie at all. Barbra fights the same fight at the front door, Helen's old position. Zombie #1 remains at the head of the scrum. With a moist splintering, the door nailed horizontally over the entrance comes down.

It's strange, the lack of ballyhoo around Johnny's return. No big entry, no musical sting. He is simply, abruptly there, the leather driving glove on the doorframe an effective reminder of who he is, in case viewers don't recognize him without glasses. Johnny's in league with Zombie #1—he is, in effect, Zombie #2—and he's here to chase our film's patricide and matricide with fratricide. (How Johnny reanimated despite his head trauma will remain a mystery.)

As we learned with Tom, Judy, and Helen, *Night* lets no good deed go unpunished. Even for Barbra 2.0, the brotherly revival is too much. She freezes and screams *no*, over and over, as Zombie #2 takes her by the collar, just like Zombie #1 taught him. Ben rushes over but it's too late. Our last view of Barbra's face is over Johnny's back, her left arm crooked over his shoulder as if they are dancing in an overfilled ballroom. Heads and hands swarm her in cavorting waves until all we see is a crescent of her upturned face, a cramped swimmer about to go under.

She dies upright in her Air Steps.

Barbra's death in *Night* is a turn so unprecedented that Russo and Romero failed to conceive of it in the writing stage. In the script, Ben drags Barb to safety and she survives the film, just as you'd expect from the character we followed from the start. Hitchcock might have influenced Romero's blueprints by knocking off Janet Leigh twenty minutes into *Psycho*. But this is no twenty minutes. This is eighty-six minutes, an overturning of expectations that feels impossible to outdo.

Somehow, *Night*'s final minutes will outdo it.

01:26:05

THE DEAD WILL WALK THE EARTH

THE ANALOGY OF ZOMBIES AND MOB MENTALITY IS an old saw today, but it didn't exist until this final onslaught. Agoraphobia was rampant in the 1960s. Most Americans lived in small towns, and what struck them most about crowds on TV was the danger: storming this, setting fire to that, sitting peacefully where well-behaved citizens ought not sit.

I have (big surprise) thoughts on zombie mobs from a specifically American lens. It's a major thread in *The Living Dead*: the uses and misuses of collected masses, the inspirational capabilities and the awful realities. I never thought I'd write a zombie story until the offer to finish Romero's manuscript—such was my deference to the master—and after it was done, I didn't expect to write another. But I did: In late 2022 and early 2023, AWA Comics published a five-issue arc called *Year Zero: Volume 0*. The appeal for me was the international premise. *The Living Dead* was, by design, strictly U.S.-based (with a coda purposefully set in Canada). This left my ideas for the rest of the world (North Korea, Russia, and South Africa in *Year Zero*) dangling beyond my reach.

It was a fleeting thing. My thoughts on zombie hordes are back on domestic shores. These days I'm not comparing Romero's legions to the Arab Spring uprisings, the Bolivian wildfire protests, the South Korean candlelight demonstrations, the U.K. rallies against Brexit. All I see is the mob of election deniers who flooded the U.S. Capitol on January 6, 2021. Photographer Kevin Dietsch, at the Capitol that day, saw it the same way, telling *People*, "It was like something out of a zombie movie. Where hordes of these rioters just kept coming and coming."

The Capitol. The same place where George Romero as Don Quinn tried to uncover the truth, not burn the ballot boxes that contained it. It would be nice to blame an exploded Venus Probe for the solipsism that has infected people we know and love, turning them, bite by toxic bite, into soldiers in an army with only one general: chaos.

United in purpose, the zombies, these neighbors, take the farmhouse.

In opera terms, it's our closing number, the whole company on stage for the final belter. A half dozen ghouls squeeze through the door like meat through a grinder. Zombie #1 crawls through the window. It feels less like an invasion than it does a scene from *The Poseidon Adventure*, the world upside down, a flood filling rooms that, moments ago, were dry.

It is here, more than anywhere, that *Night* reflects *Birth of a Nation*. In Griffith's film, slavering Black men crash their way into a country cabin with fists and lumber, a two-fold threat: the visceral threat of Black men raping white women and the existential threat of interracial copulation. *Night* lacks a sexual threat, but structurally, the biggest difference is how Griffith intercuts the siege with shots of a heroic KKK riding to the rescue, the hypothetical equivalent of Romero cutting to Sheriff McClelland's posse closing in.

There's another way to view it. Isn't there always? Following the thread of the zombi, risen by a Vodou houngan, this sequence invokes the racial panic ginned up by movies like Lugosi's Haiti-set *White Zombie* (1932). "Haiti represented the idea that Black people could be agents of world history," Raphael Dalleo wrote in his 2016 book *American Imperialism's Undead*. Here we are at last, agency fulfilled, power attained.

Ben backs away. He never backed away from Harry, the burning truck, the zombies he dispatched so efficiently. Romero rack-focuses to the cellar door behind him. Raccoon-eyed Karen slides through unseen, doing a zombie limp despite having suffered no leg injury. Her eyes are fixed not on Ben (he's not a person to her) but on his delicious, dangling arm.

She grips that arm with both hands. Ben looks disgusted. There's some satisfaction in settling scores, but this is an innocent child he can't possibly harm. Compare this to Ben's successor, *Dawn of the Dead*'s Peter. When Peter is bum-rushed by two zombie kids, he machine-guns them without a thought. (In the same scene, two notes are tacked to the wall that I like to interpret as references to Barb. The first I imagine being written by her husband: *BARBARA—MEET ME IN PITTSBURGH—MARK*. It's the other one, though, that permits us the fantasy of a good-riddance note left by Barb: *CHARLES—I HAVE THE KIDS. LEFT WITH BEN.*) When it comes to dead kids, both scenes pale next to an ad the Latent Image filmed for George McGovern's 1972 presidential bid, in which *the corpse of a dead baby* is carried away from its screaming mother into a hearse.

Ben holds Karen at an arm's length for too long, as if caught in the nostalgia of mercy, before hurling her to the sofa and ducking through the cellar door.

The last we see of Karen is pressed against that door. Her attention attracts the zombies still pouring in behind her. As you know by now, I don't cotton to most tales invented for *Night*'s characters, but I want to mention a good one. Chapter five of the Russo-Wolfer *Night of the Living Dead* graphic novel (with art by Edison George) features a startlingly poignant story told from Karen's perspective. As she lies in the cellar, her thoughts drift to her unhappy years raised by a cruel adopted dad and meek mother, forever told she was "just a girl." She kills them, same as in the movie (Blumberg's

Journey of the Living Dead posits the bracing notion that Karen ate her father's arm first because it was the arm that often struck her), only to shuffle off with an undead family that accepts her as she is. The best story of the *Nights of the Living Dead* anthology, Isaac Marion's "The Girl on the Table," takes the same tack, with similarly haunting results. (For wannabe Karen siblings, Hardman and Eastman offered a signed-and-stamped "Certificate of Adoption" at a Halloween 1997 *Chiller Theater* event.)

The farmhouse zombies do what they can to access the hot-blooded man on the other side of the plywood and plaster. They bang on the cellar door and shake the piano, atop which rolls a pair of maracas, which have been changing positions atop the piano for the whole movie. (Were the farmhouse residents a family band? There's even a guitar in the cellar.) Ben bars the door from the other side. We only ever saw Harry use one board. But there are three, and Tom's assessment of the boards as "pretty strong" seems like an understatement. Which leads into a major talking point in the fandom.

Harry was right all along. The cellar *was* the safest place.

I mean, yes? This opinion is usually proffered as a blistering hot take, though from what I can tell, it's been the majority opinion for decades. Even Romero agreed. And I hate to dissent from the man himself. But Harry was not, in fact, right. Ben's plan was never to refuse the cellar; it was to stay upstairs, where they could watch and listen for help and partake in resources (TV, radio) that probably wouldn't get a signal downstairs. Ben's final retreat to the cellar is by plan, and could have been done in orderly fashion with Barbra, Harry, and Helen in tow.

This, in essence, is the climax: Ben escapes the zombies. The desultory denouement of the final eight minutes starts with the return of the grumbling synth pulse from the Last Supper. As with the cannibal orgy, what happens next contains no drama. All that's left are a few unpleasantries that must be gutted through, penance for the decisions that led us here.

Ben stumbles down the stairs. The trowel is back in place

on the wall, tidily returned by the murderous Karen. Ben sees Harry's corpse, face-up, wide-eyed as Karen left it. Next, he sees Helen's corpse, one of the most striking images in horror history, the trowel back where it belongs, embedded in her sternum, ink-black blood streaked down her body, all contained in a small oval of light, giving our eyes nowhere else to run.

Harry sits up. Though Karen and Johnny were resurrected loved ones, too, only here does it sink in how much Romero's ghouls mirror Don Siegel's pod people from *Invasion of the Body Snatchers* (1956). Everyone you know is going to become one—including you. Few make the link today, but Romero copped to it in 1973, saying, "I'm into Don Siegel pretty hard." (*Body Snatchers* also foreshadowed *Night*'s ending.)

Ben cocks the rifle and shoots Harry. His superfluous, ammo-wasting second and third shots vent his frustration. Killing Harry the first time felt like victory. Killing him this time only emphasizes the greater failure. "When there's no more room in hell, the dead will walk the Earth," *Dawn of the Dead*'s famous tagline, applies here, though the phrase is usually misunderstood. Romero had no interest in religious rationales for zombies. The dead who walk the earth are the living. It's Ben. This cellar, this subterranean chamber, is but the first level of Hell he'll get to know if he survives.

Helen's eyes fly open. She's Helen, but not. The visual returns me to the Halloween store aisles that frightened me as a kid and retain the power to creep me out today. In 1990, American Mask & Novelty Co. put out four licensed *Night* masks and I can still see them, genuinely disturbing in their rubbery crudeness: "Graveyard Ghoul" (Hinzman-esque), "Dead John" (resembles Russo), and "Creepy Karen" (but with Barbra's hair). The scariest was called "Mangled Marilyn," one eye pale, the right side of her face puckered in scars, mouth too big and filled with teeth, a dribble of green bile on her chin.

A horrid fantasy. The Helen in the cellar is more beautiful than ever, the stripes of blood turning her into an underworld god.

Ben doesn't care. One shot this time. Helen doesn't even get to sit up.

Ben loses it. Finally loses it. A cleansing sight, proof that Ben is zero-percent zombie. He hurls the Winchester, flips Karen's table, knees aside a sawhorse. (The creak of zombies above was generated by rocking one of these sawhorses.) The surefootedness that has been his calling card evaporates like dew. For the first time, Ben seems to have no idea what he's doing. But at least he's thrown away the gun. The gun that, really, killed not only Harry, but all of them.

This freedom from the Winchester does not last. Ben scrounges for the rifle and impulsively crouches in an infantry pose, barrel aimed at the stairs. Ben is strong, but not strong enough to break from the promise—and the lie—of the rifle. Retired Marine Corps major general Merritt "Red Mike" Edson (a.k.a. "Mad Merritt the Morgue Master"), recipient of the Congressional Medal of Honor and executive director of the NRA, wrote in the April 1951 issue of the org's magazine, *American Rifleman*, "It is more important than ever that every man know how to handle a rifle. Even the home front may, overnight, become the battlefront."

He's describing Farmhouse Nation, but from the perspective of a critter caught in Harry Cooper's mind trap. Ben tried it Red Mike's way. He met violence with violence. While it had instant benefits, the long game looks to be more doomed than ever. Yes, there's always been an untrustworthy element of society, usually one on the upper floor, that needs to be watched. But not like this. It can't be like this. On August 14, 1955, Edson sealed himself into his Washington, D.C., garage—like Ben is sealed into this cellar—started his vehicle, and died by carbon monoxide poisoning.

Ben doesn't know this. He'll never know this. The impression I get from this shot, with Ben, once so big, framed so small at its center, is that he might be holding this ready pose for the rest of his damned life.

01:29:00 EVERYTHING APPEARS TO BE UNDER CONTROL

Upstairs, zombies lose interest. The victors in the battle for Farmhouse Nation pivot from the cellar and gaze in wonder at their spoils. In the RiffTrax commentary, Mike Nelson makes a credible point: "They just have no goal now that they're in. No one's in charge." The zombies reflect a reality of history's conquering forces (vividly illustrated in *Dawn* as our heroes wipe out the mall's zombies only to grow bored and irritable). They are the dog who caught the fire engine. Now what?

Three zombies (of the roughly eleven crammed into the dining room) wield wooden legs Ben weaponized from the dinner table. *The dinner table*—a phrase politicians and pundits use to invoke images of sleeve-rolled farmers spooning mashed potatoes as they reassure their family about some perceived threat to the social order. I sat around such tables growing up. Family members circled like wagons. To keep us in. To keep you out.

Now it's the undead who exist in racial, temperamental, unargumentative solidarity. Three table legs so far. One more to scrounge up, and then the table can be rebuilt.

The film's slowest dissolve makes all this explicit: The shot of the crowded dining room turns into an external shot of the Seven Pines house sitting quietly in the Pennsylvania countryside. It always looked to be made of white panel wood, but it turns out it was gingerbread, a lure of comfort to the Hansels and Gretels who found it while lost in night.

In the daylight, of course, it looks quaint, how it must have looked to attendees of Camp Deerhead. We haven't seen it like this since Barbra first spotted it. The dawn light is gentle. Birds twitter peacefully. You can almost feel the cool brush of the grass.

Romero shows us two shots of an untroubled sky. The third shot, finally, divulges that the night did not, in fact, wipe humans from the face of the earth. Over the horizon soars a helicopter, the vehicle most identified with the war raging eight thousand miles away. We cut to a shot from inside the chopper, looking down, and though the terrain is grassy fields instead of rice paddies, there are soldiers down there, twenty-one men walking an extended line to flush out foes. You can see their flannels from way up here.

One year as a teen, I became preoccupied with William Golding's *Lord of the Flies* (1954) and its saga of Ralph, Jack, and Piggy, and read it several times. I discovered that *Night of the Living Dead* and *Lord of the Flies* (the film version had come out just four years before *Night*) both involve a group of stranded characters falling prey to the desire to create hierarchical kingdoms.

You can be the boss down there. I'm boss up here, Ben says.

We did everything adults would do. What went wrong? Piggy asks.

Jack versus Ralph finds its analogue in Ben versus Harry. *Lord of the Flies* ends with one of the great deus ex machinas of literature: Jack's tribe descending on Ralph as the whole island burns, Ralph's murder disrupted only by the serendipitous arrival of a British naval officer. Here, *Night* looks to be doing the same thing. The posse is coming to save Ben from the farmhouse's metaphorical conflagration.

It's no wonder these tales appealed to me. I saw savagery everywhere. Unceasing cruelty on the school bus. Bloody-nose beatdowns on the playground. Corporal punishment in school, as well as by neighborhood parents. Everyone was jockeying for control. I was small and tried to be smaller to mouse past all these cats. My constant prayer was for someone—a bus driver, recess monitor, friendly teacher, courageous spouse—to show up like a naval officer and force the madmen to see what they'd become.

A view from the ground shows the posse to be of the same makeup as before. Though they proceed with solemnity, traces of smiles betray their pride. In this shot, one of them (played by one more ad man, George Burdell) is armed with a revolver. What are you going to do with a revolver? You're going to put it against a zombie skull and pull the trigger, that's what. Another carries a machete, which at least is handy for decapitation. (The machete carrier is Ashby Jones, a golf buddy of O'Dea's dad, who went on to become a novelist of historical fiction.) Behind-the-scenes pics show Romero, Russo, and Streiner all working cameras, sometimes shooting two at once. It was all hands on deck.

We cut to a field in which the helicopter sets down in front of the men. Like the Washington, D.C., sequence, this was a "money" shot, a way for Image Ten to look like they spent lots of cash. Like most everything else, the chopper was a favor. The KQV on the side tells us it carries the news radio station's Bob Harvey, a.k.a. "Captain Bob," a.k.a. "Turkeyman"—"the most feared fowl Pittsburgh has ever known," according to the intro of his *Batman* parody program. Captain Bob was so beloved that, after he sent KQV tapes to Pittsburghers in Vietnam, they dedicated the Cam Ranh USO radio station to him.

Captain Bob was doing a story on *Night* that day and got roped into it. Piloted by former Air Force flier Bernard "Bud" Hoffman, the KQV whirlybird (ID number N22G9U) is a mosquito-looking thing roughly the size of a car—a car without doors. There's a great photo of Russ Streiner strapped into the left seat with a movie camera in his lap, Captain Bob at his side and George Romero looking on, probably wondering if this is the last time he'd see old Russ alive. (Streiner is visible when the KQV chopper lands, as if dead Johnny rose from the grave to pursue aviation.) Captain Bob had actual dialogue—stills exist of him interviewing a posse member—but, alas, his moment in the sun was snipped.

Like the TV segments of *Night*, it all feels uncomfortably real. Realer than anything in the movies that helped inspire it. These shots feel like news footage because that's what they are: unvarnished point-and-capture records of non-actors going about their business in unaffected environments.

Back to the bridge where we first saw the posse. A police vehicle carrying K-9 units pulls onto Zoelle Lane, where others with dogs have gathered. Both the cars and dogs were courtesy of David Craig, a former WWII B-17 bomber pilot who had become Pittsburgh's public safety director, not an easy job in the age of public protests. Still he made time for a little zombie hunting. One of the K-9 units, handled by officer Robert Ebbert, was named Sigmond. A year earlier, three inches of Sigmond's infected tail had been amputated.

Sigmond and the other K-9s are released from vehicles. This is my dog Merv's favorite part of the film—he screams and chases the long-dead dogs off the side of the TV screen every time. I'm with Merv. It's invigorating to see animals outdoors after ninety minutes of scrutinizing human faces in tight quarters. There's a whole forgotten world out here.

Image Ten congregated a lot of people in this spot, from law enforcement and posse men to news media, a coroner, and a nurse (played by sound engineer Marshall Booth's wife, Ivy, an actual nursing student). Among this group is twenty-year-old Don Wadsworth, who would go on to become a vocal coach with a client list including Danny Aiello, Ellen Burstyn, Olympia Dukakis, Bob Hoskins, Tom Hulce, and Diane Ladd.

Two familiar characters reemerge: Sheriff McClelland and Bill Cardille talking at a telephone pole against which two men sit. "Hey, Vince, Al," McClelland greets. Vince, of course, is Vince Survinski. Al is Al Croft, an ad exec who has the (probably unfair) rep of being half of the Latent Image's Yoko Ono. Post-*Night*, Romero brought Croft into the Latent Image as executive vice president, along with Romero's first wife, Nancy, a move that Jack Russo says hastened the demise of the company that had seemed so indefatigable. Here, though, Croft is just a guy with a gun. A militiaman. A garden-variety villain.

"You wanna get four or five men and a couple dogs?" McClelland asks. "There's a house over here behind those trees." It's a rare instance of movie geography aligning with the real world. The farmhouse is, in fact, right behind those trees where he's pointing.

Cardille says he's staying with the posse until they meet up with the National Guard. The line carries weight. The National Guard is nearby? Well, then, it's all going to be okay. McClelland asks Cardille where he got the foam cup of coffee (posse extra Bill Messenger reported that he got drunk for the first time in his life off the beer in some of those cups) and Cardille gives it to him, saying, "You're doing all the work, you take it." Kosana as McClelland is as slurrily convincing as before, and Cardille's ability to tamp down his known instinct for tomfoolery remains admirable.

As McClelland takes off, Cardille has a short exchange with his real-life cameraman, Steve Hutsko. (Both men reprised these roles in *Night 1990*.) Hutsko says he's going to check in with the office and Cardille tells him to report that "everything appears to be under control." What should be a throwaway moment is lent gravitas by a close-up on Cardille, which disrupts the news-footage style. Beginning here is a Spencer Moore cue called "Eerie Heavy Echo (L-1216)"—the same title as the cue that began the whole film, but a whole different brand of spooky. A spooky that insists what Cardille just said couldn't be more wrong.

01:31:05 ANOTHER ONE FOR THE FIRE

Image Ten appeared to be under control as well. Their first movie was a hit. A monster hit. They didn't yet know the monster's dimensions, but they had an inkling. In the first week, the film grossed over $62,000 in just eleven theaters. Four months after the premiere, an Image Ten rep estimated their take being $1.5 million by the end of 1969. It added up; the film had made $700,000 in its first year. Per a fun-sounding publication called *Boxoffice Showmandiser*, the film had originated the idea of the "midnight movie" by 1972, thanks to a two-year run at Greenwich Village's Waverly Theater.

In a June 20, 1967, *Pittsburgh Press* article (adorably titled "Ghoulie Show Next for City's Budget-Minded Film Makers"), business editor William Allan could not have been more wrong when he wrote, "One low-budget movie probably will not have as much impact on the Pittsburgh economy as the next ladle of steel at Duquesne—even if the steelworkers dump it on the floor." Image Ten's film *had* changed the economy. That continued with Russ Streiner's founding of the Pittsburgh Film Office in 1990. The economic impact so far is in the billions.

Public opinion, too, was swinging their way, with 1971 as the pivot point. After *Cahiers du cinéma* and *Sight and Sound* put their stamp on *Night*, stateside entities like *The New Yorker* started to come around. This included Rex Reed, who, in a May 7, 1971, *Daily Mail* piece, admitted the film "spooked the living daylights out of me." (It's a long, effusive article I can barely pay attention to due to the international exposé on the same page: "Monster Rises in Cuba Slime . . . Some Say It's a Huge Log.")

Yet the *cash*. The cash owed to Image Ten did not manifest. For a long time, the gang was patient. The Latent Image had been going for five years. They knew payment schedules could get wiggly. What they didn't know was that they'd spend the next decade chasing their distributor into court. Letters in the Eastman-Hardman *Scrapbook* show how heated this got. On April 23, 1974, Walter Reade's Roger Karnbad demanded the return of 16mm prints, writing, "This, of course, is a complete violation of confidence and we can only consider it a ploy on your part using your request as a subterfuge to get possession of our two prints." This is followed by two mid-seventies letters from O'Dea (who was also an investor) asking when she might expect payments.

Image Ten wanted the rights back. They wanted everything back, including their own selves, their own spirits. In the 1975 *Cinefantastique* interview, Hardman outlined his idea of what to do with *Night* once they reclaimed it: "I'd opt to shelve it for a while, then rerelease it." Russ Streiner had his own idea: "We're also considering, when the rights come back to us, releasing it on a first-run basis. It wasn't eligible for that the first time out."

Eventually the Walter Reade Organization quit showing up at court, and in 1978 went bankrupt. That didn't stop the Lincoln Center from christening the Walter Reade Theater on December 8, 1991. President and board chairman Walter Reade Jr. had been killed five years earlier in a skiing accident, and his *New York Times* obit celebrated him by naming five notable films he distributed: *Room at the Top* (1959), *David and Lisa* (1962), *A Taste of Honey* (1961), *War and Peace* (1966–1967), and *Faces* (1968). Great movies. High-brow stuff. But the film that made the real money, the film that changed lives, is conspicuously absent.

O'Dea could send letters all she wanted—Image Ten was never getting their payday and, therefore, neither was she. For a film that, by today's conservative estimates, has grossed in the range of $40 million. On a $114,000 budget. One of the most profitable films ever made, provided you're a profiteer. Salt in the filmmakers' wounds was each time *Night* popped up inside other films and TV shows—129 times as of January 2024, a Guinness World Record—with no fees paid to Image Ten.

To namecheck a handful of the *non*-horror inclusions: *The Big Sick, Bound, Christiane F., Cold in July, Colors, EastEnders, Father Hood, Leverage, Luke Cage, A Mother's Justice, Mysterious Skin, One Hundred and One Nights, Patti Cake$, Proof, Shameless, Sid and Nancy, Tie Me Up! Tie Me Down!, The Trigger Effect,* and *World's Greatest Dad.* Experience this whirlwind in Dave Dyment's 136-minute meta-homage *Watching Night of the Living Dead* (2018), a version of *Night* reconstructed from clips from other movies of fictional characters *watching* it. Where else can you find Duane Jones consorting with the likes of Don Johnson, Gary Oldman, and Robin Williams?

In 1969, however, it only made sense to Image Ten to go ahead and pour their money—surely coming soon—into a second film. Why risk being a one-hit wonder?

So the group got cooking. Right away, the artist collective mindset that had nourished *Night* wore thin. The smart money was on something they called *Horror Anthology,* which would capitalize on *Night* and (this is my guess) give multiple directors a chance to shine. The anthology concept would eventually bear fruit with *Creepshow*, but at this heady juncture, Romero didn't want to be typecast.

It must have been surprising, if not traumatic, just how plain *bad* the filming of *There's Always Vanilla* felt compared to *Night*. What should have been a month-long shoot dragged on for a year. (A May 1969 calendar tucked into Romero's archive is packed with evidence of competing commercial and feature-film obligations. May 5: "Bubblebath commercial." May 7: "Bold Gold commercial." May 12: "Lynn and Dorian in a restaurant arranging abortion.") Everyone was high on success and low on the spoils of that success. They were at one another's throats, Bens and Harrys jockeying for control of a second Farmhouse Nation. *Vanilla* bombed; *Night* was a pounding legal headache; personnel issues were shredding the Latent Image. Things went so wrong you have to connect the dots between all the dismal quotes.

Romero: "It was an awful experience and I care very little about it."

Chris, his wife: "It got real ugly between everybody, and it was really a mess."

The Rev: "By the end, people wouldn't talk to each other, and best friends for a lifetime split apart and began talking to their lawyers."

George Romero, college drop-out, two-time director, was thirty-one years old, and already the dream had died.

Across time and space, I shared his fear. When people look at my output (twenty-eight books in seventeen years), they probably think, well, there's a guy that doesn't suffer writer's block. This wasn't always the case. For my first three books, I worked with the same halting indecision as anyone else. In 2011, I suffered what I can only call a breakdown. Suddenly the act of writing—the one joy threaded through every phase of my life—felt poisonous. I was mired inside *Scowler*, a nasty, pessimistic novel that had me tied in knots.

Though I've blocked out the inciting incident, the point is, I got sick. Physically sick. The fire of the illness hopped the fence and caught my brain. Same as it did when the horrors of my youth—fictional horrors fueled by real-life ones—crawled from the TV and wiggled into my brainpan and had me gasping for air over the toilet. The worst part was how viciously I assailed myself for being so weak. What kind of man was I? If I couldn't take this, what could I take?

These catastrophizing spirals have made me susceptible to eating issues since middle school. Suddenly, after this particular episode, I found I couldn't eat. At all. Which stressed me out. Which only made it worse. Soon I was waking up in the middle of the night dry-heaving and turning away dishes my partner made especially for my tender stomach. My brain had turned zombie against me. I was partially devoured.

I choked down protein shakes but the situation was intolerable. I began writing close friends what were essentially goodbyes. I saw no path of avoiding institutionalization. My zombie brain showed me pictures of myself in bed, being fed by a tube, alive but, for all real purposes, undead. My career was definitely finished, just like Romero's career seemed to be finished, and I didn't care. All I wanted was what the zombies wanted: to be able to eat.

The crisis psychiatry sessions I was thrown into didn't help. But the Celexa did. Over weeks, the meds kicked in, and slowly, over months and years of occasional relapse, I clawed my way back. The zombified lobe of my brain was excised, an operation that never worked in Romero's zombie flicks. *Scowler* was finished by holing up in an Extended Stay America in Wisconsin, during which I became trapped inside by a *Shining*-style blizzard.

I dug myself out of the snow. Out of the book. Out of the zombie moans in my head. I would forever after equate zombification with other kinds of benumbing miseries, a metaphor heavily employed in *The Living Dead*. (It's even better employed in Morgan Talty's 2022 fiction collection *Night of the Living Rez*, which follows life on a Maine reservation, where alcohol, opioids, and methadone have anesthetized the Penobscot population). My first post-*Scowler* project was *Trollhunters* with Guillermo del Toro, and properly medicated for the first time in my life, I roared from the gate with a ferocity I'd never felt. It was a second life, one I'm still living, albeit with periodic stumbles. But to achieve that second life, part of me had to die first.

No drug was going to save the Latent Image. One by one, everyone left but Romero and Survinski, with the Brothers Streiner, Jack Russo, and Rudy Ricci departing to open a competing company called New American Films, Inc. It was astounding how quickly it all fell apart. It always is. It hurt Romero so deeply he spent the reputational capital from the global success of *Dawn of the Dead* to make *Knightriders*, a passion project intended as a direct metaphor for the disintegration of his company. "We had made one of the best horror movies of all time!" he cried. "And we had this elysian, little, completely democratic company. And then guys just left. Those were the guys who I thought were the core of Camelot—and they booked."

Twenty-five years onward, Danman Productions fell apart too. My so-called company was only a silly hobby, but its dissolution still broke my heart. I kept herding my friends together to shoot my ridiculous epics, but we were in college now, spread across the country, and they were getting sick of it. I'll never forget a 1994 dorm-room screening of my parody opus, the two-hour-and-forty-minute *The Godfathers, Part Two,* for a group of new college friends, seeing them yawn and fidget, and realizing my movie was not, in fact, awesome. It was *terrible*. I was *terrible* at this. How had I been so blind? No fights, no lawyers. Just an eighteen-year-old kid who got boxed in the ears by reality. It was my *There's Always Vanilla*—it all ended right there.

It is a relief for me (it would be to Romero, too, if he was still here) to return to *Night,* back when everyone was friends and anything felt possible.

Heading across a Butler County field are McClelland, Survinski, three straining dogs, and five real-life cops. One is played by

Paul Coffman, remembered less for *Night* than his hole-in-one at nearby Irwin Country Club, and another by Don Barth, remembered as one of the winningest coaches in Pennsylvania high school history. Another is Joe Costello, a childhood pal of George Kosana, who didn't realize until later that his pistol contained live rounds. (The script has the posse cutting through the cemetery and finding Johnny's bones, an idea sacked upon devising Johnny's return.)

Romero hasn't excelled in maintaining screen direction throughout *Night*, but here, when it matters most, he nails it. The barking dogs head left. Ben, in the cellar, lifting his sleepy head at the sound, looks right. The viewer's subconscious understands the two forces are going to collide.

I don't know when they filmed this shot of Duane Jones, but his hair looks longer than anywhere else in the film. It's like he's been down here not for hours but weeks. In the script, in which Barbra still lives, Ben tells her, "They must be here to rescue us." But Jones doesn't require dialogue. We see him thinking, figuring, weighing. Russo's novelization has Karen biting Ben, which makes his survival irrelevant—he's going to die anyway. But the movie sticks to the script. Ben has made it through the night.

Outside, the militia platoon closes in on two zombies. For some reason, despite the barking dogs, the zombies don't turn around. This unusual zombie behavior is probably best not overthought, but naturally I'm going to overthink it. Now that living people have the size advantage, the zombies refuse to give them an excuse to fire. If the men want to kill them, they'll have to shoot them in their backs.

The men happily oblige.

McClelland directs a passing car to the barn. CITY OF WILLARD DEPT. OF PUBLIC HEALTH is stenciled on the door, the only example of the production defacing a borrowed vehicle. The washable paint did not, in fact, wash off the brand-new car, which had been borrowed from a dealership. ("They had to wind up painting both sides of that station wagon, and they were really hacked," Hardman laughs in *Reflections*.) McClelland turns to address Tom and Judy's incinerated truck. The dirt cloud from the leaving car makes the truck look like it's still smoking.

"Somebody had a cookout here, Vince," the sheriff says. Repulsive.

The posse takes down four more ghouls. The zombie played by Russ and Gary Streiner's Aunt Norma—gone. The zombie played by Jason Richards, Goth Ghoul's dad—gone. Goth Ghoul herself—gone. The zombie played by Dave James, a newsperson there to report on Cardille's cameo—gone. Friends, colleagues, family members, *neighbors*, all dropping like flies, a lifetime of mourning in mere seconds.

This militia is local yet shows no reluctance to kill. Not one of them pauses to see if they recognize the dead. Instead, McClelland orders them to burn the evidence. "Nick! Tony! Steve!" Such familiar names. "You want to get out in that field and build me a bonfire?" It's Vietnam all over again. Cover your tracks. Torch the village.

The group is on Seven Pines property now. McClelland stands beside the remains of Ben's incinerated chair. What looked forceful an hour ago now looks pitiful, the miserable result of kids playing with matches, a charred skeleton of cheap wood, black lumps of melted stuffing.

Intercut into this chain of slaughter are shots of Ben. Rising from the cellar floor. Listening. Tiptoeing up the stairs. Listening. Removing the bars from the cellar door in aching silence. Now he tiptoes into the sunlit battlefield of the dining room. Walls scuffed from zombie fists. Framed painting askew. Chairs and table feet-up like dead insects. Ben picks his way through it and approaches a window—we can tell by the sunlight cascading over his face, the bright wash of hope over a forehead perennially wrinkled in concern.

McClelland. Bandolier down a few bullets now. Cigars in his hat band unsmoked because there's still work to do, though you know he'll puff them later in alternation with an Iron City, and laugh about what a wild couple days they had. He orders a minion: "You. Drag that out of here and throw it on the fire." He's not referring to the burned chair.

Everyone's standing around. Except Vince Survinski. He's got his eyes trained on the house. Survinski was the humblest of men. Capable of doing anything Image Ten or the Latent Image required, from accounting to construction, but painfully shy. Even at the Pittsburgh premiere a year later, he hid at the edges, not wanting to be seen. Yet Romero cast him in this bit part, something Survinski must have tried to refuse. But you can see why Romero insisted. Survinski radiates a lack of pretension, a willingness to act. Every director needs a Vince, just as every sheriff needs one too.

"Let's go check out the house," McClelland says.

"There's something in there, I heard a noise," Vince replies.

The next shot faces the house. Ben approaches a window with the Winchester raised. We clearly see him. Surely the posse sees him too. Can't they? All they have to do is look. Zombies don't crouch like that. They don't hold guns like that. Romero took special care in framing the next shot, the tightest close-up in the film, Ben in wary, watchful profile, the slant of his face taking up the upper diagonal half of the frame like a planet facing the sun, strong, unknowable, eternal.

It's all a lie. He's only a man.

"Hit him in the head," McClelland tells Vince. "Right between the eyes."

A man like Vince always strives to please his boss.

Whine of the Fawn, when abandoned, denied Romero his brutal ending. This time he gets it. We all get it. We return to the profile shot for but a few frames. It's a shot so beautiful, of so beautiful a man, that a painting of it by artist-actor Barnaby Edwards hangs in my office—and now graces the first edition of this book. In the painting, Ben stays in handsome profile forever. Forever in the dark, yes, but forever looking toward the light.

In the film, Ben's face rockets away. In a wide shot of the dining room, his body falls to the rug with a thud. I told you there was a third lethal weapon yet to hit the carpet and here it is—Ben himself. We don't see the rifle, the cause of so much death, fall to the floor, but we hear the rattling snick of its gears. Before we can process this terrible instant, the camera leaps back outside. Vince lowers the gun with a little smile, eager for his pat on the head.

"Good shot." McClelland turns. "Okay, he's dead. Let's go get him. That's another one for the fire."

In chunks. I can only bear to take these last four sentences in chunks. *Good shot.* That's what you're here for, to take shots, not to keep any kind of peace. *Okay, he's dead.* He can't be, surely it glanced off Ben's skull, we had to have seen it wrong. *Let's go get him.* Don't you dare, don't touch him, he's a human, a better human than any of you. *There's another one for the fire.* The cruelest final line in cinema history, our resourceful and ingenious Ben, despite everything he did right, not just tonight, the night of the living dead, but every night and every day that led to these last several hours, when he was able to shuck off whatever unsatisfying path life had foisted upon him and be the master of his destiny, just plain a master—gone, just like that, as quickly as any other ghoul. He had the requisite rifle, same as his killers, but not the flannel. He was missing the flannel. Sure. That had to be why.

01:33:38

NIGHT MIRROR

WHAT WE NEED FROM THE NEXT SHOT IS SOLACE. A look of horror on posse faces as they grasp their error. A shot of Ben beatific in the morning sun. If we are really airing our wish list here, a 1980s-style slow-motion montage of Ben's greatest hits, or flashbacks of Ben holding his wife, playing with his kids, that sort of thing.

We are fools to long for it. Romero has punished his characters for ninety-three minutes. He's not going to stop now. The most substantial change in Savini's remake is that Ben is a zombie when he's killed, meaning that he must, himself, be killed. It's a dodge of the entire racial conversation, any conversation at all.

What comes next in Romero's film is a muddy still photo too grainy to make out. The frame zooms out to reveal a larger picture. It's just as ugly, an effect achieved by printing still photos through cheesecloth. It's a shot of three men walking through the farmhouse. There's a fourth in the background, a man in a tie, but the film grain is too swollen to know if it is Sheriff McClelland or just another ghost.

An unpalatable image. Smug assholes. This isn't their property to parade through. They did nothing to earn it. Ben, on the other hand, gave his life for it. These fatuous conquerors carry guns. But that's not the worst of it. The man in front carries a hook. A meat hook.

Because the shot lasts but two seconds, we only have time to feel our rising bile.

The next shot is of Ben, not the shot we wished for, not even close. It's another grainy photo, perhaps taken by a journalist embedded with the posse, like Steve Hutsko. It has all the qualities of a hasty snapshot taken for posterity. Ben spread-eagled. Unartfully framed. Crudely lit. There's a meaty-looking wound in the middle of his forehead.

It all happened too fast—only now does it sink in.

Ben is dead. Really dead.

In this book, I've injected a lot of grayness into Ben's character, but don't let that lessen the impact of his murder. Ben was our hero, all the more heroic for the shortcomings that dogged him. It's staggering to imagine Image Tenners shooting the shit over snacks and saying, hey, what if Truckdriver dies at the end? Man, the squares at the drive-in won't see that one coming! They had no idea. How could they? How could they anticipate the transubstantiation from Truckdriver to Ben? How could they prepare for this performance from a young Black actor they had yet to meet?

It's difficult to get one's arms around what losing Ben means. At the story level, it instills a bitter irrelevance to everything we have witnessed, like a time-travel plot in which the characters cease to exist. What good were the interracial inroads plowed between Ben and Barbra? What was the point of Ben refusing to back down from Harry? What was the point of watching the whole goddamn film? No doubt people booed screens, threw popcorn, and stormed out muttering, as vitriolic as they'd be if the ending had been Barbra waking up from a dream.

If only it were. The film is a nightmare, but in the way that I interpreted the word as a child—a "night mirror." *Night* reflects things about us few who saw it in 1968 were ready for. Medgar Evers was assassinated in 1953. Malcolm X in 1965. The story Romero and Russ Streiner often told about April 4, 1968, borders on the unbelievable. They were on the Pennsylvania Turnpike, a finished print of *Night of Anubis* in the back of the car, en route to the Big Apple to show their flick to distributors. Excited chatter. Heads full of dreams. That's when the news hit the airwaves: Martin Luther King Jr. gunned down in Memphis.

And here George and Russ were about to demo a film in which a courageous Black protagonist is assassinated. AIP, their first-choice distributor, turned them down unless they reshot an ending in which Ben lived. Romero refused. The filmmakers had, indeed, pondered multiple endings, but chose to shoot none of them so as not to be tempted by requests like this.

They were fucked. The country? Even more fucked. Image Ten was lucky to get the deal they got from Walter Reade, for whom Romero and Streiner screened the film on June 5, 1968, the same day Sirhan Sirhan killed one more civil rights crusader, Robert F. Kennedy.

Night was terrific on its own, but these fateful twists made it immortal. One theatrical adaptation I haven't mentioned is a 2020 coproduction by Imitating the Dog and Leeds Playhouse called *Night of the Living Dead—Remix*, officially licensed by Image Ten, and no wonder. It's astonishing. Above the stage hang two screens, the left one playing the original film and the right one broadcasting the live re-creation being performed below by the actors, who trade off four handheld cameras. Get what I'm saying? They restage the film *in real time*, every camera angle, all 1,076 shots, right down to the famous cellar jump cut.

But when it comes to Ben's death, they abandon their rigorous method for an emotional flight of fancy. Ben, as if sensing he's about to die, lip syncs the audio of Martin Luther King Jr.'s "I Have a Dream" speech. After Ben bites it, King's speech continues. "Let freedom ring," King refrains, again and again, over Ben's lifeless body.

It's impossible to recall with any accuracy my first time seeing Ben die. Any other movie, I would have gleefully relived the plot's highlights, like Joe Bob Briggs does in his trademark

"Drive-In Totals" segment of his April 29, 2022, episode of *The Last Drive-In*, tallying *Night* with 9 Dead Bodies, 81 Undead Bodies, 35 Dead Undead Bodies, 2 Breasts, 1 Tussle, 1 Beatdown, 1 Zombie Picnic, Dad Eating, Gratuitous Animal-Head Trophies, and Gratuitous Music Box.

No, not with *Night*. No matter how much fun my mom had with the film, chastising Barbra and jeering Harry, all frivolity evaporated each time Ben died. I'm sure I asked her, "Why did they kill him?" "They thought he was a zombie," she surely replied, but that wasn't the whole truth, was it? They thought he *might* be a zombie, and he wasn't worth the few seconds it would have taken to find out.

The offhandedness of his death is the cruelest part. My self-defense is to recall the happiest I have ever seen Duane Jones. On September 13, 2024—Friday the thirteenth to be exact—a trove of roughly 230 behind-the-scenes photos, plus 53 photos from the October 1, 1968, premiere, were uploaded to the Pitt Library Digital Collections site. The pictures had arrived as negatives back in 2019 from Tina Romero's portion of the archives. For fifty-one years they had napped between the waxy sleeves of a bygone era in an envelope labeled "*Night* negatives."

Suddenly they were live. The timing was uncanny. Following a book event on September 12, I was in Pittsburgh, and had built in Friday the thirteenth as one last day in the Romero archives. I was literally at Hillman Library, days from finishing this book, when I accessed the photos. I was speechless. These unguarded instants, lost into a new genre's dreams. This band of friends bumbling as best they could through a task way over their heads.

I was even more taken by the photos from the October 1, 1968, Fulton Theater premiere. The big revelation: Jones beaming in photo after photo. Absolutely beaming. Another shot taken outside the Fulton, completely by accident, gives a glimpse of a different movie theater down the block, the Gateway, advertising KIRK DOUGLAS SYLVA KOSCINA ELI WALLACH "A LOVELY WAY TO DIE"—a film only recalled today for being the screen debut of Ali McGraw. There *are* lovely ways to die, I think.

There are also ugly, ugly, ugly ways to die.

Night's ending distressed me as a boy. Were movies allowed to do that? Could they kill the hero? I'd never seen such a thing and, for the next few decades, rarely would. Some would say I, in my *Star Wars* pajamas, saw *Night* too early. Go suck an egg. It was the best thing that could have happened to me. I examined. I processed. I probably night-mirrored, too, but so what? I realized before most of my peers that sayings like "might doesn't equal right" are aspirational, not realistic. Truer was a saying favored by my dad: "Life isn't fair."

An artist's job is to illustrate how and why this unfairness exists. It's a lesson that took a decade to bubble up through the swamp of my adolescent intellect. Though our house was full of guns, it never occurred to me to pick one up and take revenge on my bullies. Because of *Night*, I saw even my tormentors in grayscale, noting their difficult lives and emotional struggles. The only time I made an author appearance in my hometown, a man ran up to me in the parking lot, asking if I'd sign his book. It was one of my childhood bullies. I was ready to tell him to go fuck himself. But he spoke excitedly of giving the book to his kid. He couldn't have disarmed me any faster. I signed the book.

A reasonable guess would be that this man and I had the same heroes when we were kids. He-Man, Batman, Han Solo, Indiana Jones, Joe Montana. But no. My hero was Ben. I've been saying that for decades, but what do I mean by it? I think I wanted to be decisive. I wanted to stand up for myself. I wanted to make truehearted decisions and not care what people thought. I failed, of course. Yet I consider myself fortunate to have found Ben when I did.

Fairfield, Iowa, was hardly teeming with Black people. I didn't meet a single Black person till I was a teen. But I had Ben to set my mind right—heroic but also impulsive, capable but also vulnerable, explosive but also vindictive. Today, at age forty-eight, this goes unchanged with one tweak: It is Duane Jones, not Ben, whom I consider my hero.

What Jones has meant to me can't possibly measure up to what he has meant to Black audiences. In *Birth of the Living Dead*, film critic Elvis Mitchell describes the transformational exhilaration of seeing Jones in *Night* at age ten: "It was like hearing Public Enemy for the first time."

Similar sentiment is all over Xavier Burgin's documentary *Horror Noire: A History of Black Horror* (2019). Actor Keith David: "At that time, there was not a Black character who was really a man, who took charge of his fate. Who wasn't waiting for the white man to save him." Actor Rachel True: "That was the first time I probably saw somebody Black in a movie, and they weren't a criminal, and they weren't a gangster, and they were the hero." It's *Dawn of the Dead*'s Ken Foree (who knew Jones as part of New York's Black theater scene), who strikes the truest: "For the first time, we're not just the victims. We were the destroyers and the protectors." Destroyer-protector—the perfect way to describe the endlessly complex Ben.

In the *Cinefantastique* interview, Streiner speaks of attending a screening of *Night* at an all-Black theater, one night after the almost-no-Black Fulton Theater premiere. He describes a highly engaged audience: "You could hear murmurings of 'Well, you know, they had to kill him off' and 'Whitey had to get him anyway.' 'He bought it from the Man.' Maybe the whole feeling would be different if, for instance, Superman had been Black. I think the Black community is looking for a latter-day Superman. They found him in Shaft and they find him in Ben." Ben's slender back would have to carry them: There wouldn't be a Black Superman until Grant Morrison and Doug Mahnke created Calvin Ellis in 2008 for DC's "Final Crisis" storyline.

Romero might have repeated to his dying day that he had no agenda in casting Duane Jones. But once he understood how that choice affected people, he kept making it, casting Black men as male leads in both *Dawn of the Dead* and *Day of the Dead*. When preparing the Universal film *Land of the Dead*, Romero was vetoed from casting a Black lead. In 2005. Thirty-seven years after *Night*. Where are we going? It feels like we're taking Johnny's sharp U-turn at the start of the film. All roads lead to the boneyard.

Jones considered it his duty and privilege to serve the Black community. He taught Black literature at Antioch. He directed Black musicals at SUNY Westbury; the first play he put on was the U.S. premiere of *Black Orpheus*, and one of his last was *Lysistrata*, which a March 18, 1988, *Newsday* snippet described as a "rap adaptation" of Aristophanes's play. He acted with the Negro Ensemble Company. As executive director of the Black Theatre Alliance, he was a titan of New York's Black theater scene, his hands in dozens if not hundreds of productions. He didn't have to go that route. Blaxploitation films like *Super Fly* and *Foxy Brown* were looking for actors with gravitas. But Jones had a higher calling. He wanted to inspire change. Black theater in the 1960s followed the leads of Stokely Carmichael, Bobby Seale, and the Black Panthers, and eschewed assimilation for consciousness. Jones chose a greater good over greater paychecks, just like fellow Pittsburghers Jonas Salk, Fred Rogers, and George A. Romero.

If you look at the four films Jones had major roles in, only one didn't have a Black director: *Night of the Living Dead*. This dedication to working with Black creators had to be a major reason why he took so few film roles. There weren't a lot of Black directors getting projects off the ground.

Jones might still mean as much to the LGBTQ community. His solitary nature leaves us to piece together clues. His last couple years were spent living with trailblazing dancer Joanne Robinson; SUNY staff recall Jones and Robinson being the most striking couple on campus. But he was primarily observed by colleagues and students as being gay. Anecdotal evidence supports this. His lack of public partners. The privacy he chose over a life in the public lens. His close association with Bill Gunn, whom Jones directed in the play *Black Picture Show*, who directed Jones in *Ganja & Hess*, and who starred alongside Jones in *Losing Ground*.

Gunn, who was gay, died in 1989 from encephalitis brought on by AIDS. Jones died one year earlier from "cardiopulmonary arrest" at Winthrop University Hospital in Mineola, New York.

The heart attack didn't come out of the blue. He had been hospitalized for three weeks. Greg Sims, producer of *To Die For*, for which Jones filmed a two-day cameo only months earlier, told *Fangoria* in 1988, "He was very ill when he came out and was taking medication." In a call with me, Sims emphasized that Jones was smoking mass quantities of "high-end marijuana," the only thing that helped the pain. Here's what HIV-positive activist Paul Scott, founder of the Los Angeles Black LGBTQ Pride Movement, said about cannabis and AIDS: "You can't think back to one without the other," and while the Reagans were just saying no, "marijuana was all we had." Sims speculates Jones did the cameo primarily because the production put him up in a Malibu beach house. Jones knew the end was near, Sims said. Who wouldn't want to be awed by the unfathomable ocean so near the end?

Over ten thousand people died of AIDS in 1988, the year Jones died. That's roughly thirty a day. People with HIV were more than twice as likely to suffer sudden cardiac death than the general population, and hospitals in the late eighties shied away from entering "AIDS" on death certificates for how it might divulge sexual orientation (if they recognized the disease at all). They preferred to list the immediate, not underlying, cause of death, things like cardiopulmonary arrest. The most appreciable thing about Jones in *To Die For*—aside from how good he is, still, even in a bit part—is how drastically skinny he is. SUNY colleagues, some of whom attended a huge celebration of life event for Jones in Harlem in Fall 1988, all concur.

Karl Hardman was the closest to Jones. At the 2024 Days of the Dead panel, Judith O'Dea spoke wistfully of watching the typically reserved Jones yuk it up with Hardman. If anyone knew the factors behind Jones's demise, it was probably Karl. Near the end of *One for the Fire*, Hardman breaks down sobbing: "I choke up when I think about Duane because he was my friend, and I think he got a rotten deal in life." It is possible this "rotten deal," which goes unspecified, was worse than we know.

Jones has been dead for nearly forty years. But he lives eternal through Ben, the role he all but disowned, and there's still time for other communities to surround him like a zombie horde, but instead of eating him alive, lift him onto their shoulders.

The payoff could be Jones finally attaining the goal he revealed to Ferrante, his "absolute insistence that I be seen as a total human being."

There's also still time, too much time, for the opposite reaction to take hold. You may have only watched Ben die once. If you're a fan, maybe three or four times. But how many times have we watched George Floyd die? What are such repeat viewings doing to our souls? Earlier I mentioned the *Night of the Living Dead* DLC for the *Into the Dead 2* video game, which puts you inside Ben as he fights his way to Beekman's Diner. One YouTuber uploaded a compendium of Ben deaths, two-and-a-half minutes of Ben's bloodcurdling screams—of *our* screams—as he, and we, are murdered thirteen times in a row.

Watching it made me sick.

Duane L. Jones is buried in Atlanta's Westview Cemetery under a headstone he shares with his mother, Mildred G., who outlived her son by seven years. Jones died at age fifty-one, one year younger than my mom, Susan, who died of her own cardiopulmonary arrest. Two weeks ago, my older sister, Jenny, died at age forty-nine of an aggressive ovarian cancer that spread to her brain, lymph nodes, liver, everywhere. She looked like a zombie at the end, bone-thin, unrecognizable but for the mole on her right cheek. Her only sound was a gurgled moan I recognized instantly: the exact zombie noise she made in the Danman version of *Night*. Here we were again, she the distracted actor, me the clumsy director.

"You can go now," I directed, softly. Hours later, she did.

This is the real fear zombies shove in our faces: not of being dead but of *dying*, perpetually dying, an elongated process of decrepitude.

Seeing Jenny that final day, my thoughts went to a strange place. On Thursday, December 27, 1984, when I was nine, my mom, then thirty-two, failed to yield to an oncoming car as she pulled out of the Ben Franklin department store parking lot, an error for which magistrate court would fine her $34.50. The other party suffered little but our family's 1980 Chevy was totaled, the windshield cracked from the skull impact of the sole passenger—Jenny, age ten. Somehow both Mom and Jenny survived unscathed.

Or did they? It haunts me. It feels like my mother and sister dodged the grim reaper that day and thereafter carried a debt. It makes brutal sense to me that Duane Jones, who must have evaded the violent loathing of untold numbers of racists covetous of his education and erudition, owed the second half of his life as well. It never ends. The heartache never ends.

But you deal with it. With whatever tool is close enough to grasp. Could be family. Could be a minister, a friend, a therapist, a dog. Could be a restorative hobby. Painting, running, birdwatching. Could be music. Or it could be a movie. The same movie you turned to when you were twelve and your grandpa had a fatal heart attack, the first loved one who ever died on you, and you didn't know how to feel. The same movie you found consolation in when the rest of your grandparents passed away, and all your aunts and uncles too, and a friend OD'd, and your mom died before you published a single book, before you had the chance to show her what she and her favorite film had passed on to you, and therefore to all the people who read what you wrote. And when your sister Jenny died, a long, appalling, excruciating death, that same movie was there, this time in the form of a book you were writing about it, *this* book, and the continuity of writing the book in the weeks before Jenny died and the weeks after, of writing about those other people you adored, George Romero and Duane Jones and everyone else, it opened a valve allowing you to fully feel how you loved her, and presented a model for how you could relive that love, hold it in your hand, rewind and play it, like a Blu-ray, a DVD, a LaserDisc, a VHS tape, a 35mm reel. This is the movie that taught you how to live. How to love, too; if I've ever made you watch *Night*, that means I love you. And how to say goodbye. Maybe it even taught you how to die. Take a peek at the clock. Your closing credits are not so far off.

01:33:43 IT'S TOO BAD

Earlier, I reframed Barbra's time-change dialogue as an echo of Bob Dylan's "The Times They Are A-Changin'." The closing sequence of *Night* warns that change will come at a dreadful cost. Instead of Dylan, we get the most potent needle drop of the entire film. Officially, it's our third cue called "Eerie Heavy Echo" (this time L-1214), but in this case, I prefer its title on the Varèse Sarabande LP: "O.K. Vince / Funeral Pyre (End Title)," a six-car smash-up of words that conveys the indifference of the militiamen, the assertion of the corpse bonfire as something funereal, and the plain fact that we're rolling credits, folks. Attributed to Spencer Moore, the cue is a minor-key rising-and-falling loop of lamenting strings that echoes nothing so much as the cricket noises that dominate *Night*'s soundtrack.

I try to imagine being one of Moore's musicians, knocking out this library track like the session guy I am, thinking only of wrapping the day, getting home, having a cold one with dinner. Then this happens. Not a "cue," not even really a "song." More like a sensation, a mournful cry, but a nervous one as well, the music creating the edgy feel that more mourning is still to come. No way the musicians finished the take and didn't glance around to see if the others felt it too. This unnerving graveside spell. Romero layers under it the sounds of tires on gravel, dogs barking, the pops, mutters, and squelches of the posse's radio units. Harsh sounds polluting beautiful music, the aural match of the images unfolding before our eyes.

The power of this music—of all of *Night*'s music—never left Romero's mind. Possibly the last thing he ever wrote was a foreword to David Hollander's *Unusual Sounds: the Hidden History of Library Music* (2018). "I owe a lot to a lot of people. A big part of what I owe must go to you: the composers, the arrangers, and musicians who never even saw my first film," Romero writes. "I don't know their names, nor did they ever know mine, but we made beautiful music together."

Something else inspired the chillingly detached optical pans and zooms that run beneath the end credits: Sidney Lumet's *Fail Safe* (1964), a Cold War cautionary tale that ends with a rapid-fire photo montage of New Yorkers at the instant Soviet nuclear bombs explode. My god, how well the technique works in *Night*. The photos look so real it begins to feel as if they are sourced from a hidden record of an obliterated people. Erased genocides have happened before. They are happening now.

It's shocking to compare this ending to the happy-crap of the script's last two pages, which focus on repairing the image of Sheriff McClelland. He reprimands Vince for shooting into the house. He drapes his coat over poor Barbra. In the script's final line, he says of Ben, "It's too bad . . . an accident . . . the only loss we had the whole night." It's a disingenuous end suitable only for children. Case in point: William V. Black's 2016 picture book adaptation of *Night* ends similarly. "Barbara jumps out of the Jeep and gives Ben a big bear hug," Black writes. "And they lived happily ever after!"

Jack Russo brought McClelland back for more heroics in his *Return of the Living Dead* novel, but the sheriff didn't receive his comeuppance until *My Uncle John Is a Zombie* (2016), a comedy starring, written, and codirected by Russo. George Kosana returns as McClelland, and the confused feebleness of his eighty years (he died shortly after filming) brings poignancy to the performance. Forty years after ordering Ben killed, he's being held accountable. But he's bullheaded: "There was a lotta itchy trigger fingers. Everyone was panicking." Viewers of *Night* know, of course, that McClelland was the furthest thing from panicked.

(Russo, never one to let a sales opportunity slide by, sells one of the movie's products on his website: Uncle John's Zombie Lube, strawberry-flavored, with the slogan *Give Your Stiff a Stiffy!* No, I don't care for it either.)

It's perhaps due to the enduring anguish of *Night*'s ending that three proposed direct sequels have popped up in recent years, none of them in production as of this writing. The first came from (naturally) Russo, who in 2018 announced *Night of the Living Dead, Part 2,* supposedly based on an old project by Russo and Romero with the unlikely title of *Night of the Living Dead and the Day After.* It's just not true. The project existed, but Romero had nothing to do with it.

Second was *Night of the Living Dead 2,* announced by director Marcus Slabine in 2021. Rumor was that it had been shot in secret with the three surviving characters from *Day of the Dead*—still played by Lori Cardille, Terry Alexander, and Jarlath Conroy—which made it seem a lot more like *Day of the Dead 2.* Exciting stills and a smidgen of footage lent credence to the hearsay. But Slabine had only shot a sizzle reel to entice investors—and the investors were not enticed. (Some of my info here comes from an Irish horror YouTuber called "Kilt-Man," so take this with a grain of salt.) I'll also toss in a mention here of *Night of the Living Dead: Genesis,* announced in 2015 with a trailer starring none other than Judith O'Dea as a scraggly-haired Barbra ready to tell her story from a psych ward, but it, too, was never more than a trailer.

The third is an untitled *Night* project announced in 2022 and overseen by Christine Forrest Romero and Tina Romero, which takes place at the same time as *Night* but follows Ben's wife. While authorized by Image Ten, it's not an Image Ten production, but rather a Sanibel Films one. Both the distributor attached (Amazon/MGM) and the talent (LaToya Morgan writing, Nikyatu Jusu directing) makes this an intriguing effort, though a June 6, 2025, *New York Times* piece makes it sound deadish, with Christine paraphrasing MGM's hang-up: "We don't like your rights." That old copyright bug still can't be swatted.

A final project to be mentioned is *Twilight of the Dead*, which, as of this writing, is in preproduction with a damn fine director, Brad Anderson (*Session 9, The Machinist*). It's based on a full outline Romero created with his friend Paolo Zelati, who scripted with Joe Knetter and Robert Lucas. Having read both the outline and an early script draft, I'm optimistic. It ends the Romero zombie cycle in a different way than our novel *The Living Dead*, a way that recalls how *Battle for the Planet of the Apes* ended the original Apes cycle. I mean that as a compliment. *Twilight* goes pretty hard.

That's the future. The present, meanwhile, is bright. In the eyes of Image Ten's Gary Streiner, the MoMA restoration and Criterion release kicked off a new era for *Night*. Image Ten finally owns the rights to the only great-looking copy of the film, a big deal in the HD era. They have a productive new partnership with a top licensing firm. Also productive is a palpably optimistic new attitude that un-thinks the public domain storyline: Image Ten *always* had the rights to their film, they just hadn't known how to assert them. Today, instead of taking infringers to court over bootlegged products, they have opened their own store hawking what they hope are the *best* products. It's the right move. I, for one, keep the store bookmarked.

With some trepidation, then, let's return to the past—the final two minutes of *Night*.

The faces Romero chooses for the closing photo montage are chilling. There's Gary Streiner, his age (twenty-one) enhancing the swagger of a kid allowed to carry a big-boy gun. There's our firebug Tony Pantanello and the don't-give-a-shit way he lips his lil' stogie. There's Randy Burr, a crusty old joe who looks authentic because he was—he was at the farm fixing a broken pump when he was recruited. (When releasing *La notte dei morti viventi* in 1970, notoriously inaccurate Italian theater posters known as fotobusta gave Burr top billing as "R. Burr"—erroneously interpreted as "Raymond Burr.")

Soon it's not faces that are our focus. The optical lens pans down to Pantanello's meat hook, then the meat hooks gripped by Streiner, Burr, and a third man. This is followed by a shot of two meat hooks dangling, ready for use—as the lens pans down to Ben's face. It's here the first end credits (more like obituaries) fade in. BEN: DUANE JONES. BARBRA: JUDITH O'DEA. Thirty-five seconds have passed since the shot that killed Ben. Still too fast to be believed, even though his dead body is right there.

The meat hooks were fashioned by Vince Survinski and Jack Russo. People have tried to auction off forgeries (and succeeded: one fake sold for $6,875 in 2023). It strikes me as a ghoulish thing to sell, or to own. It would feel like keeping the gun that shot Martin Luther King Jr.

The names of the rest of the six lead actors appear. In a theater, here's where the house lights come up and patrons blink at watches, rustle for coats. At home, you might hop up for that pee you have been holding or return some texts. There's nothing on the soundtrack that signals, hey, pay attention. But rarely are end credits more crucial. As soon as Keith Wayne and Judy Ridley's names fade out, Romero rapidly cuts (four seconds total) to five still photos of posse men lifting meat hooks. This is where the comparison to *Fail Safe* hits hard. The next photo is of Ben, a meat hook embedded in his heart.

Ours too.

The rest of the credits creep upward, starting with KYRA SCHON. It's easy to get distracted by all these names, which insist what we have seen is theater. But pay attention. Please pay attention. The background image depicts Gary Streiner, Burr, and Pantanello towing Ben's body from the house by limb and hook like he's a side of beef. The next photo shows a second meat hook lodged in Ben's stomach. It's hard to make out because these are bad photos. Intentionally bad photos created to make us squint and study, and if we're really doing our jobs, pause and rewind, pause and rewind.

Because don't these men dragging Ben deserve to be identified just like the other villains referred to in this book? Dr. Frankenstein, Dracula, Jason Voorhees, Freddy Krueger, Nosferatu, Dr. Caligari, Belial, the Zuni Fetish Doll, Jack Torrance, Annie Wilkes, the Lizard, Michael Myers, the Mummy, Leatherface, the Mothman, Captain Rhodes, Captain Howdy, Darth Vader, the Creature from the Black Lagoon, the Wolf Man, Mr. Hyde, Norman Bates. And the real ones too: O. J. Simpson, Charles Manson, Harold Frieberg, Jeffrey Dahmer, Heinrich Himmler, Adolf Hitler, Ed Gein, Kyle Rittenhouse, Sirhan Sirhan.

My mind flashes back to the film's fifth shot, the goddamn LeMans crawling past the sign reading CEMETERY ENTRANCE. The bullet holes in that sign gave us the most crucial info of all. They warned us we were in a place where intolerance drifts like pollen capable of taking root inside any lung that breathes it. In places like these, you are always adjacent to a cemetery filled with unwelcome bodies.

In the hard-to-find *Knights of the Living Dead*, a DVD that captures a "Zombie Town Hall" discussion at the 2012 Denver Film Festival between Romero, Max Brooks (*World War Z*), and Steven Schlozman (*The Zombie Autopsies*), Brooks says what all of us are feeling about Ben's violated corpse: "This is payback for the civil rights movement."

There are three hooks in Ben by the time he's shown on the pyre. Seeing his body, so quick and strong in life, manipulated like a broken puppet, is too much to take. The morning my sister died, I watched funeral home workers carry her body downstairs, seal her into a bag, and load her into their car. It was my duty to bear witness. This is how I watch these shots of Ben. Romero refuses to be like the news media that, a half century later, chose not to show the Covid-19 dead. Concealing violent truths leads entire nations astray. What's next? Refusing to teach students about American slavery? Oh, right. That's happening too.

Without these end credit photos, Ben never died.

No one ever killed him.

Everything is fine.

We might not notice what Vince Survinski holds if Romero doesn't zoom in to it. It's the only thing worse than a meat hook: a gas can. Though my pain here is for Ben and Duane Jones, I reserve a speck for Survinski. He went to see a matinee of *Night* after it opened, and the way the crowd screamed at his character frightened him. "I shot the hero without knowing it," he said. "I didn't know what I was shooting at in that scene until I saw the picture." He hid in his theater seat, then scurried out into the alley.

What had he done?

Time appeared to heal that wound. Survinski reprised his hero-killer role twenty years later in Hinzman's quasi-sequel *FleshEater*, in which he picks off the film's two survivors and then mugs, "Yeah, I'm getting pretty good at this." While I like both Hinzman and Survinski, the moment rests uneasily with me. Then again, nothing about *Night* ever rests easy.

The next image follows the logic of Survinski's gas can. While our threesome lays Ben upon a pile of lumber, McClelland and two others hold sticks with ends wrapped in cloth. As yet unlit, but we have seen torches like this before. Ben created several. Now he's on the losing end. One shot later, the final actor credit, RANDY BURR, appears beside the actual Randy Burr. It's the same photo as the previous one except closer, Ben's upside-down face angelic, upturned toward the sky.

In the next photo, an even tighter close-up, Ben's face shares the frame with Zombie #1, who has been finally dispatched—the top warrior of each side dead from pointless battle. It isn't the kind of photo a crime-scene photographer would take. It's as if the photographer became arrested by Ben's face, the serenity of it, and couldn't help but capture it. Magnified like this, the film grain gets thick and mealy. As Robin R. Means Coleman writes in *Horror Noire: A History of Black American Horror from the 1890s to Present* (2011), "They look like they could be the weathered photos of Emmett Till, shot in the head, being loaded into the back of his executioners' truck."

Those photos don't exist. What do exist are the open-casket

shots of Till's dead face, so beaten and swollen the fourteen-year-old no longer looks human. They were insisted upon by his mother, Mamie Till-Mobley, whose courage was at a higher level than Romero's, though both operated on the same instinct: Show the truth. "I wanted the world to see what they did to my baby," Till-Mobley said. Go look at Till's casket photo now. It's terrible but you have to see it. Even if you have seen it before. Pause, rewind. Pause, rewind.

The film is America, I said at the start of this book. It's true, though one is forgiven to wish that it wasn't. Is it night in America? Will it always be? Can we even call what we are doing living? Or are we long dead and only going through the zombie motions? The sole piece of writing I've ever seen by Duane Jones is a theater review in the April 5, 1980, issue of the *New York Amsterdam News,* and it includes a sentence that could have been chiseled onto the headstone he shares with his mother:

Does it really matter so much what men believe as long as it renders them decent?

The opposite was just as true—and Jones knew it.

Of all the changes I don't like in Jack Russo's novelization, there's one that feels braver than anything beneath *Night*'s closing credits, though it's not an effect the filmmakers could have pulled off: "Two men with machetes came forward and began hacking at Ben, severing his head from his body," Russo writes, right before both parts are heaved into the flames.

Romero's death was slower, but not by much. In early June 2017, three years after a stroke, he was diagnosed with lung cancer—"the Big C," he dubbed it in phone calls to loved ones. The Big C had set up camp in his brain, liver, and bones. Soon he was moved to a hospital, where he, in his muddled state, repeated one phrase over and over: "I want to go home. I want to go home." Where was home, I wonder? With Suz, for sure. On the film set of a great Roman epic, perhaps.

George A. Romero died at 1:00 p.m. on July 16, 2017. Only three weeks later, on August 7, I was asked to complete his novel,

The Living Dead. His funeral had been held a fortnight earlier, July 24, 2017, at Toronto's Mount Pleasant Funeral Centre from 2:00 to 8:00 p.m. (followed, on October 22, by a memorial event at the Evans City Cemetery chapel). Had I been contacted in time, I might have taken it as a sign to fly up to Toronto. As it was, I mourned alone, though reports of the funeral make it sound like the perfect mix of sober memorialization and adoring fandom.

Outside the funeral home, media interviewed fans and shot footage of bereavers who showed up in zombie makeup. Inside, TVs played interviews with Romero while a larger screen played his movies. Though the room was filled with props from his films, the posters hung up were of the films he loved, the kinds he never got to make: *The Quiet Man*, *The Ten Commandments*, et cetera. Propped on the closed casket were several plush versions of Romero that had been produced over the years as well as a bevy of rubber duckies—an affectionate inside lark between George and Suz. They brought two rubber ducks along on so many trips that people noticed and began sending them as gifts until they had amassed over six hundred.

Romero was buried with his rubber duckie, and Suz assures me that she will be buried with hers.

There was a guest book. I regret not having my own words in there; I hope my afterword to *The Living Dead* is proof enough of what Romero meant, and continues to mean, to me. I suppose this book is proof as well.

Night's final credit, a SPECIAL THANKS, fades up over a lump of cloth we only recognize as an unlit torch for how many times they have appeared in this film about leaders and the mobs who follow them. (We also hear McClelland's voice: "Hey, Randy, light these torches over here.") With a final *Fail Safe* zoom-and-cut, the torch is gassed by Survinski and McClelland, and lit by McClelland and Burr before another instant of white leader, just like the truck explosion, so tiny this time you'd have to be an obsessive to notice it.

This photo dissolves to the movie's final shot. (Some older

versions have a stylized THE END after this shot, but that was added god knows when by god knows who.) *Night* has one last surprise: This isn't a still photo but rather a motion picture shot of the bonfire going up in a thick, white fountain of flame. In his monologue, Ben spoke of the "moving bonfire" of a runaway truck. The bonfire has stopped moving: The bonfire is him.

In *Night of the Living Dead—Remix*, this climactic shot coincides with the final words of Martin Luther King Jr.'s speech, his tone of soaring hope tainted with dire irony. Free at last. Free at last. Thank God almighty, we are free at last. Then it's gone. All gone. A burbling synthesizer sting drags out over the fifteen-second shot—and then another four seconds of black.

Romero wanted to burn the farmhouse down. I understand the urge. Something miraculous happened there: one of the greatest films ever made. But if you believe in *Night of the Living Dead* as I do—it's realer to me than events that happened before my own eyes—then the farmhouse also feels cursed. Because the owners wanted $5,000 for the privilege, the filmmakers opted for a simple bonfire. It works better because we are allowed to get closer. It's lumber mostly, a few rags, a sheet. At least two bodies are visible. Sheriff McClelland is the only living person in the shot, and he high-tails it stage right. The fire is too bright. It rages harder than McClelland, or Image Ten, or anyone could have expected.

Visiting the farmhouse site today, it's easy to get lost in a dreamworld: the tidy, quiet, private home visited by ghosts of the cast and crew, their joyful messes, the long light cables snaked through uncut grass, the franks and beans dished out to anyone who stopped by to help. But break the spell. Turn around. Look at the house directly across the asphalt road and recall that we're in Butler County, ten minutes down the road from where, on July 13, 2024, Thomas Crooks killed one person and injured two while trying to assassinate Donald Trump. It's a beige residence unremarkable but for the roadside bed of rocks sprouting red, white, and blue. They are not flowers. They are signs. WE SUPPORT OUR POLICE, one reads, a sentiment that feels perilous here where *Night*'s posse once marched. THE TRUTH, reads another, citing false data that Donald Trump won the 2020 election by 494,429 votes. Anything is truth if you don't need the photos to prove it. TRUMP 2020—KEEP AMERICA SAFE, reads a third. Keep who safe, exactly? A final sign reads, AS FOR ME AND MY HOUSE, WE WILL SERVE THE LORD, KNEEL AT THE CROSS, SALUTE THE FLAG & STAND FOR THE ANTHEM.

Who won't you serve? What other icons do you worship? Who will you refuse to salute? If you could write your own anthem, whose deaths would it celebrate?

The signs are a reminder of something we should have learned in Farmhouse Nation. Never forget to look behind you. That's where they hide, gathering in numbers, before they feel safe enough to strike.

Regis Survinski recalled how it began snowing when they filmed the bonfire, which was not only the last shot of the film, but the last shot filmed. By then it was November. Everyone was cold and tired. The shoot had dragged on for six months. They were ready to be done, to burn anything they could.

The snow was unfortunate, they thought, but there was neither time nor energy to wait it out. They set the fire and rolled film. But *Night of the Living Dead* had always been blessed, and here came one last miracle. The snow, when hit by the fire, took on a certain twinkle. It looked like embers, Regis thought, and if you watch a good enough copy of the film, you get a sense of what he saw from the fury of the fire's licking edges. It's beautiful. The flux reminds me of seasonal change. Winter has come. But spring isn't far behind. It will wheel by again, a cycle as predictable as night, dawn, and day.

I don't know if real change is possible.

But some of us will still be here when the light returns.

Partially devoured but prepared to fight on.

ACKNOWLEDGMENTS

First and foremost, thank you to the four people whose early reads made the book more insightful and accurate: Adam Hart, Ben Rubin, Dan Smetanka, and Christian Stavrakis. I also want to spotlight John Vullo's late-breaking work in digging up new info on *Night*'s extras. Additional gratitude goes out to all the other misshapen monsters who provided their dubious comforts:

Richard Abate, Megan Abbott, Tara Altebrando, Steven Barnes, Laura Berry, Matt Blazi, Bryan Bliss, Arnold T. Blumberg, Steven Brezenoff, Jordan Brown, Thomas Brown, Jill Bruellman, Olenka Burgess, Dave Burian, Hannah Carande, C. Robert Cargill, Wah-Ming Chang, Rob Christopher, Jim Cironella, Nina Lorez Collins, Ilene Cooper, Thomas DelGiudice, David Demchuk, Suzanne Desrocher-Romero, Lawrence DeVincentz, Dennis Doros, Tananarive Due, Brian Duffield, Marcus Dunstan, Stefan Dziemianowicz, Barnaby Edwards, Zusha Elinson, Joyce Emerson, Michael Felsher, Tim Ferrante, Rachel Fershleiser, Ally Field, Megan Fishmann, Xabier Fole, Mike Ford, Ken Foree, Paul G. Gagne, Marya E. Gates, Peter Grunwald, Phil Giuliano, Bervin Harris, Corey Ann Haydu, Grady Hendrix, Ben Huff, Eleanor Imbody, Bede Jermyn, Elric Kane, Dana Kaye, Jennifer Kearney, Brian Keene, Amanda Kraus, Dale Kraus, Susan Kraus,

Shad Kunkle, Carl Kurlander, Loan Le, Colin Legerton, Julia Leudtke, Tony Mansour, Victoria Maxfield, Rebekah McKendry, Drew McWeeney, Jeff Mellott, Joe Monti, Phil Morehart, Aaron Morton, Lonnie Nadler, Greg Nicotero, Phil Noble Jr., Judith O'Dea, Craig Ouellette, Danielle Paige, W. Scott Poole, Graham Reznick, Judith Ridley, Debbie Rochon, Chris Roe, John A. Russo, Michael Ryzy, Robert Saucedo, Jake Schmidt, Kyra Schon, John Scoleri, Seret Scott, Greg H. Sims, Julia Smith, Nathan Smith, Gary Streiner, Russell Streiner, Erica Tempesta, Jay Thompson, Yukiko Tominaga, Geoff Turner, Jeff Whitehead, Brian Witten, Sara Zarr, the University of Pittsburgh Library System, the George A. Romero Foundation, and the lovable obsessives of the Official George A. Romero's *Night of the Living Dead* Facebook group.

I am also indebted to the hundreds of books, documentaries, interviews, articles, commentary tracks, personal appearances, blog posts, and on and on, that have delved into *Night of the Living Dead* over the past half century. Some of the most important are listed below, and the most foundational are asterisked.

**Autopsy of the Dead*, directed by Jeff Carney (2009)

Birth of the Living Dead, directed by Rob Kuhns (2013)

**The Complete Night of the Living Dead Filmbook*, by John Russo (1985)

Fan of the Dead, directed by Nicolas Garreau (2008)

The Farmhouse Seven: The Unauthorized History of the Original 1968 Zombie Thriller Night of the Living Dead, by Jeff Moreno

George A. Romero Interviews, edited by Tony Williams (2011)

George A. Romero's Independent Cinema: Horror, Industry, Economics, by Tom Fallows (2022)

George A. Romero: Zombis, política y cine independiente (George A. Romero: Zombies, Politics, and Independent Cinema), by Xabier Fole (2025)

Journey of the Living Dead: A Tribute to Fifty Years of Flesh Eaters, by Arnold T. Blumberg (2018)

Memories of the Living Dead, by Bob Michelucci (2013)

My Life with the Living Dead, by John Russo (2017)

**Night of the Living Dead: Behind the Scenes of the Most Terrifying Zombie Movie Ever,* by Joe Kane (2010)

**Night of the Living Tapes: The Official Home Video History of Night of the Living Dead,* by Geoff Turner (2021)

Raising the Dead: The Work of George A. Romero, by Adam Charles Hart (2024)

Reflections on the Living Dead, directed by Thomas Brown (1993)

A Theater Near You!: Advertising Night of the Living Dead, by Geoff Turner (2022)

**The Zombies That Ate Pittsburgh: The Films of George A. Romero,* by Paul G. Gagne (1987)

DANIEL KRAUS is a *New York Times* bestselling writer of novels, TV, and film. His latest novel, *Angel Down*, was one of *The New York Times'* 10 Best Books of 2025. His novel *Whalefall* won the Alex Award, was a Los Angeles Times Book Prize finalist, and was named a Best Book of 2023 by NPR, *The New York Times*, Amazon, *Chicago Tribune*, and other outlets. With Guillermo del Toro, he cowrote *The Shape of Water*, based on the same idea the two created for the Oscar-winning film. Find out more at danielkraus.com.